THE PATH OF LEAST RESISTANCE

YOUR MANUFACTURER'S INSTRUCTION MANUAL ON HOW TO LIVE
A HAPPY HEALTHY LIFE AND FULFILL YOUR DREAMS

JESSELYNN DESMOND

BALBOA.PRESS

A DIVISION OF HAY HOUSE

Balboa Press books may be ordered through booksellers or by contacting:

Balboa Press
A Division of Hay House
1663 Liberty Drive
Bloomington, IN 47403
www.balboapress.com
844-682-1282

Print information available on the last page.

ISBN: 978-1-9822-5667-8 (sc)
ISBN: 978-1-9822-5666-1 (hc)
ISBN: 978-1-9822-5726-2 (e)

Library of Congress Control Number: 2020920980

Balboa Press rev. date: 04/14/2021

~ DEDICA-KNOWLEDGMENT ~

This book is dedicated to all my guardian angels in other dimensions: My Brave Mother, All my Relations, Tomas Verde and the Infinite Universal Source of ALL, & to all who desire more happiness by committing to your higher self & a healthier, better life.

Thank you to all my friends I call my family —you let me run ideas off no matter what time of day or night, though you must have thought I was rambling like a crazy person at times. If I didn't have my family of friends, I'd have nothing and be nowhere. It is because of my amazing, wonderful friends that I get to show up and be the person I am for them and for me. I owe my life to my friends. Together We Rise!!

I am grateful to Pamela Brava & Dave Haddon for being the 1st people to brave my book and offer valuable feedback. Thank you David Keith Miller for being a solid friend, who made my words better with every suggestion and more in alignment with my soul and made me cry with the cover copy.

Thank you to my Oracle & Legacy Life Coaching clients with whom I first started bouncing around all these ideas and games. It was you that made me know if what I was saying was understandable and helpful and even worked! I'm grateful I can bring it all to you in one place so that it is easy for you to access, even when I am not around.

CONTENTS

CONTENTS

INTRODUCTION

This book is the summation of the wisdom I gained from a series of childhood traumas that gave me the gift to see past veils and blossom into the highest version of myself. I learned to align my spirit, body, and mind into one heart-based practice by examining and studying nature. This practice has an answer for everything, from the micro to the macro, but only if you're seeking.

As a child, nature was my only playground. Extreme poverty can't afford toys or even food sometimes. Rocks were my imaginary toy box cars and sticks wrapped in cloth were my dolls. Once my grandmother made me a fake Cabbage Patch doll sewed from scratch because a real one would have been a fantasy of luxury for my family—we drank powdered milk! I didn't know the difference, but the kids at school did, and they mocked me mercilessly for it. When I got home I threw my grandmother's labor of love on the ground in a fit and went back to playing with sticks and stones.

Nature was my best friend, the only one that never judged me or let me down. It taught me about life, how to play make-believe, how to talk with weird accents. It let me be as silly as I ever wanted to be. Why? Because NATURE'S NEAT (said with a southern hicksville accent and a giddyup—which you'll hear all kinds of crazy voices in the audiobook)!

In my opinion, humans are the most beautiful creatures in the whole world and our survival is the most important thing worth fighting for. My goal in writing this book is to raise your curiosity enough to grow your own awareness of yourself and humanity, where we came from, why we are here, what we LOVE, and give you the tools to bring out the best in you and everyone in your life! The information here is not new—you will remember your nature as more of your higher self is revealed and the veil is lifted.

The world I want to live in is the one where all beings are respected, acknowledged, seen, heard, and financially compensated for their gifts and talents. People living their dreams have very different experiences of life than a person that isn't because of their vibration—and everything is vibration. When you raise your vibration, you change your life, positively impacting the world.

In 1999, my entire life had changed for the better. It all began when I made a very important decision. I was working a dead-end job at a company that went out of business but didn't tell any of us store managers until we were escorted out of the building by police early one morning. I had given everything to that job.

I became a makeup artist and would do Oracle readings at the cash register using the names of the makeup customers would buy to give them insight. After being kicked out with the other employees, I sat in my car that freezing morning contemplating what I would do next. It was at that moment that I made a promise to myself: I decided I would only take jobs that were of my highest calling and purpose by fulfilling my creative passions.

That evening a friend asked me to come to her party, but not as a guest. She offered to pay me to do what I did for free for her and other friends: give Oracle readings. I have been a professional ORACLE ever since. That party was the first time I heard back from someone that they got value from this *weird thing* that I did. In high school I was friends with many conflicting groups because of my ability to "give advice," which I later learned is called *divination*.

Not long after that party, a group of our friends got together to create a consciousness elevating music and art festival we called *Lightning in a Bottle*. 500 people attended our first event. In the early years, we had an all-hands-on-deck approach to make it happen and I had both a production role and performance role in the festival. I loved performing, creating, building, and set design. As the company grew, I got to simply perform. The performance part of the *DoLab* was the brainchild mastermind circus that Dream Rockwell named Lucent Dossier.

As our work gained more visibility, offers of additional work started pouring in. Both the production and performance departments of the team were getting booked separately for bigger clients. We tried to make it work to stay together but after six years we split the company. I am grateful to call them my family and have worked with both groups ever since. They have changed my life and taught me that anything is possible when you follow your dreams.

Looking back, I think the only choice we had was to create a safe place for us to live out *our dreams*, which then turned into the place where millions have found theirs. There were only a handful of festivals back then, now there is one every day of the week. It's fun to think we were at the forefront of that ripple effect. Before Lucent/The Do Lab came along, there wasn't a place for someone to have a profession as a hula-hooper, now there are thousands.

I didn't have an easy life growing up. My mother became very ill when she was eighteen and doctors didn't know what it was. They gave her treatments for things she tested negative for and misdiagnosed her for six years. Some of those treatments almost ended her life on many occasions— each time arrangements were made for my care. When she was twenty-four they finally decided upon Lupus as her badge to wear.

The only thing my mother wanted in the world was to have a child, but the doctors told her she would be unable to have a healthy baby with all the steroids and medications she had to take to stay alive. They said her child would be *mentally retarded and possibly deformed* and she most likely would *not survive the birthing process*. She refused the abortion her doctors prescribed her and followed her gut instinct. I am grateful I got this instinct from her! Her strong desire to have a child, her belief and her willingness to do what it took to fulfill her dream, were literally my saving grace.

She met my cute Mexican dad and got preggers. My grandmother was scared he would try to kidnap me and take me to Mexico to live with his family there. She was known for her very sharp tongue and would ask my dad if there were any red-haired people in his family because she saw a red-haired man going to her bedroom—I was born with red blonde hair.

My grandpa was the most kind amazing man and always would give my dad soup, sandwich and a beer every time he came over. My parents broke up before I was born and my dad didn't have much time to see me working two jobs. I never knew or saw him until I was eleven and then not again until I was twenty-six. I always felt cheated out of the possibility of growing up bilingual or knowing the other half of myself—my Mexican Family and culture—and where I came from.

I was born two months premature without any deformations or mental retardation, although as my family often tells me, I was dropped on my head as a baby. Because of my mother's poor health, she gave half custody to one of my aunts and the rest of the time I was a ward of the court (a city kid). Throughout my formative years, I was in and out of foster care while my mother was in the hospital fighting off death. I lived with my aunt for a bit until her husband got cancer and she couldn't take care of me anymore. After that I was back to being a city kid in foster care.

Many of the foster care families I lived with were only doing it to get a monthly paycheck from the government and were abusive. I was only one of four to seven foster kids in one household at any given time and was treated badly by the biological kids because they didn't understand what was going on and they were only following the lead of the foster parents. The real kids got preferential treatment and the fosters became the slave horses left to do all the chores and receive harsher punishments for the same infractions.

In one of the homes I lived, I was kicked in the soft ribs so hard that as an adult you can still see the indentation where it hardened in that trauma state. I was sexually abused for several years by a "friend of the family" until I finally told on him. I was molested by a cousin and raped by an unknown person at a party, all by the age of eleven.

In sixth grade, my best friend's dad met my mom and they fell in love. Being an only child, it was a dream come true that my best friend became my sister—or was it? Days after the wedding my sister confided in me that her dad had been abusing her. He soon started abusing me and made our lives a living hell. He used the classic isolation technique to keep his tyrannical throne. We were grounded for every little thing—mistakes on homework, water spot found on a dish/cup, toothpaste splatter on the bathroom mirror—which continued for three years. He told us physical labor would make us better people. During this time we weren't allowed to visit friends or go to family gatherings.

After some runaway attempts, he decided to allow us to have one friend over at a time while he was there, but only if they were helping us perform the physical labor punishment tasks. We were so grateful we didn't notice how weird it all was. Looking back, it was pretty smart of him because he didn't have to pay anyone to landscape the yard, install a swamp cooler on the roof, install tile flooring, or renovate the garage into a room, etc.

When the abuse worsened we tried to commit suicide. The third and last time, we downed a couple of bottles of my mother's pills and several bottles of liquor we found in the house. We called all our friends to say goodbye and one of them called the police just in time. My mother thought we were trying to kill her by taking the medicine that was keeping her alive, so we were severely punished. Since it's against the law to commit suicide, we were given one year of probation and six months of community service, which actually got us court-ordered out of the house and away from him for a while.

I figured out that doing after-school programs would keep me away from home until the evening, and there were programs year-round. I signed up for as many as I could, including cheerleading, soccer, drama club, debate team, choir, madrigals, wrestling, tap, ballet, jazz, Key club, lifeguard, and acting in all the school plays.

There was a light at the end of the tunnel that we had never seen until this point when my sister and I awoke to weird sounds (heavy breathing, gasping for air, furniture moving around and things falling on the ground, both male and female grunts, and groans) in the living room and figured they were probably having sex. We were disgusted at that thought but couldn't fathom anything like that, because they weren't affectionate toward each other after six months of marriage.

The next morning, we woke up, got ready for school, and on our way out noticed my mom looked funny. I said, "She looks like a dead frog", and my sister and I laughed. My step-dad said "Maybe she *is* dead" and we laughed again, continued out the door to the bus stop on the corner. A few minutes later my step-dad yells "Girls, get in here!" and we thought we were in trouble again.

We came in to find him pacing back and forth smoking a cigarette (previously only smoked *outside* of the house) and mumbling to himself over and over again, "She's dead, she's dead." It took us a minute to understand what he was saying, then everything slowed down and my heart sank to the floor as I ran to her. I tried to perform CPR but her body was already in the stages of rigor mortis.

I noticed her pillow was on the floor and her mouth and eyes were wide open. Her arms were crossed over her chest and it looked as if someone had held her down and covered her mouth. In reading one of my mom's journals, I discovered they hadn't had had sex since the first year of their marriage and that he was also abusing her.

It was just a few days before that awful morning that my mom signed her life-insurance policy over into his name instead of mine. They had many fights about this throughout their marriage where he would scream, "When will you finally trust me to take care of you?" Apparently it was a wrong choice because as soon as he got the money from her life insurance, emptied her bank account and took off with my sister, leaving me on my own. I never saw or heard from him again. I still couldn't believe that my mother was gone from my life and I was truly all alone in this world.

I was never offered or received any therapy because we were way below the poverty level. I carried this heavy torch by telling my story to anyone and *everyone* that would listen and feel sympathy for me, which I hadn't experienced before. It wasn't until my late twenties that I eventually grew tired of and even despised being felt sorry for, so I stopped telling "my story'" except when certain situations called for it (friends feeling sorry for themselves, so that sharing my story could help them gain perspective). I had this groundbreaking thought that if I am still in pain or suffering from any of my past abusers, I am letting them win. Enjoying my life and becoming successful was the best way to win!

Not everyone is a seeker, but I became one out of necessity in order to help me unravel all the events from my childhood. Until we seek and find for ourselves, we remain reliant on others for answers. Everything changed when I began to choose differently. I went on my own journey and discovered that all those traumatic events from my past have become the greatest gifts I have ever received.

I wouldn't be the woman I am today if everything didn't occur exactly the way it did. I created fun games and exercises to help me transform all my pain into goodness. If I had known then what I know now, I could have saved myself years of wasted time and suffering. You must be a seeker too, because you're reading this book.

My whole life, people have always wondered why I was so happy all the time. In school, people often thought I was hiding something due to my jovial attitude, when I was just grateful to be away from home. If I can be happy now, so too can you! I am still the happiest person I know as an adult, committed to living the most fulfilling life possible. I have always wondered why there was no instruction manual for being a happy and healthy human when it's probably the most important thing one could ever have or do, so I wrote one. Nobody teaches us how to live our lives effectively and efficiently while having fun at the same time! Not until now, that is.

When I started my journey, the Internet was not an accessible thing, so the library or friends were the places I went to for books and learning. I even interviewed my teachers in school and people living at old folks home on different subjects to get different perspectives. Nowadays, information is everywhere. There are books, lectures, podcasts, blogs, vlogs, Youtube, Google, and Wikipedia, to name a few. Books used to take a long time for me to read until I studied the brain and developed techniques for efficient learning and how to read quickly.

Learning how the body, mind, and spirit coalesce allowed me to progress faster, creating more free time. The more free time you have to work on projects that make your heart sing, or to be still/quiet to find your own voice, causes more joy in the world. The more fun you have in this life gives others permission to do the same. People would rather work with and be around happy people. Lift yourself up and you lift up the world.

This book is the culmination of all the downloads from my life experiences, clowning, and Oracle sessions. I am a seer, able to see a person's highest self and feel their spirit. I am an intuitive, claircognizant, clairvoyant, clairsentient, psychic, Spirit Sheppard, and receive messages from benevolent guides offering solutions for people to remove blocks.

I am dedicated to innovations that get me and my clients closer to our goals faster. This book has become my success story. If you have a strong will, nothing is impossible. From a very young age, I saw there was always someone that knew how to do the things I wanted to do, so I watched those people, took on their habits, and took the same actions to bring the same results into my life.

It is my highest joy to lift people up and make a difference in this world. I am committed to you finding growth and gratitude for all your past and future experiences. I have dedicated my entire life to have the most possible fun in every situation! I can have just as much fun at a wedding as I can at a funeral. If everyone had more fun at their job and in their lives it would make all the hours you spend at work with those people more fun, or at the very least, bearable.

We feel good doing things we are naturally good at and things we love to do. Those are our gifts to the world and healing for all. It is important to recognize and understand what those gifts are, to be of service, and make the greatest impact. It's possible to create fun games in life, work, and play. You came to the right place if you want tools to get out of your own way. If you want to have more fun, this book is for you. If you want to have a breakthrough in *any* area of your life or get in touch with your inner voice, this book is for *you*.

INTRODUCTION

If you want to do a deep dive into personal growth, spiritual ascension and physical transcendence, you'll want to use the P.O.L.R. Living Workbook in conjunction with this book so you can do all the exercises along with each chapter where you can find on our website https://www.polrliving. com/. I could only fit one exercise in almost every chapter.

You can use this book like an oracle—sit quietly for five minutes, ask the Universe "What is it that I need to know at this time?" and flip to the page. You may want to read the book first to understand the concepts, but I can assure you using the workbook at the same time will allow you to easily maneuver through life to make great strides and unfold a deeper understanding of yourself, your greatness and your ability to conquer anything. Either way is perfect, because you are perfect and listening to yourself is the most important part of this whole process.

Because the world we live in and the current state it's in—the only way to avoid extinction is UP—we *must* **all ascend together** or none of us will. It is my greatest hope that something opens the door to your higher self, causing you to be a catalyst for others as we ride this Earthship into the stratosphere together. Out of the love that I have for you and all life everywhere—may this book be a blessing and gift in your life.

Peace for *all* beings & blessings to you and your loved ones—in service,

Jesselynn

CHAPTER 1

THE PATH OF LEAST RESISTANCE

*The path void of difficulty or unpleasantness; the easiest course of action aligned with soul's purpose.

Before embarking on your journey in order to take the path of least resistance, one must know everything about it, what the meaning is, what the writer means, and then what you make it mean. A funny thing about humans—we are meaning-making machines. We have a meaning for almost everything most of which are unconscious. An unrecognized facial move on another person's face or a delayed response may cause you to create several meanings from something simple—all of which are not true unless confirmed.

Throughout this book I have done my best to accurately describe and define my meanings for you, however, if you get hung up on a particular word, consider that I mean for the best possible outcome for your higher self which serves your life purpose. Let's start with getting down to the nitty gritty meaning of the title THE PATH OF LEAST RESISTANCE that will be referred to from now on as POLR.

P.A.T.H. ~ (Acronym) Personal Agreement to Honor

In order to go anywhere or do anything you must know what path to follow and where it leads. You do your research, map it out, and create your plan of action for any stops or sights to see along the way. Whether you're going a few blocks away or on a long road trip, you have a specific route you'll choose to take and honor that. In life, though, the path is not always clear. We hit roadblocks, diversions, branching paths without signs, collisions when we cross the paths of others. The destination may be shrouded in fog, or wholly unknown; a promising road may peter out in the trackless desert. We can find ourselves looking back on our lives thinking, "How did I get here?"

There is power in knowing and honoring one's path to take. This book is a step-by-step guide in doing just that. This path is a fun one, so buckle up and get ready to take the biggest journey you'll ever make—your very own life path. Make it sacred and honor it.

RESISTANCE - Referring to the negative aspects of this word which comes in many forms: the stopping of energy flow to something, an argument or judgment that it should be different, the pushing against with force; all of which cause suffering, pain, and trauma. Resisting *what is* drains your energy, wastes time and doesn't solve anything. Bypass all of it and go directly to the solution, allowing the unfoldment to inform you of your next move with grace and ease.

This book is a guide to living in accordance with nature in the most fun way possible! The path of least resistance is the one that nature takes. You can easily see it in the way that water flows or electricity runs through a conductor. Learning to get into your own natural flow creates less resistance, which makes it easier for you to do the things you've always wanted to do. We are nature, more than half your body is made up of water and we are electromagnetic beings. Resistance to your own nature is futile.

RESISTANCE TO GROWTH

You cannot have positive changes in your life when you have resistance to what is happening now or what has happened in the past. Each problem or circumstance is colored by your own perception. How you interpret and hold your experience will either allow positive changes or stunt your growth.

Use nature as a teacher to remember that anything happening or that has happened is done *for* you, not to you. Thinking you are the victim of your experiences will leave you mired in powerlessness, seeing only lost battles that you endlessly re-fight, and re-lose, in your mind. Believing everything in your life was done *for* you allows you to see positive possibilities and search for the gift even in difficult circumstances.

A plant doesn't complain about the pot, soil, sun, or water, it simply does its thing with what it's given. The plant has no opinion about whether the pot is too small or the sun too far away, unlike us humans who have opinions about everything and can stay mad or sad about things that happened decades ago. Plants don't have opinions or egos. Your ego is the only thing that separates you from nature and nature has everything under control. We are nature and also have this innate ability even when we feel like our lives are unlivable.

When we act in accordance with nature, we free ourselves from the chains of our ego. Our ego has kept us in a prison. Being imprisoned—behind bars or not—is something that you may have created but that you can alter by changing your beliefs. You may one day find the pot you were planted in no longer suits your needs and move to a much larger or different pot. The choice is yours, but be OK with where your seed sprouted.

All great things begin internally. Take time to know who you are and why you are here. Even rock bottom can be a solid foundation on which to build your life.

Point blank: resistance stops all growth and keeps you in the same place. Resistance focuses on the past, instead of looking into the future. What is it inside us that wants to resist so badly? Nature doesn't do this, so the more we can be like nature, the happier we will be.

The sun continues to shine no matter what it burns or destroys. The river keeps flowing even when it hits an obstacle. Rain is, well, rain, and it falls on those who welcome it and those who don't. So why do we try to outdo nature in this way? Because of the ego. It wants to be right. Sometimes our ego thinks things should be a different way, other than what nature (God) intended. This resistance is not only futile but it creates suffering in your life and affects the people you love.

When we look at the world around us we can easily see that all nature just keeps growing and evolving, as we are born to do as well. This does not mean that every day is a perfect day. But it does mean in every moment you have the option of making choices—knowing that there is always more than one choice in every given situation. It's up to you to inquire and discover which path is the one of least resistance and for the highest good of all.

This runs so deep in our third-dimensional world of duality (light/dark, good/bad, right/wrong) that we must address all possible outcomes in every facet and in all aspects of self. We will utilize tools for the mind, body, and spirit such that we can live in harmony in every area of our lives. A good life is where all areas are balanced and thriving. When you use the tools, concepts, and games in this book, you'll restore balance, harmony, and joy to your life.

Events in life will present obstacles and knowing that there is always an option to choose the path of least resistance allows you to fully explore all of the options that are available to you—critical thinking is paramount. You will not change anything if you continue doing things the same exact way; you'll have to get creative. The moment you choose to focus on finding the solution to the situation instead of resisting what has happened, you profoundly elevate the quality of your life.

Whatever happened happened, you cannot change it. Accept it and switch your focus to the future. You can use tools to get out of traditional programming, limited thinking, and social pressures to become a solution-based heart-centered ideologist, as well as a happy person in this lifetime!

When you are weighed down with the constant struggle against all the things you're resisting, it becomes extremely taxing on the mind, body, spirit, and can even negatively affect your health. A person that is taxed for a very long time becomes disillusioned and therefore set in their ways creating a closed-off mindset, unable to think of new possibilities because of the sheer stress of trying to survive. It is often hard for them to ever get out of their limited world or see any other solutions to their struggles. This can cause depression, and even suicide. The increasing rate of suicide in the US is alarming.

In school, we aren't taught the secrets of using natural laws, play, and open-minded thinking to create a harmonious life. I wrote this book because I felt it was time for a change. We deserve to know these powerful secrets.

A helpful tool to use when you find yourself resisting something you want is BreathPlay. BreathPlay is playing around with different breathing patterns to work through challenging thoughts, moods, or circumstances.

There are different patterns and techniques depending on the outcome you'd like, but all of them are beneficial. Incorporate the EMOTIONAL RELEASE BREATHPLAY EXERCISE at the end of this chapter to transmute negative emotions. You can do this practice daily and it is great for helping you get out of your own way. How much you get out of it is directly correlated with how much you put into it. You may also try an online BreathPlay class I facilitate in the comfort of your own home. Current class/retreat schedules are posted on the POLR LIVING website https://www.polrliving.com/.

LIVING A LIFE CHOOSING THE PATH OF LEAST RESISTANCE

P.O.L.R. LIVING was going to be the name of this book. POLR is the place directly between two magnetic poles; right in the middle lie the most possibilities, growth, and life, and where the path of least resistance lives. If you look at our earth ship that we live on—the north pole opposite of the south pole—both are VERY challenging to live solely at either pole. The center of mother earth is the equator, where the weather is nice and there is more vegetation and animal life. In the juicy middle is the place of least resistance, growth, life, and is the *heart* of the earth.

The human body has two poles: your head and crown chakra, and your tailbone and root chakra. Living from decisions made solely from either your head or sex organs would prove to be challenging. Your heart is the place in the middle, the sweet spot; living from here will *always* give you the most growth, possibilities, nourishment and is where your path to living a life of least resistance lives.

Everything in existence is constantly moving and shifting to seek balance. Balance is a lifelong practice rather than a destination. Your heart brings balance when you use proper tools and techniques coupled with the heart's intelligence. When this happens, life flows more easily.

We are meant to live a life full of love, for our heart was destined to reign in our royal throne body temple. Heart-centered living is where we achieve the juiciest life. Once we get back to our original selves we have more power, clarity, sustained energy, life, focus, intuition and inner/outer strength.

This book teaches you to live in your heart—the highest version of yourself—and how *not* to be triggered by your natural prehistoric brain and instincts. This is the part of your brain that runs all the functions you don't notice or even have to think about, like breathing or the function of your immune system. You will learn how to be in touch with your own flow, listen to your higher self, and become super electric (aware) in order to align your spirit, body and mind.

Be prepared to play games and have more fun than you've had in a long time! Understand that by living in accordance with the guidelines in this book your magnetism, confidence and libido will increase. Be ready to live the life of your dreams! I officially welcome you to the Path of Least Resistance Living!

GROUNDING

I am not talking about a form of childhood punishment here. This is a practice of personal recalibration to center your thoughts, feelings, and emotions. It's one of the most important things you can do for your well-being.

Life throws so many curve balls at us that it is easy to become ungrounded. When we are ungrounded we tend to resist even the littlest things because the input is too much to handle from an unstable platform. Once you ground yourself you can see situations as they are in a way that will help you make better decisions that are not emotionally based. Most people do not truly understand what grounding is or how to do it.

We are electro-magnetic beings. Even the electrical currents in your home or any place that has electricity in it must be grounded so that people entering it will not be shocked or electrocuted. This grounding also protects you and your appliances from dangerous electrical surges should lightning strike. We are no different. Learn to ground yourself to protect the people you love from the emotional shocks and lightning that occur when you are not grounded.

It is important to ground your own personal energy every day to protect you and everyone else that may be affected by a massive surge. Grounding into the earth is a great way to release excess voltage and give it back to mother earth for her to process for you. Try the next two techniques to start your day and whenever you feel stressed, emotional, or out of balance.

GROUNDING MEDITATION

Find a place where you can be undisturbed for at least five minutes. It is best to put your bare feet on earth or if indoors; sit tall or lay down with your eyes closed. Take three long, slow, and deep breaths into your abdomen. Upon each exhale, relax your body even more deeply. Visualize your tailbone growing roots just like a tree and penetrating deep into the earth all the way to the very center. Wrap your roots around the golden core of the earth and feel the energy transfer.

Continue breathing slowly and deeply. Imagine your roots expanding and gently dump any unneeded or unwanted energy deep into the earth's core. Feel the support and grounding of the earth. Take a few breaths to fully feel whatever comes up. Now, put your focus on the very center of your head, the spot directly between your ears where your pineal gland sits. Take a few breaths here to really feel it, pretend if you have to—then softly open your eyes to a half gaze, keeping your focus on the very center point of your head. Take five full breaths here and then gently close your eyes again. Put your hands on your heart and thank the earth for supporting you in your grounding process.

EMOTIONAL RELEASE BREATHPLAY EXERCISE:

If you find a particular negative emotion getting in your way or holding you back—this practice will set you free. If there is more than one start with the the strongest feeling first.

Find a comfortable sitting position in a quiet, private and dimly lit room. Elongate your spine stretching up into the heavens, breathing through the nose deeply and slowly for three full breaths, allowing your thoughts to come and go while your body relaxes. On the fourth breath in you will squeeze your Kegel/PC muscles (sex organs) and your abdomen towards your spine. In this posture you will contract and hold tight the entire area from your anus to your navel while lifting your spine up towards the ceiling. This is called Mula Bandha, which translates to root lock. Holding this position, you will breathe up the energy from the center of the earth, up through your core, into your heart where the energy will hug it from the inside.

Take the emotion you want to release and find where you feel it in your body. Notice where you feel the emotion (ex: fear) building in your body. Take a moment to feel it and then hug it from the inside. Focus on sending love there while breathing in white or violet light all the way up through your spine. With each breath hug & squeeze your root lock (sex organs) and your heart from the inside. If you are in pain or suffering, you can hug wherever it is that you want to hug.

Once you found the spot, hold your breath and continue to squeeze and hug it. Hold it for as long as you can, then forcefully blow it out through a tight round mouth—as if you're blowing through a straw. Still in root lock, you'll take the deepest breath possible in through your nose. As you inhale, imagine white light coming in from the top of your head. Pull it all the way in and fill up your heart and the spot you identified, holding it for as long as you can. Then, let out the air through your nose as slowly as you can and relax your muscles down into the floor.

Take as long as you need to process through each step, your body will let you know what it needs. Wait a few moments to see if the emotion is still present. You may have to do this several times for certain emotions. Once the feelings have subsided move onto the next one. Do not rush this process.

THE PATH OF LEAST RESISTANCE

The path of least resistance is a life lived in your flow in accordance with nature and your own personal guidance system. Adopting practices from this book will help you every day to step into your own natural power and ultimate divine birthright. You are beautiful, divine, one of a kind, and part of nature. Your specialness is unique and is celebrated. May you get out of your own way so that you can shine as brightly as you were designed to. Congratulations on choosing the path of least resistance! You are well on your way and there's no stopping you now.

Nature's Neat and so are you!

CHAPTER 2

YOUR SOUL'S PURPOSE

"When one person discovers their mission in life to serve, a thousand others can theirs."

The universe is magnificent and powerful. The universe never makes mistakes. It doesn't have to repeat itself; it is already perfect and supports the highest good for all. This is why it is essential to know and be aware of what it is you are putting into the universe at all times. Each of us are unique expressions of the universe, therefore we are all also magnificent and powerful.

Nature makes one of everything. This is because nature only makes masterpieces. *We* are nature. Every single living thing is a masterpiece in the museum and mosaic of life. There is no other, there never needs to be another one of us because we each have a piece of the puzzle within us.

However, we all need to work together because there is only one Earth made up of millions of systems. The ocean and forests are two different systems that include other systems inside of them. The food chain is a system. We harvest plants to eat and then put our waste back into the environment, which feeds the plants that give us oxygen to breathe.

We exhale carbon dioxide, which is one of the very things trees need to live, making us just a part of that system. Systems have to work together or they become broken. When things aren't working in your life it's because there is a breakdown somewhere in the system chain. You must investigate the complete system in order to discover where the weak link is to restore order and become sustainable. Regenerative sustainability is the only way humans can continue to thrive on this planet.

SHINING BRIGHTLY

There is an expansive multiverse inside each and every single one of us from the macro to the micro. We have our own energy just like the sun, and we are meant to shine like it too. We are the tiny stars in this human galaxy, and when we do not shine, we forsake nature. Shining is our purpose for existence. We shine the brightest when we are doing things in our lives that light up our hearts and fill us with joy. When our hearts are activated and happy it fuels us with energy and magnetism which others are attracted to. It is our duty to activate this endless energy source within us, so that we may be the light for others when they have gone dark.

Choosing to shine brightly helps others find their light. That's just how nature works. When humans live their purpose, they shine brighter and are healthier. No matter how great the challenge, everyone can access infinite positivity and find their light-hearted center. Your identity—who you think you are—goes far beyond what you can imagine for yourself. You can find your endless light, just like the sun. It is why we are here. Everything in nature points to this fact because after all, NATURE'S NEAT!

Your duty is to find out who you are, why you are here, what your purpose is, and to express it unapologetically! Your purpose can be discovered by anything that is coming up for you in this moment wherever you are. A plant grows where it is planted just like we do. Our purpose begins with where we are planted and then flowers from being in service. Ask yourself, what purpose is trying to emerge? Why was I planted where I am now? The universe doesn't make mistakes, so why were you planted in a specific place? Why were you born into this specific family? What did you gain from each of those answers?

Wherever a plant sprouts, even if it's in the middle of a street, on the edge of a cliff, or in a vast garden, it was the perfect environment, at the altitude, terrain, and under the specific conditions it adapted to. We are no different than nature. Just like that sprout, you had all the nutrients, the right soil and temperature, all those happenings, all those discoveries, and all those traumas that occurred in each specific region *for your growth.*

All of this, so you could produce the most beautiful fruit possible. Your fruit is going to be the juiciest, most delicious fruit but only after you discover what your purpose is. You must align with your purpose in order to have these positive changes in your life. You must be on a constant journey of discovery. Your purpose will continue to unfold the further you dig. Like digging for treasure or mining for gold, more of your purpose will unfold.

As you grow spiritually you'll refine your purpose down to the exact words that describe your true soul's purpose and nature. When I first began my journey I knew my mission was to help make this world a better place for all to live in. As I grew my spiritual practice and acquired numerous new skills and techniques, I have been able to refine it to what it is today. The overlying mission is always the same and now every word is hand-selected for premium quality and to fit to a tee what my soul's purpose is, which has been revealed to me through my meditation practice.

You then take on new skills to become a healer and a teacher, which satisfies your soul's purpose because you are living your passion plus being of service by helping humanity in the best way possible. Each soul is different and yours needs to be explored in order to find your specific underlying mission in this world by following your creative passions. Sometimes you have to try a lot of things to find out what that is, but it's the thing that lights you up and has the greatest positive impact on humanity that fulfills your soul.

Your soul's purpose is your personal underlying mission statement to the world. It is very specific to you and your desires. It is the very thing that lights you up and is the reason why you are here. If you don't know your soul's purpose yet, that's okay. You will have a better idea of what your heart wants with time as you practice the techniques in this book. If you have already found yours, that's great! If you don't know yet, complete the SOUL'S PURPOSE EXERCISE at the end of this chapter.

I've had clients that thought they knew what their purpose was, but after further self-discoveries and inner personal work they awakened to their real soul's purpose. The first go at writing their life's purpose mission statement was more of a self-serving one and as the person expanded their awareness, their true soul's purpose was revealed. Maybe as a child you always wanted to be an actor, and then after becoming an actor you find you want to do something even more meaningful.

BE OF SERVICE

Your thoughts, desires, and emotions are a guidance system to discovering your soul's purpose. What passions do you want to share with the world? Being of service is a human necessity and part of our nature. We not only desire to feel needed, but service is a way to show our love to the people we care about. Being without community goes against our very nature; we need structure, support, and connection. We cannot accomplish something truly epic solely by ourselves.

Helping those in need creates positive dopamine hits in your brain. Dopamine is a chemical the body produces that makes us feel good. We get higher dopamine levels when we hug someone we love, pet a dog, help others, or spend time outdoors in the sun. Being of service is one of our soul's purposes and lights us up. In this state you are able to generate the life force you need to feel good and to shine brightly. When you are lit up and on fire, you'll notice how the universe positively responds to you.

Using your gifts and talents to be of service creates healing for all. That is the reason you have the gift or talent to begin with. When others witness you shining your light, it gives them permission to do the same, which is where the healing occurs. The more present and more authentic you become in all the areas of your life, the stronger your intuition grows.

You gain power when you are able to distinguish, in the small thoughts and conversations in your head, between the ego and the inner voice of intuition. Your intuition will whisper which actions to take to move forward with your goals, whereas the ego likes to yell. Most of us have been trained to listen to the loudest voice, but attuning your ears to the softest one will take you farther. You can train your ears by meditating daily, even if it starts with five minutes working your way up to twenty.

When you fully realize your soul's purpose, you will experience all the love and freedom you have been searching for. Out of all the 1.2 billion competing sperm at the moment of your conception, the particular sperm that was the seed of your being broke the barrier and made it here, for a reason. You are here *on purpose* because you have a purpose.

It took me to the ripe old age of three to know what I wanted to do in life; to be an entertainer. I had to follow that path until my intuition guided me in another direction, which is why you are reading this book. Everything that happened in between then and now had to happen to make this book possible.

You may not have known what you wanted to do until more recently or you may still be searching. If you are still trying to figure it out you can do the exercises at the end of this chapter. BreathPlay is a great practice that helps one get in touch with the inner self and has thousands of health benefits that naturally come along with when you do it. We can thank Wim Hof for much of the scientific proof that the oldest medicinal practices known to our current civilization, Ayurveda and Yoga, didn't have research and studies to prove.

Our purpose is to make something beautiful because that's what nature does! What do you think the world needs most? What is your deepest joy and your greatest talent? Somewhere nestled between them is where your life purpose lives. What legacy do you want to leave behind? The important part is following your bliss to discover what your heart wants. Pay more attention to your positive attributes which help to lead you to what makes your heart happy.

We must let go of our past to plant seeds for our future.

DISCOVER YOUR HIGHEST SELF

Singer, musician, and activist Nahko from Medicine and the People says in one of his songs, "If I want to know God I must know myself. If I want to see God I must see myself. If you want to love God then you must love yourself." He was stating that everything is God and loving yourself and everything on this planet is part of loving God.

Your highest self yearns for love and healing for all. When you live your purpose you align with your higher self. Commit to the highest possible version of yourself in every moment that you can. What do you have to lose? You and all the people you love have everything to gain. The moment I made that decision, my life took a magical and delightful turn from the horrid path I was on to this epic ride into the never-ending sunset. My life purpose is to contribute to the elevation of humanity, utilizing my gifts and talents to be of service.

UTILIZE YOUR GIFTS & TALENTS

I believe the fastest way to complete happiness is utilizing your gifts and talents in such a way that you are financially compensated for them. There is an old paradigm of thinking that says, "If you are a jack of all trades, you are master of none", meaning it is better to pick only one thing and be really good at it than to develop multiple talents. I vehemently disagree with this saying.

When we love to do something, we are usually really good at it and therefore have the desire to improve. In his bestseller Outliers, Malcolm Gladwell states "In order to become an expert it takes 10000 hours of deliberate practice." That is approximately 10 years of dedication to make you a master in any field. You can incorporate all the things you love to do while in your current job or situation until you figure out something better to do.

When I was still in the corporate world, I had a job managing a store in the Beverly Center in Los Angeles, California. This was a place where people of all ages could come in and get makeovers, do their nails, get fresh face masks, and talk for hours. After I did makeovers for people they would bring up to the register the items they wanted to purchase. Each piece of makeup had a cute and fun name, so I would do an Oracle reading for them using all the names of the items they bought. I was able to incorporate my management skills, makeup artistry and psychic abilities all in one place. I had constant repeat customers, excelled at my job, and became the youngest sales manager in the company, all while having the most fun doing it.

The more of your gifts & talents that you bring to your profession, the less competition there is. If you only pick one thing to do for a profession—such as the occupation of a photographer—there will always be someone better or worse than you. When you are more than just one thing, say, photographer/director/clothing designer, hardly anyone can compete with you. If you honor all the things, or at least the top three things, that you love to do and include them in one single profession, you will be happier. The game is to bring more of you to everything you do.

OLD PARADIGM THINKING

Many of us have been told what to do for so long that it can be hard to know what is a true desire and what isn't. We have been taught never to question authority. For example, we used to think that one could never be successful unless they graduated from college. But some of the most successful people, like John D. Rockefeller, Walt Disney, George Burns, Charles Dickens, Henry Ford, Mark Zuckerberg, Russell Simmons, Steve Jobs, Bill Gates, Jim Carrey, Richard Branson, Elton John, Ray Kroc, Ringo Starr, Princess Diana, and Ellen DeGeneres, have all created a "New Paradigm" of thinking that broke that old paradigm. All of them either dropped out or never went to college.

Nowadays, in certain industries, even with a college degree you still cannot find a job. Just because people have been thinking one way for a long time doesn't mean that methodology is the only way to do things. The world is changing so fast that college educational books are outdated before you can read them. The cost is too great to keep the information current, so your education suffers.

The past is filled with things we can learn from but until we release the power the past has over us, we cannot be truly free. To let go of our past we must also let go of our "old paradigm thinking" to make room for the new. The first step is to identify *all* of yours. This includes any thought or belief that was once considered true in the past. Many "Old Paradigm" thoughts could get people killed in the past until the "New Paradigm" came along.

Examples of old paradigms replaced by the new:

- The world was flat, now it's round.
- Women had no rights, now in many areas of the world, we're boss ladies.
- Mothers stayed at home to take care of kids, now daddies can do that.
- Only men could be Rabbis, now, in some temples, women can be too.
- In many areas of the world gay people were killed; now in more progressive areas they can get married legally. The current Pope Francis says "Being homosexual is not a sin."
- Marijuana was considered the Devil's lettuce, now, in some states in the US, it's medicine.
- Witches were burned at the stake for having knowledge of plant medicine and now scientists and doctors study nature's healing properties.

COMMIT TO YOUR PURPOSE

When I was managing the beauty store, one of my employees wanted to go to a workshop but it conflicted with her work schedule. I reminded her that she had the ability to create what she wanted in the situation: to find someone to cover her shift. After she called every one of her coworkers to ask if they could cover her shift and no one was available, I let her know that if she needed to call in sick to work, she should do that because the workshop would give her tools to build her future.

She felt really bad about it and did not want to call in sick, so she showed up for her shift anyway. It was at that moment I realized how often we call in sick to our own lives. We shun our own desires, wants, and needs because we get trapped in commitments (that are often based on fear) which bring us only enough to get by but don't lift our spirits or build upon our future goals. We must think outside the box and get creative to solve the problem.

In 1999, the company I worked for was bought by its competition and shut down. It was then that I promised myself that I would only work jobs that aligned with my highest joy and calling. In the beginning it was one of the hardest promises I ever made but has had the biggest payoff. I had to work through all my old paradigm thinking and programming as well as my family's fears that I would not succeed.

I grew up in a culture that perceived anybody pursuing the arts as an idiot. They thought I would starve. I went through several phases of pursuing my dreams, kept true to my promise and it all worked out. Just like it always does. In fact, the only thing guaranteed to have a 100% track record of being true is that EVERYTHING ALWAYS WORKS OUT in the end! Why waste time and energy worrying or getting upset when you could just look for the solutions and get right to the good stuff? Committing to your purpose guides you right to the juicy parts.

If you want to be successful you must create a job for yourself that fills a need and that you also LOVE doing. Doing the things that get you excited fills the need for your soul to shine. I found a profession that allows me to do all of the things I love to do: entertain and perform, act, sing, clown, heal, Oracle, direct, choreograph, speak publicly, design clothing, make films, and write. There can never be anyone better at those things combined than me. I bring all these elements to everything I do.

The goal is to find or create a job where you can utilize at least three of your strongest talents in one place. Complete the STRENGTHS/

WEAKNESSES EXCERCISE at the end of this chapter to discover yours. Start with three and work from there. My list of strengths include bringing joy to others, inspiring and motivating people, seeing people as their highest selves, telling stories, making people laugh, giving love, and being present. People hire me to be myself. My old paradigm thinking never imagined this could be possible. New paradigm thinking makes it possible for anyone and everyone who does the work to make it happen (See OLD PARADIGM in chapter 7 CHOOSE POWERFULLY).

Doing the work fuels you to keep going and get creative, and makes life more fun, including the work you do. It doesn't feel like work when you are doing what you enjoy. By engaging in creative play you will discover new things about yourself. 65% of children right now will be in jobs that don't exist yet, so why not create your own right now?

(Now is the time to call in ALL your blessings-go make that wish!)

WISHING WELL

"There's nothing capricious in nature and the implanting
of a desire indicates that it's gratification is in the
constitution of the creature that feels it".
~ Ralph Waldo Emerson ~

It's very difficult to pass by a wishing well and not place your bet. You must possess both the coin and the wishful intention to then throw it into the well. When you throw the coin, the object of value, down the wishing well, you release your grasp and expectation of the wish. It can only come true when you release your expectations of how and when it's going to show up. That is why it is important to make sure your intentions are pure and that you are specifically intending to bring a certain thing into your life. Then, the wish comes true.

For example, instead of wanting an exact type of car, focus on the reliability of getting around the city or how you *feel* driving down the road in your car. Now this vehicle can show up in a totally different way—it could be a motorcycle or a motor home instead. Don't think that your intentions were never fulfilled because you didn't get that new Mercedes that you wanted. Maybe that specific car may have not aligned with your highest self or your soul's purpose.

ALIGNING WITH YOUR SOUL'S PURPOSE

Things will start appearing for you that are more in alignment with what you're trying to manifest, and the more aligned you are with your purpose, the easier things will come to you. The more sincere you are and dedicated to deepening your daily practices, the more accelerated your progress will become. You must let go of your wants at some point and trust that the universe will provide. When you don't, you keep sending messages to the universe that say, "I want this, I want this, I want this," however the real message is, "I don't have this, I don't have this, I don't have this" because of the sheer nature and desperation of not having it.

The universe will support your "I want" affirmation and continue to make sure that you do not have it! You must be willing to come from a place of abundance and trust that the universe will show up for you instead of putting out a constant barrage of wants, needs, and desires. When you say "I want" you are telling the universe that you don't have it. It is better to thank the Universe for things you want and even better to focus on the feeling you get by having the thing you want. Focusing on the "feeling" you have when you imagine already having it and then releasing your expectations of getting it, will bring it to you sooner. It may not be a trip to Mexico, but it could be another destination that is even better than what you originally thought. You must clearly put your intentions out into the universe and then forget them. Make a practice of becoming more in alignment with yourself so your intentions can come to you faster. Not doing this is pure resistance, so you end up blocking your own blessing.

You would not have the desire to do something unless you were 100% capable of achieving it. Whatever it is that you desire with all your heart can be yours if you are willing to put in the work to make it happen. If you do not know what you want to do in life yet, you must try new things and explore new territories instead of being complacent or telling anyone "I don't know what I want."

If you don't know what you want, it's a clear sign you must get out of your routine and do things differently. Try whatever comes to the periphery of your experience until you find something you enjoy. You can focus on your strengths and what comes naturally to you or get wild and creative. Think back to when you were a kid: what made you feel the most fulfilled, happy, and powerful? Try a week or two of saying "YES" to everything, especially when you may have initially said *no*. You'll certainly discover new things.

STRENGTHS / WEAKNESSES EXERCISE:

A strength is something that you are naturally good at and didn't have to learn. That being said, you can *always* grow and improve yourself in any area just as nature does. You could be a morning or night person, good communicator or listener, problem solver, leader, or team player. You could have a positive attitude, self-confidence, strong work ethic, or the ability to work well under pressure, to accept and learn from criticism, or be easily motivated.

For instance, I am super shy, I have to work extra hard in this area because it is a weakness for me, so I put it on my WEAKNESS list. However, because of all my efforts put toward this, people perceive that being outgoing is one of my strengths, so I write that down on the STRENGTHS column, despite how I may initially feel about it.

In your journal, create three columns. Label the left side STRENGTHS, the right side WEAKNESSES, and the middle column BETA, for anything you're not sure of yet—things you may or may not be good at until you test them or get feedback from people in your life. Maybe you thought you were good at something but your partner doesn't agree, or you receive mixed feedback and further testing and confirmation is needed. After testing each BETA item, you will either know right away if it is a strength or weakness or you will have to give yourself time to get feedback in order to decide if it ends up on your left or right side column.

After writing down as many of your qualities and abilities as you can think of, take a good look at all three lists. It is really important to know what your strengths, weaknesses and possibilities are, so you won't waste time and energy with the things you are not good at, nor want to get better at. Everyone has strengths and weaknesses, it's just how nature designed us.

A rose cannot provide its own sunlight or water whereas a human's abilities are harder to detect because our species is so varied. Knowing these qualities can help you in all walks of life. Even the most depressed person can still make someone else smile and that is a strength! If you are having a hard time with this, I suggest you ask your family, friends, coworkers, and anyone that knows you to give you some examples of each. It may be harder to look at yourself in this way at first, but that is what family and friends are great for.

FINDING YOUR SOUL'S PURPOSE EXERCISE:

You would not have the desire to do something unless you were 100% capable of achieving it. Whatever it is that you desire with all your heart can be yours. Keep this handy and add to it as you try new things and explore new territories. Answer these questions and list as many as you can. Write complete and full sentences starting with "I" statements—make it pretty and easy to read.

What is my highest joy? I am happiest when I am _____.

What are all the things you love to do? I love to _____.

What things make you feel the most powerful? I feel most in my power when _____.

What things make you feel the most fulfilled when doing them? I feel fulfilled when_____.

List all the ways you love to show up for your loved ones. I love to do _____ for my loved ones.

Is there a common feeling you have when doing all these things? What are those feelings?

What is trying to emerge in my life? What patterns or messages keep coming up?

What is your purpose or the reason you are here on this planet? I am here to ____.

Why did you incarnate in this body with this family and have the exact experiences you've had? I incarnated into this family to teach me _____.

CHAPTER 3

UNDERSTANDING YOURSELF

"God uses synchronicities and serendipity to light our path"

Once we understand the complex nature of what makes us who we are, how nature affects us, what our impact is, and what our values are, we can obtain the tools necessary to free ourselves so that we may nurture our soul's purpose. This is the heart of the matter, quite literally. You can only think about one thing at a time because thought is either coming from your ego and mind or your heart and intuition. This is why it is so important to be present, so you can choose powerfully in each moment.

Everything that is in your life right now exists because it provides more information so that you can make a more well-informed decision for your next move. For a successful life journey, you need to have full understanding of your situation. Our consciousness was not designed to inhibit us. When we do as nature does, the ego becomes a tool and cannot run the show.

An ego in charge makes you weak. Nature doesn't have an ego; it is mighty powerful as it is. The only thing separating us from nature is our ego.

Understanding all the similarities we have with nature is a way to grow beyond our limiting beliefs and confusion from the ego, and gain understanding of our own nature within. If you wanted to start a business, you would first do market research to find out which companies are already doing similar things so you could formulate your business to be better or different. Neglecting proper research and not having complete understanding of the market beforehand could cause your business to collapse.

You also wouldn't want to reinvent the wheel. Your research would highlight details that would help your company thrive and give you tools to use to create a successful business. Similarly, in our own lives, we often don't take into account our own place in the universe. We tend not to do our own market research.

Let's start our research at the micro level by plunging deep inside the one of the smallest particles: the atom. We wouldn't exist without them, after all.

"I am a miracle made up of particles."
Aloha Ke Akua ~ Nahko & Medicine for the People

ATOMS
Definition: //adm// ~ Noun
1. The basic unit of a chemical element.
2. A source of nuclear energy
3. An extremely small amount of a thing or quality. (www.OxfordDictionaries.com)

WE ARE ATOMS

From the quantum or micro to the macro and mega there are lessons to be learned all along the way which provide insight to living a more joyous and fulfilled life. Nature has answers to ways of being that we have previously been blind to. I wanted to find something in nature that behaves most like humans and I came up with the mega-powerful, all existing, 99.99% empty space—atom. On the microlevel each of us are made up of billions and trillions of them, so it makes sense that we would behave like them.

The properties of atoms are similar to human nature. Atoms attach to one another from the force exerted by the nucleus, essentially the heart of the molecule. When we follow our hearts, we attract everything we need. Atoms are obsessed with finding other atoms to connect with so that they can gain structure, sustainability, and strength. You can only be attracted to people and things that provide strength, structure, healing, and stability in life; just like the atoms we're made of. I believe this to be true for the person you are attracted to because that's exactly how nature works! NATURE'S NEAT!

Those feelings are designed for you to act on that connection and find out how you can help each other create those things. We need structure. We cannot achieve greatness alone. You too can be like the atom and connect to people that enrich your life, if you act on your heart's desires.

Imagine you are a very large atom floating around in space searching for another like-minded atom. You may see someone who you think looks interesting, attractive, or happy and you notice yourself attracted to them. What if you went over to that person and started talking with them to investigate *why* the attraction is there? The very desire to connect is not an accident. It is your spirit's way of informing you to communicate with that person for some unknown but important reason. Taking action is where the *why* will be discovered.

That desire is your intrinsic understanding of the strength, healing, growth, and structure that person can create for you. If you're either attracted or repelled; you'll notice a charge around it. If it's neutral then there will not be a charge. You have heard the phrase "birds of a feather flock together." Anything you like or dislike about someone is because there is a part of you that contains that quality. There is a GIFT in it for you both if you choose to find it and address it within yourself.

Those feelings are designed to have you act on that connection to find out *why* you are either attracted to or repelled by another. For now, let's just work with the feeling of attraction until you get the hang of it. Later, we can assess why we feel repelled by someone.

What if we approached our lives in this way and acted on this with everyone we met? What would that look like? Use nature as your compass. Acknowledging the connection or spark is the first step.

Your thoughts, desires, and emotions are meant to be used as a guidance system. Your task in this game is to act on it. Allow yourself to have fun with this, so you can get out of your way and see what happens. The ego cannot be present in this task.

Honoring your instincts increases your awareness and strengthens your intuition. The first step is to be bold and connect with people you feel called to, in order for the universe to show you the magic. Trusting in your natural instinct to connect, connects you further with nature, that person, and your higher self.

CONNECTION

Connection with another human in any way, shape, or form is an opportunity for growth, yours and theirs. We connect to relationships, people, things, and ideas for many reasons and they each have something valuable to teach us. Some connections cause sparks, so be careful. The answers to many questions about who we are can be found in every connection we have, if you're looking. They can also be discovered in the ones you don't have and want.

You can build confidence and learn how to be more playful by connecting with new and old friends. Teamwork, new skills and comradery can be learned through your co-workers. Taking on a lover is an opportunity to learn sensuality, communication and intimacy. It's important to keep the connection pure by being honest, compassionate, and kind because you never know what state a person may be in when you are connecting with them.

Humans need feedback, touch, and connection. In fact, science has proven that without it, we die. One of the first discoveries of this truth was in the 13th century. Holy Roman Emperor Frederick II conducted a rather cruel experiment to see what language children would naturally speak if they were never spoken to, nor were they allowed to be touched. The experiment concluded abruptly when all the babies died from not having any human connection.

Start asking yourself what lesson can be learned in every connection. These lessons are everywhere. Connecting with those you desire will uncover magic of all kinds. I learned a new recipe which then became one of my favorite cookie recipes—vegan gluten free persimmon—all by chatting it up with the mail lady. When you investigate your attractions, you just never know what will come from any of those connections.

When you become more conscious of all of your connections it opens you up to more possibilities. You can think of it as being *online*. When your computer isn't connected to the Internet you can't do your work. Being connected to your circuitry allows you to have access to all that life has to offer. There's a reason why we are connected to certain people, and there's a reason we're not to others. The feeling of connection can be good or bad, but the feeling is there for you to discover the lesson to be learned.

Communicate with them and find the magic together. I have even gone up to someone and said, "I just got this feeling that I had to talk to you for some reason" and then began to ask questions about them to get more information. Every time I inquired, I found the gems, whether they were from my hometown, have the same birthday or profession, or know a bunch of my friends. Perceiving and honoring the connection unleashes serendipity and reminds us that we are on the right path.

PERCEPTION
Definition: //per·cep·tion// //prsepSH()n// ~Noun 1. The ability
to see, hear, or become aware of something through the senses.
2. A way of regarding, understanding, or interpreting something;
a mental impression. (**www.OxfordDictionaries.com**)

PERCEPTION IS *EVERYTHING!*

Perception without application is simply a hallucination. Your perception runs everything you do, every thought you think, every outcome, and every experience you have in this world. We are either being programmed by someone else or we are writing our own code to erase the old protocols and create new commands. Everything is available to show you yourself so you have the ability to create whatever perception you want and look for those reasons that support what you want to create.

For instance, if you are chanting the mantra "Everything is working out—best case scenario!", you have the ability to not only receive what the universe provides but you also have the ability to go get it and make it a reality for yourself. When you change how you see the world, you have the ability to make the change happen. In every situation you always have the opportunity to make it your best possible case scenario with the tools you have available to you. Do your part to ensure the best case scenario using the exact perception and action that aligns you with the Universe/God/Universal Energy Field/Ether and is the Law of Attraction. It is called "being in the flow" or "flow-state" which we will go into in further depth later in the book.

It requires time. What holds you back are all those little things that you disregard or discount because you're either lazy, don't have the tools, or just aren't using the tools. Laziness feeds the negative aspects of the subconscious. Intentionally choosing the best actions to take will create the best possible outcome for yourself. It is what generates having the best possible scenario in all situations.

DO IT RIGHT—THE FIRST TIME!

Take the extra time to do things right the first time or you will have to waste double the time and energy to do it right anyway. Save yourself hassle and tweak it to make it right—from the very start.

Little adjustments make a huge difference. Even taking the time to maneuver things in your car when you're traveling with a lot of stuff such that you can both reach everything easily and see out of all your windows creates peace and ease, and saves time. Before I learned how potent this practice is, I used to slop my stuff in the back of the car, piling it all up until the windows were fully blocked. I had to pull over every time I needed to find something, and I couldn't change lanes easily. I ended up taking a much longer amount of time with all the stops and added blind spots, instead of taking a little time initially to arrange my things more safely.

Be aware of the lies we tell ourselves due to *being in a hurry* "I'll do it later." We *always* have time to do it right the second or third time, so save yourself time and peace of mind to do it right from the beginning.

EVERYTHING GETS BETTER

Nature is constantly evolving and so are we. We also have the ability to consciously make out lives better; especially by nurturing ourselves. All of those little actions of taking care of yourself send messages to the universe to also do the same for you. If you're not there for yourself, how will the universe know how to be there for you?

Whatever actions you take are the actions that support what you're committed to. You can commit to your success in every possible moment or scenario and ask yourself, "How can this be an even better experience?" It's a quick and simple, yet effective reminder. Each action you take to support this new habit sends messages to your subconscious that you're worth it. It feeds your mind, body, and soul because it's the highest possible version of yourself, for yourself.

Actions that support your mind, body, and soul bring you closer into alignment so that you don't have to work so hard or have feelings of regret, guilt or separation. It works when you work it. I challenge you a solid week of committing to yourself in every possible moment where you're bringing awareness to everything that you're doing and choosing the best case scenario. In order to change your life you have to assess what's going on and how you're showing up, and re-evaluate the way that you're doing everything. This simple game allows you to go through all the ways in which you do things to find all the leaks. These moments you don't follow your best case scenario or highest version of yourself leak your energy and feed your subconscious with negative messages.

SENSITIVE SUBCONSCIOUS

You'd be surprised how sensitive our subconscious is and how easily influenced we are by the people we surround ourselves with, or what we watch and listen to, as well as the actions we take. Everything we experience is recorded, including our memories, which are all stored in our DNA. That includes everything we watch on TV, with its permeating blue light that makes it nearly impossible to look anywhere else. We are imprinted by the shows we watch. Television programs trauma, drama, the protagonist, the evildoer, and that there's always someone else to blame. This is why they call it programming. Programming is used to control the narrative for the mass public to consume.

Game of Thrones was a show that attracted viewers of all kinds because of its great acting, amazing costumes, and beautiful locations. It was also extremely violent and focused on revenge; it was really good war propaganda. While watching the show, it generated feelings of wanting to kill or having people be killed. Everyone seeing the show banded together in the celebration of death, violence, and murder. Meanwhile, the subconscious of the watcher was being programmed to get us comfortable and even excited about war and violence. We wonder why there are mass school shootings when we let our children play all those shoot-to-kill video games and watch violent TV.

This awareness can be really seen and felt when you cut out all TV for a period of time. It's wonderful how sensitive we are but it's imperative we be diligent in what we expose ourselves to, no matter how seemingly benign it may be. Ideally, you'll even want to control all types of information you are putting into your head in watching particular shows—the same way you'd do for a child.

Choose your own programming or someone else will.

REPROGRAM YOUR REALITY

Luckily, we can reprogram our subconscious in many different ways once we are aware of what is going on. It's crucial to rewrite your own script so that you can have the best life possible. It's time that we take control of our thoughts, our subconscious, and our future. The more heart-centered the life we live, the easier it is to access all of the gifts available to us. In my youth I was abandoned, misunderstood, and abused. As I grew into adulthood I kept gathering evidence of those beliefs which kept shaping my reality unfavorably.

I had beliefs imprinted from the traumas and abuse in my childhood that as an adult I kept finding to be true because I was always looking for evidence to prove them right. Some of the beliefs were: No one loves me, Authoritarians abuse their power and can't be trusted, I'm a bad person, etc. The list went on and on but you can see that your child's perspective becomes your adult perspective until you question it. I didn't even know that I was being negatively affected by those ideas/beliefs.

Change your perspective and you change everything in your existence too. You can only see what you see, until you see something new. Luckily there is always more than one way to look at something. Look at every moment, no matter how intense or challenging, to see how you can make it the best-case scenario.

OTHERS' PERCEPTIONS

Not all perceptions are created equal. Any perception that only looks at one side of the coin is either lazy or self-serving, therefore limited. Limited vision is not only unsafe, but it usually ends up making people feel bad. Acting on judgments of others causes harm to them and you. We humans cannot see anything in someone else that we don't possess within ourselves, so we are constantly reflecting onto one another our thoughts, beliefs, patterns, and ideals. Often during an argument between two people, they both feel that the other is the problem when they're actually upset at the other person for having the same characteristics as they do.

We are all reflections of one another. I had a boyfriend who would constantly accuse me of cheating on him. He'd check my emails and search my phone for text messages and never found anything. We constantly fought for no reason and I somehow always had to defend myself and make it up to him, even though I hadn't done anything wrong. But in situations like this, it's important that we step back to take a deeper look at how we may have behaved that way in the past. This helps us take ownership of our issues and address them. As I've said before, the universe brings situations into our lives so that we can learn from them.

I decided to take some time away from my partner to really delve into myself to ask some big questions. I didn't want to let this slide by without due diligence investigating his side of the story. I wanted to see where I had cheated in the past so I could heal it within myself. In sixth grade, I had cheated on my Spanish final, but later realized, as an adult living in Southern California, that I could have really used that skill.

I really only cheated myself out of the ability to be fluent and communicate easily with those around me, especially because I am half-Mexican which I didn't realize until I reunited with my dad. I also cheated myself out of confidence and self-worth by not believing that I could do well on the test, which had its own implications later on down the line. Then when I came back to thank him for accusing me of cheating and I shared with him all the gold I got from it, he broke down and cried, letting me know he was the one cheating.

All this is to say that, even in challenging circumstances, we can take the opportunity to heal a part of ourselves, our ancestry, and our relationships by taking sole responsibility for the moments when we've also behaved badly. We all make mistakes at times and as we get older we get to be more of who we know we are inside through learning from those mistakes or challenges. Everything that happens is a gift when we choose to look at it this way.

FAMILY IS THE MOST CHALLENGING LESSON

Years ago, whenever I went back home to visit family, I had a horrible experience with one of my aunts. I have been extremely challenged and triggered by this person ever since I was a little kid. I always tried my best to avoid her because she was always mean to me.

Growing up, we had only seen each other every four to six years and then maybe once a year when I was in college. As an adult I tried to connect with her for her birthday, however both our perceptions of each other continued to color our relationship, which sadly was never great. Even though as an adult I had years of experience with the tools to build a relationship with her, I was still in trauma and would get triggered every time I saw her. I felt I had to defend myself from her constant attacks. It was only until this last visit where I was able to use all the tools in my toolbox to be loving and calm, and able to listen to her perspective.

She used to get all the attention from the family, but when I graced this planet and she grew older, she got less attention and was no longer the baby in the family. I was a rambunctious kid with a massive amount of energy and I still am for that matter! I was a lot for anyone, especially someone who doesn't have kids and is also very mellow. Everyone has a different perspective and it's important to recognize that.

On a family road trip, when I was around six, she was sitting in the front while I was in the back seat, right behind her. For some reason, she reached behind the front passenger car seat and pinched my leg so hard that it bruised and tore the skin. I thought I had gotten bitten by a spider because she never even looked back at me. I can not remember why she did it exactly; I assume it's because I may have been screaming, talking loud, or just being a childish brat. It sure worked and shut me up for the rest of that road trip.

This moment was a turning point in our relationship and in how I saw her. She had gotten physically violent with me whereas no other family member had at that time. It impacted me greatly. I avoided her as often as I could until I got older and stopped being afraid of her. The imprint was already made and my perception of her from that point forward was, "She is mean, I can't trust her or feel safe around her".

As soon as I was able to drive as a teenager, I wanted to visit her and get to know her better. She is family, after all. She lived near the beach and I thought it'd be fun to make a road trip with a friend to see what her life was all about. It didn't go well. Since it was an 18-hour round trip, I had a friend come with me to split up the drive. After we arrived, my aunt told me that I wasn't allowed to have any friends over. Because we were already there, I brought my friend to the clubhouse instead of my aunt's condo, thinking it would be fine because it wasn't technically her home. When my aunt came home she was so upset that I had a friend with me, she slapped me and kicked me out. We didn't talk for years after that incident.

GENERATIONAL CONDITIONING

I grew up in a time when it was socially unacceptable to spank your children and was considered physical abuse. Society had learned new ways that worked better so that we didn't have to use physical violence as a punishment anymore. I had been taught that it was not okay for anyone to touch you without your permission or hit you, not even your parents. This became my perception. So when my aunt pinched me on that road trip, and when she slapped me, I received it as abusive behavior because of my conditioning (perception).

My aunt grew up in a time when it was socially acceptable to spank and hit your kids. Parents would use anything they could grab right at that moment or even keep the tool in a special place for beating time, such as belts, spatulas, sticks, and more. To her, it was nothing and she didn't even remember the pinch. She refuses to see that there is any other perspective besides her own. When we don't have better tools to use, we go with what we have. She and I were raised with a completely different set of rules and beliefs which created clashing perceptions. Seeing another's perspective creates some peace.

When I went back to visit my aunt/mom who was being cared for by this aunt, I apologized for all the misunderstandings. She quickly became infuriated, calling me names and telling me that she hasn't considered us family for years and then asked me to leave her house. She doesn't remember doing it and believes I made it up for some reason, all because we have very different perspectives.

We were both hurt and felt betrayed in the past. I could only see certain things about her and she could only see those things about me, always coloring our perceptions because we constantly look for those things. I recognize how I kept propagating the stories from when I was a kid because anytime I had an interaction with her, it sent me into a triggered state. Pain and trauma triggers more pain and trauma until one person can step out of it and see what's really going on. Unfortunately by the time I was able to step out of my old patterning and apologize, she had already given up.

PLAY THE O.P.P. GAME (OTHER PEOPLE'S PERCEPTIONS)

It's important to know what or whose perception is correct. In order to know that for yourself, you must be consistently making heart-based decisions and actions by not reacting from fear, anger, or sadness.

Any perception coming from the heart or done in love will have the highest good. You will know it's from the heart if everyone feels heard and understood. Even another's wrong perception of you can be a gift and an opportunity for you to grow. Everything in your current field is there for your growth. Pointing your finger at someone in blame points three fingers back at yourself. In times when it's confusing and you do not know who's finger to follow, you can easily decipher it yourself by playing the O.P.P. GAME.

By playing the OPP game in the case with my aunt mentioned above, I was able to fully investigate where I have acted out and reflected those names she called me. She can't trust me and thinks that I'm a liar. I can see now where I lied to myself all those years and therefore created this seemingly irreparable relationship. So many misunderstandings compiled upon perceptions and blame. Yuck! Until you shift your perception you will continue to get the same results and see the same patterns occurring in your life.

Another OPP opportunity; I had a roommate who constantly interrupted me. She would also yell across the house things which I could never make out because I was in another room. I wasn't even sure she was actually talking to me because she talks loudly on the phone and to herself. When she first moved in, I would run out to the living room asking her to repeat what she said and most often it was something that had little or nothing to do with me. While other times I inquired about something she'd reply "I already told you." I used to work from home and since writing is a very internal and quiet process, I was unable to get any work done with her around.

Even when I do something very mundane like washing the dishes, I am still working out the details of my book and need that time to myself to think. The constant barrage of chatter caused me to lose my train of thought over and over even though I asked her to be considerate of my space and not interrupt me during my work day. Asking her didn't work, so I had to start wearing headphones as well as a fluorescent orange sign above my desk that read: "PLEASE DO NOT DISTURB ME WHILE I'M WORKING! Do not talk to me or ask me questions. Pretend I'm away for 8hrs at an office job. Thank you~Management". Unfortunately, that didn't work either.

The final straw happened when I had a meeting at my home with someone to help me with my book, and the moment my friend walked in the door, she railroaded our conversation to talk about something that happened to her that day. It was hard enough to get people to come and help me with my book, and on both occasions, she hijacked all their time to talk about her problems. She was the only roommate in 14 years that I had to kick out in under a year, whereas all my other roommates had stayed for at least three years. I was upset and annoyed at the constant disrespect until I turned the projection into self-reflection in the OPP GAME.

I wrote lists of all the times I railroaded, interrupted and hijacked people's time. In my self reflection, I discovered that I was being very selfish, self-absorbed, thoughtless, and rude. As a child, I constantly interrupted people, and I remember my mother yelling at me for it. She told me to wait for a time when the conversation quiets to interject. I often find myself having to interrupt people, but I wait for a good time and then also ask, "Is this a good time to talk?" Especially when calling someone, because you are catching them in the middle of something they are doing, it's crucial to ask them if they have a moment to talk before you start in on your needs.

Looking at all the ways I have done the same things it has allowed me to have compassion and forgiveness for my ex-roommate—she is a wonderful person. I had to heal that part of myself by diving into my soul wound. I was doing those things because I felt desperate and alone and believed that no one listened to me, coupled with being an excited little kid wanting to share things right when I thought about them.

I was also only able to see the problem in her because it was a problem inside of me too. I was immature and didn't have the tools to be any different then. When you are a kid you generally just think about yourself, just as I was by getting upset with her for not giving any thought to my needs. I was able to put myself in her shoes and then was able to rectify the situation from this newly self-reflected state.

I like to play this game for all forms of criticism and names I've ever been called. I take whatever people say to heart so I can assess the situation for myself even when I know in my heart of hearts they are wrong. This does not mean for you to take it personally and then hold a grudge, nor does it mean to get depressed and suicidal. It means it's time to get to work. It is simply a piece of information you didn't have earlier and now you can use it as a tool for healing. Heal yourself and you heal the world.

We funny little humans have the superhero ability of compassion. When we look from our hearts into another's soul we can ultimately understand any way of existing. We've all at some point gotten upset, flown off the handle, or said or done things we didn't mean. It's important to recognize what's true and what the heart wants in order to prevent breakdowns in communication. You can consciously choose to lift yourself up above reactive behaviors from yourself or others, which creates the space for all those around you to do the same. Forgiveness is essential. Understanding other people's perceptions is putting yourself in their shoes, which helps you both understand one another better. When we allow our light to shine as bright as we can, we become the star we are.

STAR
Definition: //stär// ~Noun
1. A self-luminous heavenly body held together by its own gravity, in which the outflow of that same energy then balances energy generated by reactions from within the interior to the surface.
2. The principal person in a production.
(www.Merriam-Webster.com)

WE ARE STARS

We are, in fact, made up of the same materials as the stars inside the Milky Way Galaxy: carbon, oxygen, nitrogen, hydrogen, phosphorus and sulfur. It's no wonder we are as powerful as stars because we *are* stars. A star's responsibility is to shine. One star's shimmer doesn't dull another's brightness.

You are a unique star here on earth and it is your responsibility to act as such and shine the brightest that you can. Do you think a star uses partial energy to shine? Do you think that a star says "Naw, I'm too tired, I'll shine tomorrow"? No way! A star illuminates the sky as brightly as it can because that is its very nature. It is our nature too! We are meant to shine as brightly as we can so that another may find their way to the light. In this movie called "Your Life," you are "The Star."

Results from behaving like a star include increased magnetism, renewed and heightened energy, spreading bright brilliant light, guiding others to find their purpose, attracting attention, lifting others up, influencing the future and designing your personal destiny. Who are we not to shine? For those of you that believe in God, it's like kicking Him in the face, because it is our duty to shine. When you illuminate your entire being you have full potential, power, and presence where you can use your intuition to guide you to one synchronicity after another.

INTUITION
Definition: //in·tu·i·tion// //int(y)ooiSH()n// ~Noun
1. The ability to understand something immediately, without the need for conscious reasoning.
2. A thing that one knows or considers likely from instinctive feeling rather than conscious reasoning.
(www.OxfordDictionaries.com)

STRENGTHEN YOUR INTUITION

Strengthening your intuition is not something that just happens automatically or by doing the exact same things you have already been doing. You must choose to trust yourself to grow it consciously. It is an active practice made easier by using the tools in this book. As for courage and optimism, intuition can be cultivated.

Every single one of us was born an intuitive being and has this ability and there are many ways you can use it. In caveman times, our ancestor's six senses were essential for survival. Most of us are familiar with the five senses: sight, hearing, smell, taste, and touch, which correspond to the five sense organs of the human body, namely, eyes, ears, nose, tongue, and skin. Anything outside of your normal senses is considered paranormal. Those sensations are called the sixth sense and are directly connected to your intuition.

Until this sense is exercised and regularly practiced it may feel like you don't have this ability, but I assure you, we all have it somewhere deep inside. As a kid I had "seen visions" & "known specific facts" that I would have no way of knowing and never had seen with my own two eyes, however my sixth sense (third eye) showed me images and gave me information to help my soul along its journey. These gifts and talents are most often misunderstood and shut down by those that do not experience them.

Try these tips to improve trusting your intuition (inner voice):

- Pay close attention to your daily thoughts and feelings, spending more time on the positive and constructive thoughts and no more than 60 seconds on any negative one.
- Tune into someone you care about and guess how they're feeling. Validate with them whether you were on target or not. You can say something to the effect of "It feels like you are upset, is that correct?"
- Meditate. Meditate. Meditate. I don't care how you do it, just do it every day, even if only for 5 minutes. A meditation practice allows you to start hearing your inner voice and interpret those messages. There are several meditations in this book, however just holding space to silence the mind is a great start.
- Practice balancing all six of your senses and see what each is trying to communicate instead of relying on just one. If you're eating, try to distinguish each ingredient in the dish by taste and then smell separately. Do blindfold touch/taste/smell tests with friends. If you are a wine drinker, this is a great game to play with friends to discover all the notes in each glass of wine.
- Connect with animals to experience a connection that doesn't have an agenda with you.
- Take action on your inner voice by testing your hunches.
- Practice free flow journal writing.
- Look closer for messages and signs everywhere. Pay attention to what's in front of you and keep track of synchronicities in your journal.
- Pay attention to your dreams by keeping a dream journal. Then interpret the messages from your higher self.
- Get creative. Make things with your hands.
- Consult Oracle cards with your favorite theme (spirit animals, sacred geometry, Angels, etc.). My current favorite is the Isis Oracle deck.
- Get into nature and see what it has to say. Hug a tree. Get into a staring contest with a flower.
- Go on vacation and let yourself be guided by the messages or intuitive hits you receive instead of planning every move out.

- Practice psychometry. Meditate holding an antique to see if you can discover any facts about the object or who it used to belong to. If nothing comes to you off hand just pretend and then look it up or find out the answer—you may be surprised. This is either a natural talent or one that comes from being an avid meditater.
- Garden and talk to plants. They are a direct connection to source.
- Read books and take classes to further develop your psychic abilities such as Sonia Choquette's Trust Your Vibes, Shakti Gawain's Developing Intuition or Caroline Myss's Sacred Contracts. Go to www.MagicalMysterySchools.com for the full spectrum of Spirit, Mind, & Body education classes. See the RESOURCES page.

Meditation is by far my favorite tool to increase intuition because it's free, I can do it in the comfort of my own home (naked—if I want to), and there are countless ways to do it that will surely fit any mood you're in or outcome you want.

Others keen on meditation:
"To the mind that is still, the whole universe surrenders." ~ Lao Tzu
"Stillness is the altar of the spirit." ~ Paramahansa Yogananda
"Quiet the mind, and the soul will speak." ~ Ma Jaya Sati Bhagavati
"Meditation is the art of doing nothing." ~ Naval Ravikant
"Meditation is not evasion; it is a serene encounter
with reality." ~ Thich Nhat Hanh
"Suffering is due to our disconnection with the inner soul.
Meditation is establishing that connection." ~Amit Ray

MEDITATION INCREASES INTUITION

In nature, you can only see your reflection in a pond when the water is still. It is only when you are still like the water that you are able to see your own true self, your pure nature. The truth of everything reflects back to you when you are quiet enough to hear the messages. Still water is like a person in meditation. To distinguish the difference between all the mind chatter versus your intuition, you need to get quiet and sit still long enough as you lovingly wipe each thought away—creating a cleared cache to receive downloads.

Meditation not only increases your intuition, it improves your mental and physical wellbeing as well. Billion dollar business executives boast that it boosts business. Meditation is mandatory for athletes, Navy Seals, CIA operatives, and even schools in Canada because of its peak performance traits, so why not try it for yourself to see what all the hullabaloo is about?

MEDITATION INCREASES PRESENCE

I encourage you to try any of the meditations from the www.POLRLIVING. com website. It's a terrific resource when you're on the go so you can do it anywhere! A great time to meditate is right in your car right after work and before you greet your family again. Put on a quick ten minute meditation so you can be more present in the ways you'd like to show up for your family before going inside.

EMOTIONAL CONTROL

In every moment there is an opportunity to grow. You can manage your wellbeing and state of mind in any circumstance. You can achieve mental balance even when something crazy is going down by simply managing your emotions.

Neuroscience shows us that every emotion, thought, and feeling creates an electromagnetic pathway in your brain. The more often you experience that same emotion, the stronger the neural network gets, which is why it becomes more difficult to alter course and change behaviors after doing something the same way for a long time. Many people are addicted to their emotions because the sensations from that repeated feeling is familiar and comforting.

In every moment, there is an opportunity to read the language of your soul that your body is trying to communicate to you, which is your emotional guidance system. We have the ability to change the way we feel by changing the thoughts connected to it. Everything you feel is connected to a thought and every thought you focus on is a choice.

Heartmath Institute discovered thoughts are electric and emotions are magnetic. You can synchronize your breath, mind, and body to create new electrical grids. Your breath is connected to your spirit as the great yogis and Ayurveda teaches. If you don't believe that, then stop breathing! You'll notice right away it's not an ideal choice. People can live without their brain, or without their body, but they cannot live without their breath. You can bring awareness to deepening and slowing down your breath when you feel stopped.

Fear is the most common emotion that stops you from everything you want to do in life. Notice when you are in a fear state how shallow and shortened your breath is. Never act out of or make decisions based on fear unless your life is being genuinely threatened. Most people live their whole life reacting because of a fear of something. It might be a fear of how hard something will be, so they continue to do something they hate instead.

Once you understand which feelings or emotions stem from different parts of your brain, you can then choose your own feelings. When you hide to protect your fear or insecurities you actually just magnify them, storing up more energy that will make it harder to free yourself from fear. Few can look at fear objectively. We are not our fears and can choose different actions in spite of fearful thoughts—this is courage.

Fear is commonly thought to start in the amygdala, otherwise known as the lizard brain, which, when activated and engaged, cuts off access to your heart. The reptilian part is the oldest part of your brain and is responsible for many of our survival instincts. It is also the hardest part of the brain to alter without the proper tools. Something as simple as a loud sound can trigger your lizard brain into a flight, fight, or frozen state. The moment you feel yourself tightening up, make a conscious decision to let go. It's the opposite of what you feel you want to do in that moment. Now, obviously, if there are real threats in your environment, e.g., a bombing, gunshots, etc., you may want to take cover, flee, or fight, but use sound judgment.

When you close your heart you are protecting your ego, which is the weakest part of you. Some people protect themselves so well that they never experience growth or any real connection or intimacy. The tendency to hang on to fear builds the energy behind it and keeps you stuck. Allow yourself to first examine every emotion and feeling as a spectator instead of identifying with it or immediately claiming it as your own. Question everything until you know what's running your life. Allow your consciousness to access your energy first instead of your lizard brain.

When you think you can't open any more, dig deeper and choose to open up and the rest will follow. When you are activated in a negative way (triggered) it is a sign that your heart is closed. When your heart is closed, there are no solutions, only more problems. Unfinished experiences will linger until they are resolved. When you resist, you get stuck. Often you'll find yourself on a negative thought loop. Spinning out is your mind's way of trying to solve the problem when it doesn't have the answer. Only your heart knows the real answer. Dramatic or impactful incidents can create impressions on your psyche. These psychological imprints are called Samskaras. They exist below the level of normal consciousness and are said to be the root of all impulses as well as our innate dispositions.

SAMSKARA
Definition: //sam·ska·ra// //sam' skär// ~Noun (Sanskrit)
1. A purification ceremony or rite, marking a major
event in one's life. (www.OxfordDictionaries.com)
2. In Yogic philosophy, the mental impressions left by all thoughts,
actions and intents that an individual has ever experienced in
this and all lifetimes combined. (https://www.yogapedia.com/)

Samskara (a word in Sanskrit, the mother of all languages) is an impression caused by a blockage or trauma and is where we get the term "scar" from. You could say it is a scar on your soul or spirit. When a Samskara is activated or triggered, everything presents itself as evidence to stay in protection mode.

Clinging to or pushing away energy is wasteful. Your heart is capable of opening even further than you think is possible. We keep recreating situations and triggers until the scars are healed. To achieve this state, simply allow the experiences of life to come in and pass through your body without taking them on yourself. If old energies have come back up it's because you were unable to process them before. This is your opportunity and a clear sign to let them go now.

It's actually easier to let it go than to hang onto all the pain and trauma wrapped around it. Fill your heart with gratitude and allow the Samskara to be released. Stored pain causes suffering and kills all growth. Giving gratitude for the trauma before you know what will come of it, speeds up the universe showing you reason for it. Trust that all is happening for you in perfect time.

In order to understand any emotion, you must break it down from why you want to feel it and how it feels in your body. All emotions are created from your thoughts. You can ask yourself "What would I be thinking if I was feeling happy or excited?" Start with that and then reverse-engineer by working backward from there. What feeling or emotion are you having? Now name it. Ask yourself what thought you are having right now as you feel this feeling. Use the Emotional Release BreathPlay technique for this as well.

WE REPEAT WHAT WE DO NOT HEAL

We repeat what we do not heal. History repeats itself and so do we. We re-experience the emotions and sensations from the past lessons we did not learn. It is our spirit's way to heal in this life so we can move on in the next phase wherever that may be.

We continue to attract painful situations and experiences similar to those in our past until we heal ourselves from the initial pain and trauma of our past. This pain may cause you to feel lost or empty and unaware of where to turn for help. Those thoughts and feelings we have about ourselves that we don't like, we tend to hide. We don't want anyone to find these things out about us, so we tuck them far away, even from ourselves. They can be scary to face, so to cope we repress those qualities so deep in our souls that we can only find those traits in another reflecting them back to us.

By using the tools in this book and practicing the art of powerful choosing, you can work through anything. Past negative emotions will no longer have power over us when we create new neurological pathways in our brains. We are a series of habits but we can reprogram ourselves. The world reflects to us, allowing us to see the pain again, so we can heal it within ourselves. Once you heal the original wound, it no longer has power over you. You can turn your wounds into wisdom. Anything that comes up for you within your experience of life is there for you to heal and grow from.

Emotions are such a powerful force. Your emotions are there to show you many things so that you can experience healing and get the best and most out of every situation. When you unlock your emotions and your full potential, you thrive with vitality and enthusiasm, free from obstacles blocking your path.

First, we must identify our limiting patterns, behaviors, and beliefs. Many of our limited ways of being come from family and loved ones, and some come from TV programming. It's important to ask yourself, "Is this what I really believe?"

Most of my preprogrammed, limiting beliefs came from my family and people I looked up to as a kid. They would say their truth and I automatically believed it because it was right for them and that's just how I thought life was. I never questioned them until I started my deep dive into self-mastery.

It wasn't until I was in my thirties that I questioned the phrase that repeated in my head since childhood, "Desmonds can't sing," and realized that I didn't actually believe that about myself, despite being a Desmond. I spent twenty years behaving as if this was my reality, preventing myself from singing all those years just because I overheard my beloved favorite aunt's declaration about our family as a kid and went along for the ride. Unfortunately, this is what happens until we begin to question.

The thing is, truth changes as you obtain more information. I pray the information in this book helps you to know a more fulfilling and rewarding truth. Know thyself and discover the true you. Millions of people around the world have realized a newly empowered life, thanks to knowing themselves and taking action on their dreams and goals. You can, too! What are your projections for your new life?

PROJECTION
Definition: //Pro·jec·tion// //prjekSH()n// ~ Noun
1. An estimate or forecast of a future situation
based on a study of present trends.
2. The presentation of an image projected on a surface,
especially a cinema screen. (www.OxfordDictionaries.com)
3. The act of visualizing and regarding an idea
or the like as an objective reality.
4. Something that is so visualized and regarded.
5. Calculation of some future thing.
6. The tendency to ascribe to another person's feelings,
thoughts, or attitudes present in oneself, or to regard
external reality as embodying such feelings, thoughts,
etc., in some way. (www.Dictionary.com)
7. The forming of a plan: SCHEMING 8. Transforming
change (www.Merriam-Webster.com)

PROJECTION

Projection is a very helpful self-healing mechanism where we identify what's wrong or right in another person, even though the issue is within our own self. The images we see come from our little box, our thoughts, beliefs, and ideas called the mind. We must use self-reflection to heal all those issues we have with others as if it is our own, so that we can finally stop repeating the vicious cycle of victimhood and blame. We project on others what we need to heal within ourselves.

TURN PROJECTION INTO SELF-REFLECTION

Every time you project, you point at something or at someone else. Every time you point your finger at another, there are three pointing back at you. Turn that same judgment towards yourself so you can identify where you have been the same way, then address that. Every projection is an opportunity to heal a part of yourself that is begging for it or you wouldn't be able to see it in another in the first place. Take the opportunity to turn projection, yours or others, and turn it into self-reflection—just because you can!

Even when I was very young I was interested in the study of the human mind—especially the minds of psychopaths. I felt that maybe they just didn't have all the information they needed to use their powers for good things and found it fascinating that they didn't feel like they were a bad person. Everyone tries to do the best that they can in every situation with whatever tools they have available to them. We are of this world and are just like the earth, other planets, and the stars. We have the same ability to heal and cleanse ourselves in all the aspects that we are, which is why we project onto another what we need to heal.

CLEANLINESS IS NEXT TO GODLINESS

The earth has many rituals for cleansing, fire, flood, and even ice, as the fossil records suggest. It has live cleansing organisms such as bacteria, protozoa, fungi, and worms. Our bodies are no different. As the earth self-regulates and cleanses itself, so shall we.

We must clean and align ourselves *daily* so that we will not destroy relationships or cut off possibilities for growth. Begin each day with a clean slate—otherwise it's energetically colored by the previous day or situation. Cleanliness *is* next to godliness. We must also cleanse our Spirit just as we clean our homes and physical bodies. Besides a shower, a great way to clear yourself or your space is a smoke ritual.

SMOKE RITUAL

You must only use pure ingredients to burn (No synthetic perfume incense), such as palo santo, sweet grass, sage, copal, frankincense, or myrrh. First smudge yourself from head to toe—including under your feet. Going clockwise starting at the front door of your home wafting the smoke all the way around your house, in every room—be sure to do extra on windows, doors, and mirrors, until you end up at your front door again.

If you feel called to use these words during your smudging, say them with power in the tone of love:

> "This body is of the Light. This body is of God.
> This body is of the Light. This body is of God.
> All others must leave now, and forever.
> This home is of the Light. This home is of God.
> This home is of the Light. This home is of God.
> All others must leave now, and forever."

VICTIM MENTALITY

This is one of the most significant problems in the world today. We must get away from playing the victim role and take responsibility for our lives. It is not because of someone else that you suffer, it is your own response to the situation and the beliefs you put in place because of it.

Victim mentality gives you a list of excuses so you don't have to look at your own behavior and how it contributed to the situation. It provides you with a list of reasons why you're not receiving your happiness, or why you're not getting the things that you've been praying for. You must take responsibility for your part in making or allowing situations to happen to you.

What did you believe about yourself that you allowed someone to treat you that way? Many people don't have any idea what that responsibility really means. People get stuck in the pattern of blaming other things like your astrological sign, your parents, your partner, your job, or the financial circumstances you were born into. This mentality will keep you a victim and never let you rise above to receive all the blessings that you deserve as your birthright.

You must be willing to dig yourself out of the victim mentality in order to harvest your fruit (see CELEBRATIONS & PRESENTS GALORE Chapter 8). Victim mentality lives in the soil. The soil is already there. There's no sense in hashing over, getting upset, or refusing the soil you were planted in. Get over it. It's time to focus your energy on things that you *can* change and disregard the things you cannot. It's futile to think otherwise. If you are sick and tired of being sick and tired, you are most likely standing in your own way.

No one and nothing could ever hold you back other than yourself. You are the only cause for your growth or your stagnancy. There is no one else to blame, and no other person is powerful enough to stand in your way. You must ask yourself important questions to get out of your own way (See CHOOSE POWERFULLY Chapter 7). It's the same idea that when you throw a piece of trash "away," there is no actual "away" place. The idea that problems are "out there" is absurd because there is no "out there." There is only "you." If you heal what is in you first, it heals "out there" too.

You must be accountable for how people view you and receive your energy and be responsible for what everyone says and does because they are in your experience. We are constantly co-creating everything. Healing yourself is not only good for the divine, it's also for the highest good for everyone and everything. It is your responsibility to heal everything that's goes on in your life if you want to change it. Anything coming into your awareness is up to you to clean up and clear the energy. You are the creator of your experience; therefore, it is your obligation to heal it. Otherwise, you'll be living like in the movie "Groundhog Day," repeating it forever.

You can control your experience of life or you can continue down the same road, as most people do by pretending not to have control over anything.

Remove the "victim veil" to learn what is real and what is not, so as not to be controlled by the falseness. Both victim mentality and time are constructs made by man, not nature. Nature does not live by the limits of victim mentality or a clock. We must get back into alignment with our nature because NATURE'S NEAT!

Nature's Neat, & so are YOU!

CHAPTER 4

NURTURING AWARENESS

AWARENESS
Definition: //a·ware·ness// //werns// ~Noun
1. The knowledge or perception of a situation or fact.
2. A concern about and well-informed interest in a particular
situation or development. (www.OxfordDictionaries.com)

Awareness has many layers, like an onion. You may be aware of who you think you are or how high you can reach, but I can assure you that it's not even close to the infinite potential inside of you. I am constantly striving to be better or more efficient in every moment, which requires my constant due diligence: consciously being mindful and thinking about being aware in order to have awareness.

Every person and even generation might have their own way of saying something. For instance, millennials say, they're "woke." In order to be aware, you must be awake. If you are asleep physically, emotionally, or spiritually, you are cut off from your ability to be fully aware. Full awareness comes from paying attention to your surroundings, moments, and to the people in your life.

In every moment there is the opportunity to be consciously aware of everything that is going on, your emotions, the past, your internal world, etc. As you read this, you can read and understand it, but until you integrate it into your life these are just a bunch of words and concepts. Consider that all the people in your life are there at the perfect time, and all you must do is figure out how they fit into your puzzle. Consider that everything you experience is to show you yourself.

Every moment could bring an opportunity for you to heal the past and change the future according to how you respond or take action. To do this, you must have a great awareness and be physically, emotionally, and spiritually awake. Awareness is not found in what you do, rather its discovery is in "how you do it."

Every action, whether it be as mundane as doing the dishes or shaking someone's hand for the first time, can be an act of love if you bring your awareness to it. This awareness is also called mindfulness. We all have free-will, you have the power to choose.

"This is a free-will zone ~ If you didn't have the freedom to choose It wouldn't mean anything." ~ My dear friend, Alicia Marie ~

We are constantly making choices, but choosing with full awareness is where great power lies. You can choose to be aware or not, it's as simple as that. Awareness allows you to know when you are in the shadow or in the light, and both are very informative.

AWARENESS OF BOTH DARK & LIGHT

Light creates purpose and coherence. Dark creates distortion (confusion, forgetting, anxiety, feeling lost) so that light can find its path by creating structure. The darkness teaches us many things when we bring awareness to it. When there is shadow, you must acknowledge the darkness and seek tools to guide you back on track. If the world has turned you away from the sun, you can turn yourself into the light by choice.

Remember, creation has two children, light and dark. It is impossible to see only light, for when light hits things it creates shadows. Shadow is creation's other child and should be treated as such. Shadow is sacred and is there to serve us, too. You can investigate why the shadow appears in order to bring it into the light again and continue on your journey.

You will never be able to remove either light or darkness from your life, but with your awareness you can learn how they work together. You can't see your own shadow when you're in the dark. As soon as you turn on the light, a shadow appears. The closer you are to the light, the bigger your shadow gets; in fact your shadow completely surrounds you.

FAMILY AWARENESS

All families have a way they view life. I grew up in a family where nice behavior often wasn't the reality behind closed doors, but to the world, the neighbors, or anyone else, we looked like the perfect family. That's what I was born into and what I get to heal. It taught me to be aware of all my actions and words and how they affect people. I was always aware of how my actions or words would make my family look. It created a hyper-awareness on top of the fact that I had to be the perfect kid so I wouldn't be a burden on people.

My running program was that I must be a joy to be around so people would love me. This underlying awareness tainted my entire life experience until I became aware of it. Imagine how hard it would be to keep up that perfect behavior in all relationships! It would have been nice to be awake then, it was exhausting.

AWAKE
Definition: //a·wake// //wāk// ~Verb
1. Stop sleeping; wake from sleep. 2. Not asleep. ~Adjective
(www.OxfordDictionaries.com)

This chapter introduces you to the many wonders this book has to offer, but we will go further into each of these concepts in the following chapters. For now, I want you to bring your attention to how your brain works and what contributes to your levels of awareness. This way, as we continue through the book and dive deeper, you will be able to easily swim along.

FIGHT OR FLIGHT

Our lizard brain has our bodies react to stress like it's life or death.

To survive over the millions of years humans have been on this planet, we developed a fight or flight (FOF) reaction that is controlled by our autonomic parasympathetic nervous system. The fight or flight response causes a physiological chain reaction in the body that starts when we perceive a danger that threatens our survival. If a lion was chasing you, FOF would kick in and you could instantly run faster than you ever have before. You would be more agile, swift to react, and quick-thinking.

What happens to the body during a (FOF) fight or flight response? The nervous system causes your adrenals to release the hormones adrenaline, noradrenaline, and cortisol into your bloodstream, which increases the heart rate and raises blood pressure.

In modern times, this system still kicks in when we're stressed or are encountering a difficult situation, even though most of us don't have to run from lions anymore. A person who is constantly stressed out may be in this

FOF state all the time. Having this high level of cortisol streaming through your veins all the time lowers your immune system, decreases bone density, causes inflammation and weight gain, increases your cholesterol, and puts you at risk for heart disease.

Unfortunately, sometimes our FOF is triggered when our ego feels threatened, and it reacts the exact same way—as if we were about to be eaten by a lion. The difference now is that the body may release adrenaline and cortisol when we encounter something as simple as another person saying something that hurts us. It's important to be able to recognize when your natural FOF response springs into action. Do not let your ego trigger the FOF and cause sickness in your body or limit what is possible for you and your future. I will talk about some techniques to interrupt the FOF response later on.

Most people cannot see beyond the FOF response because they are not aware it is even happening. Some may even be aware that it happens but might not know how to manage it or even what it looks like exactly to get a hold on it. When a situation triggers our ego or an unresolved trauma, FOF kicks in, making it very difficult to see past those feelings of anxiety, anger, or panic to the big picture. (See Big Picture Thinking in Chapter 9). We fall victim to our natural responses, creating unnecessary suffering until we gain awareness of our reactions. We are creatures of habit and routine. The tools in this book are to help you not fall victim to your natural automatic responses and create new habits of awareness so that you may nurture the exact life you want to live.

Choosing not to react when in a fight or flight state gives you time to acquire the tools or knowledge to respond intelligently and make a well-informed decision in a situation that may feel highly emotional or scary. Something that has already happened cannot be changed, but the present is not the past. You have to be aware of this so you can get out of the trap of your brain's automatic responses and make space for a new response in the present. This ability to choose is part of our nature and therefore a wonderful thing to be aware of. With more awareness, you may choose to react from your heart or a deeper intelligence instead.

When you take every upsetting situation at face value and don't investigate your natural reactions, you will experience unnecessary suffering. That is where most of us go wrong. When we have an awareness around it, we can choose something different or better. (See Choose Powerfully, Chapter 7). I am not asking you not to feel your emotions or to just blow off bad feelings by brushing them under the rug. What I am asking is *very different* and I'll discuss this more later.

SLOW DOWN YOUR MIND

We live in a fast-paced world with a "click-now" mentality and we're getting technology devices handed to us at a very early age. We don't have time to talk on the phone anymore, let alone drop by to visit each and every friend or family member like we used to. Using full words or phrases in speech or text takes time and feels like a chore. In our verbal speech we use abbreviations such as TMI and LOL. Some of us even abbreviate small two- or three-letter words due to this feeling of not having enough time, such as: For=4, be=B, see=C, are=R, you=U, why=Y. Since everything is speeding up in the world, it is integral to slow down your mind and listen to your heart so you can see straight.

When I was a kid, if I strolled by a friend's house and it looked like they were home, I would stop and visit. I took my time, never rushing, and my mom never worried about me. It seems like the world is speeding up the older we get. Time especially flies when we are having fun.

We have new gadgets to help us do things quicker and more efficiently, and all of it right now. It's important not to get caught up in the "I need everything RIGHT NOW" mentality, so you can have a clear understanding of what is really going on in the moment, as well as the proper mindset to plan your actions accordingly.

We can access different parts of ourselves by changing the speed of our brain waves. Our brains have five wave states: Delta, Theta, Alpha, Beta, and Gamma, each with a very distinct purpose to help us behave, think, move, and process the world we live in. We also have the ability to modulate and vacillate between these waves for optimal growth. How good we get at moving between wave states determines how well we cope with daily stresses, rational or irrational thoughts, or performing any task at hand. When I was a kid, I was either having a brain freeze or a brain fart, both of which cut-off access to my memory, and I wouldn't be able to continue my sentence or regurgitate the information requested. My brain was moving faster than my mouth.

BRAIN WAVES

Gamma (30-100Hz): The Gamma frequency is the fastest and is associated with bursts of insight and high-level information processing. Seasoned meditators such as Buddhist Monks have been reported to experience Gamma waves well into 200Hz and 300Hz.

Beta (12-30Hz): Beta brain waves are present in normal, everyday consciousness where people are alert and able to use logic and critical thinking. Higher levels translate into stress, anxiety, and restlessness—that's where the inner critic lives.

Alpha (7.5-12Hz): Alpha brain waves are present when you are deeply relaxed or daydreaming, usually with the eyes closed. You can go into this state when you take a bath or relaxing shower, or when you go lay down for bed. You can access this relaxed, detached awareness of your subconscious mind through light meditation. When you are in an Alpha state, it is an optimal time for reprogramming your brain with new thoughts or mantras. Higher levels heighten your imagination, visualization, memory, learning, and concentration. This is the state I use for most visualizations.

Theta (4-7.5Hz): You achieve this through both light and deep meditation as well as REM dream sleep. It is the state where you can consciously heal yourself or others. I have several friends that are Theta Healing Practitioners and it always amazes me how effective their work is. Theta is the silent realm of your subconscious mind and where you experience a oneness with the Universe and a deep spiritual connection. Vivid visualizations, great inspiration, profound creativity, intuition, as well as your mind's deep-seated programs reside here. You can access this state through certain types of breathwork—take one of my classes online https://www.polrliving.com/. I use this state when working with my clients and for quantum learning.

Delta (0.5-4Hz): This is the slowest of these waves, which puts us in the deepest relaxation so that our bodies can get restorative sleep. This is where awareness is detached and your unconscious mind, Universal mind, and collective consciousness lies. This state is often achieved by monks because they practice meditation all day long, although they have the ability to go even lower according to new studies. In this state you can regulate your body temperature and other bodily functions, master matter, levitate, etc. We have several cycles of this state in a full night of sleep and our brains secrete DMT. There are photographs of monks sitting in snow meditating and all the snow is melted around them.

MEDITATION TO HARNESS YOUR BRAIN WAVES

Meditation is one of the most powerful tools to gain control of your brain waves, and your daily experiences, to decrease suffering and to increase awareness.

There are many ways to go about meditating. You can meditate instead of medicate to alleviate pain. You can train your mind to do anything, especially if you practice meditation regularly. It has been my salvation.

Meditation has proven to reduce stress, increase self-awareness, improve willpower and confidence as well as make changes in the brain to improve self-control. Children with ADD and ADHD can be taught how to meditate before being prescribed methamphetamines to treat the issue. Meditation calms and focuses the mind, making it a far better solution than giving kids drugs to do the same thing. Often children raised taking doctor prescribed legal speed have addictions and emotional issues as an adult.

People who meditate regularly have more gray matter in the prefrontal cortex, which is responsible for making decisions, emotions, muscle control and all your senses, so having this part of your brain more developed will benefit your entire life. The health of your mind, heart, and body improves with regular meditation and it helps to stabilize metabolism, lower blood pressure, improve heart rate and breathing, and regulate brain waves. Tension and tightness seep from muscles as the body receives a quiet message to relax. You can use a simple meditation to transition between the brain wave states listed previously. Breath and mind work in tandem—as the breath lengthens, brain waves slow down.

If you have never meditated before, start with simple meditations first. For beginners, concentration can be extremely difficult; even an advanced meditator has to gently go back to the stillness after a thought pops in. Go to a quiet place without distractions and make it a special time for you by lighting a candle and/or incense. Set an intention and ask for guidance. You can play meditation music, binaural beats, or simply sit in silence.

I recommend sitting with your spine perfectly straight with your eyes closed, feet firmly on the ground if you are in a chair or cross-legged. Simply allow yourself to relax and become aware of your body, the space around you, the sounds, and the scents. When thoughts pop up, let them go gently and without judgment. Slow down your breath and be sure to take full inhales into your abdomen and fully exhale all the stale air out each breath.

Focus on your breath filling your body up and then empty out. Sit here for as long as it feels good, or you can set a timer. Begin with at least 5 minutes every day in the morning right when you wake up and before you go to bed. You can add another time midday depending on your stress levels. The more you meditate, the less stress and anxiety you will have. Download the P.O.L.R. LIVING MEDITATIONS from the www.POLRLIVING.com website to make it really easy to sit back and relax while tuning in. The goal is to do it every day and work your way up to thirteen minutes and then 20 minutes twice a day. My current practice is 30-45 minutes twice a day. There are days when I add another session to manage my emotions, ground, or relieve stress/pain management.

AWARENESS + INTENTION x ACTION = TRANSFORMATION

Consider that everyone and everything that is coming into your life at this time or has come into your life in the past is here for the healing of not only you, but the planet. I'm not asking you to believe this, I'm asking you to play a game of what is possible. Awareness is a multi-layered onion, which is to say, it can make you cry at times but there is so much to discover as you peel away each layer. In the uncovering process, you become a new person who then delves even deeper into more layers that uncover even more levels of complex richness than you ever thought possible.

This exploration can feel like a never-ending black hole in which you lose track of time and your senses, but exploring it will bring you so much satisfaction. Being aware of something you'd like to change on its own isn't as powerful as adding your specific intention to it, followed by an action, which creates a new reality. Stronger awareness builds your intuition.

Adding your intention and an action around your awareness causes the transformation to happen. Generally, the first thing you think about in a given situation comes from your gut instinct or your intuition, and then ego steps in to create confusion. Your heart knows what it wants. I want you to know the difference between thoughts coming from your heart or your ego. Expanding your awareness will do just that.

Consider that everything happens for a reason, and it's your job to figure out what that reason is. In every situation you can use questions to gain even more awareness. When you find yourself in an overwhelming situation, ask questions like, "Why was I supposed to be here tonight?" "Who was I supposed to meet?" "What did I learn?" etc.

Keep questioning until you have complete understanding and all your answers. You either affect or infect people. Some people are awake and live in a constant state of amazement. Most people are asleep and live in blame (the victim mentality). Being in this unconscious state makes it so that you can't live your life the way you want to. It is a sickness that can turn into a terminal disease. It is our responsibility to heal that disease so that we can free others from that same sickness.

YOUR INNER GUIDANCE SYSTEM KNOWS

A good friend of mine and I were discussing intention versus ego and confusion. We came to the conclusion that if you have to ask, then you already know the answer. Your heart always knows what it wants and your mind/ego likes to create confusion. You might think that you don't know the answer, but I can assure you— you are the ONLY person that does. Everyone else's answer is only *their specific answer.* Only *you* know what's right for you in that moment. If you have to ask, you already know the answer.

Asking is the mind's way of getting validation from someone else, when only your heart can answer it. For example, maybe you are considering a big career move or dealing with a family situation. When you are with your trusted friends and the question comes out—"Should I move to Colorado?" "Should I go on this vacation?" "Should I break up with them?" "Should I ask for a raise?"—your heart already knows you want to, or you wouldn't be bringing it up in the first place.

Recognize that the very reason you're asking another person you trust is to gain confidence in what you already know you want to do. Humans need constant validation on almost everything. When our intuition is strong, we can be free of asking others to validate us. If you have to ask, you already know what you want but aren't aware which idea/thought is coming from your heart or ego. Your heart is aware of and always knows what it wants. Ask yourself "What would love do in this situation?" and you'll have your answer. Usually the option that is best for you is best for all involved when it's coming from a pure loving state. It's good practice to be mindful of what your heart wants.

MINDFULNESS
Definition: //mind·ful·ness// /mīn(d)f()lns/ ~Noun
1. The quality or state of being conscious or aware of something.
2. A mental state achieved by focusing one's awareness of the present moment, while calmly acknowledging and accepting

one's feelings, thoughts, and bodily sensations, used as a therapeutic technique. (www.OxfordDictionaries.com)

PRACTICE ACTS OF MINDFULNESS

If you want to grow your understanding and awareness in life, you can achieve this by practicing acts of mindfulness. It's amazing how few people do this despite how simple and effective this daily practice is. Perhaps the phrase is confusing to you, or you may not know where to start practicing mindfulness with all the distractions we have in the world now. You can begin by starting with the easier ones and then include more as you evolve or are willing to take on more.

ACTS OF MINDFULNESS

As your awareness grows you become more mindful. This mindful state provides freedom from overreacting or unnecessary suffering and generally increases your quality of life. A person living a mindful lifestyle is healthier because it relaxes the FOF and increases immunity—there have been several studies done on this. Here are some games to increase your awareness of your daily actions. Becoming more aware of the little habitual actions we all have can help you strengthen your "awareness muscles."

UH's & UHM's AWARENESS GAME:

This is an awareness "game" to play with friends & family where each person tries to catch the other one saying "Uhm" or "Uh." You can create your own rewards or punishments depending on who you are doing it with. You can also just play on your own. Because of my efficacy addiction—the way I did it was to combine one of my other goals; getting fit, into the punishment. Every time I would say the mindless word, I would drop down and do five pushups. Using empty words such as "uh" or "uhm," or for you Frenchies, "beh," does not contribute to any conversation or speech and it is better to simply pause and say nothing until you know what your next words will be.

Ego is very excitable and always wants to speak first, but it doesn't have anything of real value to say, so all that comes out is "uhhhhhhh." Using these words comes from an unaware or mindless place and wastes time and energy. Because these words do not come from your mind or heart, they take away from what you are saying and don't make you look as intelligent as you are.

Take a moment to think before answering questions or communicating to others, it lets them know you take it seriously and are respectful of their time. Mastering this will make you ready for public speaking. Once you bring your awareness around it, you can remove them from your vernacular altogether. Consider opting to avoid them in all conversations so that your real message comes through powerfully and with grace.

FOOD MINDFULNESS

As you sit down for every meal, imagine all the people involved that it took to get your meal on your table, such as the farmers that grew it, the drivers that trucked it to the stores, the grocery cashier that rang you up, and the person that prepared your meal. I like to send love and gratitude to all those people in my prayer before I eat and bless my food.

Look at your food. Pay attention to the color, texture, taste, etc. What part of your body has the same color as that food? Imagine as you eat that specific thing that it is feeding/healing the part of your body associated with the color/texture. For example, when I eat cauliflower or walnuts I imagine my brain improving its memory.

Eat slowly. Try chewing each bite at least 30 times or more before taking another bite. It's better for your digestion and allows you time to absorb more of the nutrients you are putting in your body, as well as other things that may press on your mind.

OBJECT AWARENESS GAME:

Make it a practice to always put things back where they belong or where you got them from. You'll have to be mindful of where you got it from so you can be mindful again in putting it back in its place—especially for things that are not yours. No one likes taking the time to search for things, especially right when we need them.

LEAVE IT BETTER MINDFULNESS GAME:

Leave every area you occupy better than it was after you were there. For example: When living with roommates and you cook a meal for yourself, be sure to clean up all the spilled food and oil splatter on the counters, stove, and floor so your roommates don't have to clean up after your mess. Pick things up off the floor or ground that do not belong there as you spot them. The trash clutter in your periphery takes a toll on your subconscious as "The Tipping Point" book explains. Take out trash, recycling, or compost as it's needed. Everyone appreciates a clean space.

STUFF AWARENESS GAME:

Bring mindfulness into every room in your home. Tidy your home by creating the perfect spot for every single item you own. When you have things thrown carelessly into corners and drawers, you begin to develop the same kind of clutter in your life too. Completing this task throughout your entire home may take a little more time, but it will save you years of time looking for things and save you money from having to buy double when you can't find something. I wouldn't have been able to do this without the book "Spark Joy" by Marie Kondo. This one act of mindfulness has profoundly changed my life for the better.

Everything in your home has an energy to it, from the item itself to the way you feel about it. It is either contributing to or taking away from you until you address it. If there is something in your home that doesn't feel good or doesn't have a purpose, it's time to consider fixing it, giving it away, or removing it from your house.

For example, that cracked tile at the front door that bothers you—fix it; the vase that your ex gave you or the outfit that doesn't flatter you that brings yucky feelings—give it away. Often a friend will be better suited and very happy to receive the item—a "perfect fit." If you have negative feelings about any object, it's a good indicator to get rid of it. If it has a purpose, such as a vacuum, even though you may not like looking at it, since you prefer to have a clean rug you keep the purposeful object. You don't want anything in your home that takes away from you or triggers negative energy.

TRIGGERS
Definition: //tri·ger// /'trigr/ ~Noun
A small device that releases a spring or catch which sets
off a mechanism, especially in order to fire a gun.
The cause of an event or situation to happen or
exist. ~Verb (www.OxfordDictionaries.com)

AWARENESS OF TRIGGERS

Triggers can be deadly— they cause a chain reaction of behaviors, most of which are unconscious and keep you in pain and suffering without any way out. The trigger is the most dangerous part of a gun because it is so easy to press. Once it's pulled, it cannot be undone.

There are many different types of trigger locks for guns to help prevent accidents and the mishandling of firearms. Locking the trigger for safety ensures that only people qualified to use it, can. You must also prevent your emotional firearm from going off to eliminate any further casualties. By the end of this chapter you will be armed with the knowledge on how to do this in your life so that you stop hurting yourself and others.

Being aware of your personal triggers before you react is a way to put a lock on your psychological firearm before inflicting damage or injury on anyone.

In our lives, we have developed many triggers from past experiences that we unknowingly continue to fire off at the people we love and care about until we become aware of those triggers. A trigger often first feels like an annoyance, followed by a negative emotion or reaction such as anger or withdrawal which can cause a downward spiral that fires off more triggers for you and others.

Consider that whenever you are triggered it causes others to pull their trigger too. Think of it like you are psychologically pointing a gun at someone's head. We all know what happens when one person pulls their gun out: everyone else who has a gun does so too. This is no different.

Triggers are negative thoughts, feelings, unpleasant emotions like irritation, frustration, or anger, and reactions that we feel due to another person's actions, a series of events or personal issues. Triggers are also caused when you are in your FOF and feel threatened in any way. We might be triggered by a difficult boss, family members, a nosy neighbor, or situations such as watching a scene in a movie that reminds us of a past trauma, or finding that we're overdrawn at the bank. Triggers bring up old emotions from painful times or bring up painful thoughts that may cause us to act from our emotions in some way. We might yell or say angry words, withdraw from our partner, or have a panic attack when we have a triggering incident.

Usually, when we're triggered, we're not in real danger, but if you are in danger or are being threatened, disrespected, or injured in any way, you must immediately get out of that situation and call for help or get to a safe place.

If you are affected by something that happens or by something that someone does in a negative way, it means it is the shadow side of yourself that needs to be looked at. Your negative reaction is a trigger. When something happens that doesn't affect you, and there's no trigger or charge around it, then it is simply information. Triggers exist to give you the gift of remembering a part of yourself you have hidden away for so long. Often triggers stem from unresolved trauma and pain.

When you developed the initial trigger, you were a very different person than you are now. In traumatic situations, we tend to push certain traits away until we discover them again as our future self to heal it. It is important to accept that old part of yourself, so you may be free from that pain and suffering.

If you feel an emotional charge around any situation or person it's an indicator to address unhealed wounding or trauma. By healing it in yourself you will not be triggered anymore and therefore the person who triggered you before will not have to deal with the gun pointed at their head and may also be free of it too. They will no longer be negatively affected by your old triggered reaction when it is no longer a trigger for you. With proper and effective non-violent communication skills there is no need to raise your voice at anyone to get your message through.

One of the earliest triggers I can remember was when I was around five or six years old. I had just left foster care, where I had been for a year in California, and was sent back to Nevada to stay with my favorite Aunt Barbara. I never liked wearing shoes. It was the middle of summer and her driveway was black asphalt. It was so hot you could fry an egg on the ground. I had been begging her for an ice cream cone and she finally made me one.

I wanted to eat it outside underneath the tree in the front yard. She told me I couldn't go outside unless I had my shoes on. I was so angry that I threw the ice cream cone on the ground. I cheated myself out of my own treat because my ego was triggered, which put me in fight or flight (FOF) mode and I reacted without thinking. I lost my treat when I lost my cool and I was the only one that lost something and suffered. Every time you get triggered and react, you not only lose your cool—you lose your treats too!

When you lose your cool, you cheat yourself out of the things that you desire and want. All for what? It's simply being a victim of our nature. This happens every time we react from our triggered ego.

We retreat into the FOF mode instead of taking a breath, focusing on the solution, and taking action from there. We must learn to take pause, gain awareness, and react from the heart. I know I was only a little girl at the time, but that lesson stayed with me my whole life. Dissolving triggers harnesses the ego and empowers your spirit, body, and mind to engage. Mastering this technique aligns you with your whole and complete self and is beneficial for everyone involved.

IDENTIFY YOUR TRIGGERS

In order to stop being triggered you'll have to assess what your triggers are, how they come about, who in your life makes you most susceptible to being triggered, and what states of being are more likely to lead to you being triggered. When I am hungry, tired, not speaking up for myself, or upset by something or someone is when I am easily triggered. When we take care of ourselves and our needs it is easier to avoid being triggered altogether. Become aware of what triggers you by completing the FOF Freedom exercise. The more often you identify your triggers, the easier it is, not to have them at all. Once a trigger is dissolved you are free of it because you have identified and healed it.

FOF FREEDOM EXERCISE (fight or flight): Simply begin to notice what triggers you and write them down. Every time you become triggered, notice it but *do not react* in that moment—give yourself a pause to think. Let the other person know you need a minute and they'll see you are being responsible with your emotions. If you have to leave the room—do it, otherwise take three full deep breaths before responding or continuing about your day. Every time you experience the FOF state, make a note of it in your journal. Write the date and answer the following questions for each trigger:

> What just happened?
> What emotions did the experience make me feel?
> Is this how I truly feel inside?
> What is the best possible outcome in this situation?
> What would make me happiest moving forward from here?
> What could I learn from this experience?
> What outcome does my heart want? What would love do?

Continue to answer these questions for every single trigger, until you know your baseline. Most of us, including me, have been way off track for so long that this might seem wild and crazy at first. You have been doing things the same way your entire life and perhaps there is a different way. They say the definition of crazy is doing the same thing repeatedly and expecting different results. All I'm asking you to do is to try something new for 90 days.

IDENTIFY OTHER PEOPLE'S TRIGGERS

Learning what triggers other people will allow you to prevent another person's bomb from going off in your face. I grew up watching the TV show MacGyver. He was able to make any tool out of whatever was lying around in order to save lives. He could turn a paper clip, string, empty toilet paper roll, and a can of hairspray into a bomb. MacGyver could defuse any bomb in seconds and you can too once you learn how. When you start recognizing triggers, you prevent your own bomb from going off as well as others.

Doing this practice for 90 days will get you into the habit of recognizing your own triggers and makes it easier to identify when other people are triggered as well. As you practice learning to disarm your own triggers by using the tools in this book, you can help others when they are in that state. You do not have to take on other people's junk, be it their fears, insecurities, victimhood, scarcity mentality, poverty consciousness, or anger issues. The first order of business is to *not be triggered by other people's triggers*.

As soon as you identify the trigger in someone else, you can investigate where the real issue lies and address that. Then you can respond to the person's needs by holding them accountable for their greatness rather than responding to their trigger or the words coming out of their mouth. Whatever the person says during that triggered state is coming from their ego and is not the real issue. Do not negotiate with their ego for you will not get anywhere, it's like talking to a wall. Going in circles with a person's trigger or ego will most likely cause you to be triggered. That means both of you end up losing.

There is nothing worse than a lose-lose situation. You must quickly locate the need not being met so you can focus on the solution, to get them out of being in that triggered state. With practice, you will become really great at defusing human bombs, yours and others. Being able to turn negative energy around in any situation quickly is really fun to do and a great skill, and now people call me in to mediate for them. It is also a great way to master the energy in a room and I love being of service in this way— helping people hear one another.

For example, imagine you have been working late every night this week and have not had time for your partner. Your partner keeps requesting that you make time to be together. You're extremely busy and stressed out about the extra load they gave you at work; one of your co-workers is on vacation and you have to pick up their slack too, so it just doesn't work out this week to make that date. You get home and finally make the first meal of your day, but don't do the dishes because you zonk out right after you eat. The next morning you and your partner get in a fight about the dishes not being done.

It is important to own up to your actions and apologize for your wrongdoings. However, continuing to argue about the dishes is responding to a personal trigger and not addressing the real issue. Identifying the trigger allows you the opportunity to cut straight to the solution. It is crucial for you to be aware of where you are out of integrity within that relationship, so it can be addressed first.

You'll want to begin your conversation with acknowledging you made a commitment to make plans and haven't yet, but would like to schedule it now. The conversation becomes productive and efficient rather than just squabbling about the dishes for hours and potentially digging up a bunch of other things from the past, and then going to bed angry. Most fights or disagreements in relationships are not actually about the things that you end up spending the most time arguing about.

I had a roommate that started growing his hair out. He began leaving hair all over the walls of the shower. This was a trigger for me because I showered to get clean, *not* to find another person's hair as artwork on the walls where it would stick to my wet body if I didn't remove it all myself first. I also like to have a very clean home, especially my bathroom. It really bothered me that he wouldn't just remove it after his shower—the trash can was two feet away. How lazy could he be?

I have long hair too, but I gather all the hair that ends up the bathroom wall and throw it away at the end of the shower. Needless to say, I was triiii-geeeerrrrrd and he didn't even know it. When you are in a triggered state, you cannot find solutions. I reacted differently each time I took my shower, all of which didn't work. A month of silence passed until I finally had the sense to remember that if I am still experiencing suffering around something, I am still in the triggered state.

I didn't say anything initially because I thought it was such a small thing. When I couldn't take it anymore, I burst out in a very uncomfortable and unimpressive way. My tirade was not well-received and fell on deaf ears. Then I tried the passive-aggressive approach by leaving my hair all over the bathroom walls too. I don't think he even noticed. When I had exhausted all possibilities, I got quiet. In my meditation I asked myself what I wanted the solution to be and immediately went straight there. I was able to have a conversation with him that was not coming from a triggered state.

Most people focus on the problem and who's to blame. But when I took the time to realize that I was triggered and wasn't communicating well, I tried a different approach. I said, "I'd really love to have a super clean bathroom, because it makes me feel so good. When the bathtub is clean, we can take baths and soothe sore muscles especially after the long hard days we work. When it is dirty, we don't feel motivated to take care of our well-being. How can we support each other with this? Is this also something you desire? How can we help each other provide what we need to have a happy home and take care of our well-being?" My roommate immediately started throwing his hair in the trash and not on the walls and we even developed a cleaning plan for the house. By identifying the trigger and working on approaching problems with a more solution-oriented approach, you can focus on the solution.

PARADIGM SHIFTS

A paradigm shift is an instant change in your belief(s), approach or thought system which expands your awareness. The shift usually comes about when you receive new information, knowledge or experience that doesn't fit into your previous understanding. We can go our whole lives thinking one thing, and then in one moment have it shatter by thinking something entirely new. Once you see something, you cannot unsee it.

PARADIGM SHIFT PARABLE

A lovely couple is riding in a convertible with the top down on a winding road in the mountains on the most perfect, beautiful, and epic day. They are having fun, singing all the words to their favorite songs, when a speeding car screeches around the corner and into their lane, almost hitting them. The guy swerves his car to avoid hitting the couple and screams "PIG!" as he passes them. The couple are not only startled by the potential accident but offended by the man's rude behavior. They continue around the next bend and crash right into a group of pigs. The pigs and the car go off the cliff.

That snap judgment call ended in death. Luckily, most paradigm shifts are not life or death matters, even though they might feel like it. Moments before that couple died, they had a paradigm shift. The couple did not have enough information until it was too late. Do not let your lack of information end your life or dissuade you from your goals and dreams. Paradigm shifts happen all the time. Ego *loves* to be right, so it tricks us into thinking things to keep the ego comfortable but does not serve us and is often false.

ALWAYS BE LISTENING

Oftentimes we are too hasty, judgmental, or insecure to consider that something might be missing. We are often unaware there might be more information to the equation before making a snap decision or judgment call. Those snaps can cost you lost time, suffering, and dis-ease. There is almost always more information to every story. The key is to really listen, so you know where to look for the information.

An argument usually consists of two triggered people not listening to each other and trying to retaliate. Generally, when each person takes the time to sit and listen to the other, they learn where the other person is coming from. The moment you obtain the missing information, you can create possibilities for solutions from there. You create your own paradigm shift by gathering more information from the person you experience a misunderstanding with.

Did you know it's possible not to fight? Wouldn't you love to skip the pain, hurt, anger, and trauma, not to mention acting like a fool? Fighting, unless for literal self-defense or sport, is not classy, graceful, or any behavior you want to be proud of at all. Expanding your awareness is the weapon for peace.

THOUGHTS TURN INTO THINGS

Conscious awareness of your thoughts allows you to greatly influence your life in the direction you seek. Your thoughts bring your focus to what you do or don't want to create. When you start becoming aware of your thoughts, you can then decide which thoughts to act on. Which ones are going to propel you forward and which ones will slide you backwards?

It is important to remember that you do not want to repress or ignore all negative thoughts so that you only think positively. Just become aware of how much time and energy you spend on them. Whatever you focus on you bring about because thoughts do turn into those things.

The reason you should not spend more than 60 seconds on a negative or bad thought is that your brain creates a neural pathway to activate in your circuitry. Over time, continuing the same thought creates deep ruts that are harder to climb out of. Spend more of your time on thoughts that propel you forward—or are solution-based.

Negative thoughts are self criticism/doubt, judgment, helplessness/victim mentality, worry, and gossip. Sadness, thinking about world issues, or having concern for a family member are perfectly normal. However, if you become obsessed over any of those things and you can't stop thinking about it which causes you stress or sleepless nights, it has then become a negative aspect and is unhealthy.

ATTITUDE OF GRATITUDE

Gratitude brings you right into the moment and increases awareness for all those who partake in its benefits. It is important not only to focus on what you want, but also to celebrate all the blessings in your life and things that are going right now. There is *always* something to be grateful for. Gratitude is the highest vibration and is very "sticky."

Bringing your awareness to things you are grateful for will increase manifesting more of them. I like to list all my blessings in my head during my daily shower. When I get out, I am not only physically cleansed, I feel mentally focused and able to operate from this high vibration. It really is a great way to start your day. You can keep a gratitude journal listing all the things you are grateful for and add to it often. Keep it bedside to read it right when you get up and just before you go to sleep. Focus on what you are grateful for, not what you don't want.

PROCRASTINATION AWARENESS

Let's talk about this later...Procrastination rarely, if ever, accomplishes anything positive. It usually brings you and the people involved in your procrastination down. It is intentionally ignoring your higher self and is a very childish way to respond to things. You can either procrastinate or honor yourself by taking immediate actions to support the things you say you want.

Time is either working for you or against you; it can either be a gift or a curse. Do you really have the luxury of limitless time in this life? Upon their deathbed, people regret the things they didn't do, rather than the things they did. Would you want someone else to end up achieving your dream before you even get a chance at bat? Don't let life be a series of missed chances. Ideas are like atoms, they're everywhere. The person who takes action on that idea is the winner.

Have you heard of the Hundredth Monkey Theory? It is a hypothetical phenomenon in which a new idea, thought, or behavior spreads rapidly by unexplained means reaching critical mass once one member of a group acknowledges it. Now is the *always* the *best* time to act! Now is a gift called the present. If you have been thinking about something for awhile, chances are 100 other monkeys have been, too. You must honor the idea as if it is a gift and act the moment something comes to you—otherwise someone else will.

It is coming to you at the perfect time for a reason and at the exact time you need it. The exact moment of inspiration is when you'll have the most Universal energy behind you to make it happen faster, utilizing all the resources available in that current time to accomplish it. I know a person who makes a living selling his *inspired ideas* to companies that have the means to carry it through. Once you have become aware of your procrastination, ask why it came to you and what you're supposed to do with it next.

EVERYTHING MOVES IN CYCLES

No matter how you feel in this moment, this too shall pass. Days move into nights. Nights become days. Days become seasons, seasons turn into years, and history repeats itself over and over again. Everything has a beginning and an end, which creates a circle or cycle.

Our lives are made up of a series of concentric circles colliding and sliding in and out of one another. When there is light, it is easy to stay on your path. Within darkness you may lose your way unless you have the tools to help you find the light again. There are many events or wildcards in our lives where we have no choice in the matter, like the weather or the world turning, and they can affect you in different ways. Knowing where you are at in the cycle will help you greatly.

STRENGTHENING AWARENESS

When we align our spirit, body, and mind with our purpose we are unstoppable. We, too, can write our own code, with or without handicaps. Humans can reprogram themselves to be better and more efficient in every area of their lives. Humans are designed and programmed to survive. There are so many tools available to help us thrive in the world. There are training programs (Mind Valley), teachers and classes (speed reading), nootropics (Adrafinil), plants and herbs (Ginkgo biloba), music (binaural beats), and meditation, just to name a few.

Utilizing all that life has to offer us to help us along the way makes it easier for us to accomplish the things we came here to do. One of the best ways to strengthen your awareness is to take actions from each area (spirit, body, and mind) to support your goals. For instance, you want to get a new job so you align your spirit, body, and mind in this process by taking actions from each of those areas to ensure success.

You'd first apply for the job which is your body, then you start visualizing techniques every day for your spirit, and you could start connecting with others at that company to see how they like it, or do research on how to start your own similar company to engage your mind. We will delve deeper in the coming chapters but having all three parts of yourself on board gives you more confidence and a better shot at whatever you are trying to achieve, and strengthens your awareness.

CHAPTER 5

ASK & YOU SHALL RECEIVE

Universal Law: The Universe will answer any question you ask.

ASKING THE UNIVERSE

What is the Universe? The Universe is a magical place of duality where anything you can conceive can turn into form. It's everything living and non-living throughout the infinite galaxies and is another name for God, energy, or the Creator. It is important to have reverence for the Universe because you yourself are a microcosm of it and without each piece to make up all the systems that create our known Universe, it simply wouldn't be the same.

I grew up in a strong Catholic family. I never liked going to mass, especially when it was in Latin. I thought it was really weird to be a part of a religion where we ate the body of the man that we worshiped and drank his blood, claiming we loved him more than anything or anyone in this world. I remember asking my pastor if it was okay to eat my favorite teacher and drink his blood because he was the best teacher I ever had. When he told me that would go against the church's teachings, it left me quite confused. I didn't know what cannibalism was back then and the whole thing just didn't make sense to me. I could only eat this one man, Jesus, that died for our sins, so that we could be like him. It's no wonder now that I am a vegan.

Upon being chastised and made to feel guilty for asking questions like that, I begged never to go to church again. I wanted to learn about other religions that made more sense to me. My mom made me promise that if I completed going to Confraternity of Christian Doctrine School (CCD) and got confirmed within the Catholic church, I could do whatever I wanted. So I did. The most valuable thing I got from the Bible in all its forms is "Ask and you shall receive." It's written many times in different chapters: Matthew, Luke, Mark, James, John, Philippians, 1 Kings, Psalms, Job, and Jeremiah. They all reference it in one way or another. My third-grade teacher, Mr. Perkins, said, "If you don't ask, you'll never get." When we move into adulthood, we sometimes forget all about this or we become programmed not to ask for what we want anymore.

Growing up, my mother couldn't afford school pictures, field trips, summer camp, museum days, or even school lunches. The rest of the extended family seemed to be doing OK and because my mother was very stubborn and independent, she didn't tell them how bad off we were. It hurt my feelings terribly when several aunts, my grandma, and a cousin around my age all went to Israel one year and wasn't invited.

Instead of being able to go with them, my mother put my name on the tree at the grocery store hoping some kind stranger would buy me a new pair of shoes I desperately needed. I had been going on two years wearing the same pair and I had to cut holes out of the toes as my feet grew. It's strange to walk around with your toes gripping the concrete over the front of your shoes. My toes were always dirty and people made fun of me.

Growing up in poverty, I created a game from the understanding that in every store I entered, someone was getting that service or item for free. It could be the people that work there, the owner's friends and family, or perhaps homeless people as charity—so why couldn't it be me? Not to say we shouldn't pay for the things we want if we can, but nothing is set in stone and sometimes there are other options if you ask. For instance, I always ask for a discount because you just might get it.

When my mother didn't have money for food or school supplies, I would ask store workers if I could have them for free. That would embarrass my mother and she would scold me right there inside the store, but you'd be surprised how often it actually worked. Afterward, she would say thank you and make up some excuse for why we didn't have the money at the time. After a while she would just stay in the car or outside of the store and let me go in to ask for things.

I found that just by my complete boldness in asking, some people would say yes. Others saw that I actually needed it and gave it to me simply because I asked. Boldness gets you further than meekness. Why not ask? You just might get it. Almost everything I have is because I asked for it. Being direct and focused on your goals gets you closer to them. If you don't ask, you don't get anything and you stay in the same place.

It is integral to use nature as a guideline to know what to do in all situations. Nature gets everything it wants. Just listen to your heart and train your mind to work for you, not against you. For those of you that have grown up doing things the hard way, let's now try doing them in the most fun way possible! The more we know what we are, who we are, and what our purpose is, the better we can communicate to others. The process gets easier with practice and if you aren't getting the answers you want or need you can re-approach it another way or ask another person. There is always someone somewhere who has the exact thing you are seeking—they may have extra, or they bought it randomly, but the point is, you both get what you need by asking for it.

I have 40+ years of experience in asking embarrassing questions, which can often offend others. I like to use the great example of the bargaining determination of a child. You know how kids keep asking the same thing repeatedly until they wear you down to saying yes? The conversations often go something like this:

KID: Can I have a cookie?

PARENT: No.

KID: Can I have a cookie, now?

PARENT: No, we are going to eat soon.

KID: What about now?

PARENT: No, honey.

KID: What about now?

PARENT: No, I already told you. I'm not going to tell you again.

KID: Why?

PARENT: Because you have to have dinner first.

KID: I'm not hungry for dinner. I want a cookie first.

PARENT: No.

KID: I promise I will eat my whole dinner if you give me a cookie.

PARENT: No!

KID: What about now?

PARENT: Okay fine, but you better finish all your veggies, or no more cookies!

If you are coming from a place of love, and your "yes" is stronger than their "no," it's only a matter of time. A "no" is only a "No for right now." Each moment is another opportunity to ask again. Things change from moment to moment and it's important not to be discouraged by hearing a little *no* in regards to your goals, hopes and dreams.

PLAY THE RELENTLESS "WHYS???" GAME

It's not a coincidence that "whys" and "wise" sound exactly the same. In order to gain wisdom you must seek the answers to all the worldly "whys" to know the truth or a better way. The answers to your "whys" make you wise right before your very eyes.

It is only through asking "why" as a kid that we learned, and we asked all the time. Some children are taught to stop asking because it's a bother or nuisance, but some parents have the patience for it. My mom certainly didn't, and was hardly around to ask in the first place, so I had to figure out most everything on my own.

For some reason, as an adult we stop asking "why." Playing the "why" game in *your* life will bring you massive understanding and benefit every area of your life. You'll get new information and acquire a deeper understanding of yourself and others. Asking "why" stops you from living in autopilot so you can live a richer life and not exist solely from your programming or how your parents raised you. Oftentimes people say "I will never be like my parents" but turn out just like them because they never questioned why they do the things they do and what they believe.

Start asking why and you will get many unexpected presents and gifts. You will get down to the bones and reasons why you do everything. Why do I like that? Why don't I like it? What does it remind me of? If something is working and you like it, ask, what are the dynamics or energy at play? Who are you showing up as that's different or opposed to who you are at your day job? Understanding the differences in each area of your life will give you answers on how to do things differently in the areas you want to elevate to create a more fulfilling life.

THE GIFT OF ASKING

How good does it feel to be generous with someone you love? How good does it feel to be there for a friend in need? At a time of need, how good does it feel when a friend has your back? Being able to help or to be helped is a gift. Stepping up to help someone shows how much you care. When we get to be of service, we shine brighter. Being asked for your help is a sign of respect and trust. When you ask another for help it shows vulnerability and it can even deepen the relationship.

Often, we just don't ask for help. When we don't, we cheat the people we love out of the gift of giving. How many times have you not asked for help, especially when you really needed it? I say ask, ask, and ask again. The worst thing that could happen is they say no, and with practice you'll get really good at crafting your ask in an unrefusable way.

Feeling free to ask, however, is not the same as being the kind of person who always asks for help with EVERYTHING but isn't willing to do the work on their own. Some people search for all the answers outside of themselves and need to be validated constantly. They often bounce around from one guru or practice to another and claim none of them work, but it's really because they aren't doing the work themselves. Such an abdication of responsibility that can lead to codependency and exacerbate other bad habits.

A person that asks for things all the time is usually so unaware they aren't even listening to the answers they receive. If you recognize yourself in that description it is important to stop talking, listen to your inner guidance, develop self-discipline, roll up your sleeves and get to work. If you have anyone like that in your life you can lovingly let them know you'll no longer be enabling them to play small and will encourage them to get the answers on their own as your answer may not be right for them anyway.

ASKING FOR HELP EXERCISE:

If you have major resistance to asking for help, you may want to try this exercise to fully dive into all the aspects of what is really going on within you. You may discover that you are imitating a pattern in your family or perhaps your resistance stems from a fear of looking bad, but you will only learn its origins through self-investigation. In order to change anything, one must gather the current facts and assess where to go from there. Looking at all the information from all sides will better inform you to make the best decision possible.

It's important to remember the "feelings you had" around your answers and use your emotions to guide your next action. Remembering how you felt when you could or couldn't help someone can help you see the other side of asking. It's not as scary as it might seem. Remember, it's important to know that a "no" doesn't mean anything except "not right now." Oftentimes you can ask at another time and it changes to a "yes." It's actually easier to ask than not ask.

In your journal, answer these prompts:

Write down as many experiences as you can remember where someone asked for your help and you said yes or no.
How did it make both you and them feel?
Were you too busy or just didn't want to?
Were you happy to help in your field of expertise?
Did you refer someone else if you were not able to help?
How did it make you feel being able to help them or not help them?
Was it a positive or negative experience for you?

Was it positive or negative for them?
Did anything come up for you in saying "no" or "yes" that
you or they benefited from?
List as many gifts as you can recall that came out of the
no or yes, for both you and them.

ASK THE RIGHT QUESTIONS

When asking the question why, it is important that you ask empowering and not disempowering questions. Being in a rut of asking yourself those disempowering Murphy's Law kind of questions like, "Why does this always happen to me?" will keep your life small and stuck in suffering. You must have sincerity in your questions or you will get insincere answers. Learn to love to ask questions. We can achieve anything if we try. Nothing is out of our limit.

Now that you know the importance of asking, you must learn to ask the right questions. Dwelling on the wrong questions leads to confusion and keeps you further from your goals. The right questions lets you receive your answer straight away. Asking questions to those not qualified to answer your questions can throw you off course. The process gets easier with time and practice.

It is easy to see if your line of questioning is on the right path because you're getting the answers you want. If you aren't getting the answer you want or need, you can approach it in a very direct but different way. Don't waste your energy asking people who can't help you.

For instance, if you're speaking with a customer service representative because you see a charge on your bill that should not be there and you can ask them till you're blue in the face to take it off but, they say they can't, that is an indicator you are asking the wrong person your question. Ask for a manager or someone that has the authority to help you. There are all sorts of people in every situation who can either lead you to your answers or push you further away. If a person tells you that something is impossible and you feel differently in your heart, let them own their limitations and you can own all that is possible.

Old paradigm thinking trains us to *not* question. The key is to keep asking more and more people until you get the answers you need. Answers are everywhere, so keep asking.

POWERFUL QUESTIONS EXERCISE:

You must be willing to accept the answers. It's nice to get yourself into a quiet space without distractions so you can really be present with your inner guidance system. Asking powerful questions will give you a whole new framework of questioning for success.

Disempowering questions keep you in your body, in pain, and continue the suffering. They aren't even the real questions you have or want to know, they are just bad questioning habits. Why would anyone in their right mind want to have a discussion with all that is wrong with the world? That is a dead-end question of gloom and doom. What you really want are solutions when something challenges you, not a barrage of more problems. Disempowering questions are:

> What's wrong?
> Why did this happen?
> Why me?
> Who did this?
> Who's fault is it?
> Why is this happening to me?
> What should I do?

Empowering questions will get you out of your pain body and to a solution faster. They are the most accurate and heart centered questions to dig right to the truth of the matter, and allow you to have more time to enjoy life instead of remaining stuck. Until you ask your guides, higher self, and/or your heart what it wants, you are only answering the pain body's questions. Praying is asking for help. If you don't ask, you'll never receive it. Empowering questions are:

> Is this good for me?
> What am I doing when I feel most alive?

What is my gift to share with the world or others?

Why is this happening *for* me?

What is the gift in this situation?

What if God or the Universe was *really* on my side?

What if God or the Universe *really* wants me to be happy?

If this experience were to last forever—what quality of myself would need to emerge in order to exist?

"Pain pushes until vision pulls."
"Asking for H.E.L.P. (Hello Eternal Loving Presence) is a prayer."
~ Michael Beckwith ~

VISION BOARDS

The person to always ask first is *yourself*. You must identify what you want so you may go get it, or ask for it. Start with a brainstorm for each area of your life you want to address. Once you do that, you can collect images that represent each thing. If you have never taken a shot at a vision board, now is the time to do it! It's fun to do with friends, family, or even on your own. You can have everyone you invite bring old magazines and newspapers and you can have a little vision board creation potluck party. It is a great social event and fun to do with your family.

Our brains respond well to symbols, this is why seeing images of what you want on your wall, day in and day out, actually help to you bring them into your life. Taking action to collect and gather symbols and images of things you want in your life, brings awareness to all the parts of yourself that you'd like to nurture. It's important to get quiet and experience what it feels like inside your body as if you already have it.

I used to have several different vision boards for each category, but they took up too much real estate on my walls. After that, I went to one board for all my desires. Now, thanks to the Internet, I am back to several different Pinterest pages for each area of my life, so I can get super specific in each area. You can get as detailed as you want, including images that depict your exact feeling when you have everything you desire. Use the PILLARS OF POWERFUL PRESENCE to define each area.

PILLARS OF POWERFUL PRESENCE

The world is a teacher to the wise man and an enemy to the fool. Confusion is that wonderful state right before clarity. Presence is made up of many factors. It's not just one thing that makes a person powerful when they walk into a room, it's layers deep.

To gain a deeper understanding of presence you must first know what in your life is not working and where you are unnecessarily suffering or having energy leaks. You must bring awareness to each area of your life to identify what is not working so you can create solutions. There are eight major areas that I call The Pillars of Powerful Presence.

It is important to have the pillar for each aspect of your life flowing and working properly to experience life as whole and complete. Harmony and growth in each of these pillars correlate with how happy and effective you are in your life. Bringing efficacy and fun to the areas in your life expands your powerful presence and increases your productivity and satisfaction overall!

The benefits don't stop there. Getting all your pillars in good working order will do wonders for your Spirit, Body, and Mind, which have the ability to completely heal when given the proper nourishment. As you set up each of the 8 Pillars of Powerful Presence in your life for success it will feed and grow all the other areas of your life, too. In aligning each of these pillars we heal ourselves on a cellular, emotional, and spiritual level.

Allow yourself to honestly assess each area of your life so you can improve your interactions and outcomes with others and the world. You can systematically go through one at a time to start the work of healing and repair. I suggest starting with the pillar that needs the most attention, which may appear to be the most difficult. No matter the current situation, you can always upgrade any area of your life.

THE 8 PILLARS OF POWERFUL PRESENCE

What areas are you ready to make a change in right now? When you heal and cleanse each of the pillars you are more available to all the light that shines within you and possibilities galore.

1~Family & Friends _____
2~Career & Finances _____
3~Physical Environment & Home Life _____
4~Love & Romance _____
5~Fun & Recreation _____
6~Health & Body _____
7~Personal Growth & Education _____
8~Spirituality _____

Next to the name of each pillar, rate your level of satisfaction in that area of your life. Zero means you are completely unsatisfied and ten means you're highly satisfied. You'll know the areas with the lowest numbers are the ones to choose to start work on immediately. Just like in school you'll raise your curve immensely by making shifts in your life to raise the lower numbers up first, rather than going for the most satisfied areas right off the bat.

ACT AS IF YOU ALREADY HAVE IT

Explore your feelings every time you look at your vision board. How would you walk down the street, or drive your car differently, if you already had that thing? Is your head held higher? Do you skip? Are you smiling from ear to ear? If so, do this *now*. There is no need to wait. How are you different while driving in your car, now that you have this thing? Now that you just signed that big contract, do you let people over in your lane or not? What if someone cuts you off? How would you respond differently? Start walking or driving like that now, don't wait! See it, feel it, love it and yourself, then let your expectation of it go.

PAY ATTENTION TO GET POWERFUL ANSWERS

The Universe will answer any question you ask, that is how powerful its energy is. In fact, the Universe will even answer your questions in a way that you can understand. Once you start asking questions, it is important to pay attention to all the signs, intuitive gut instincts, and dreams that come up.

Pay attention to the lyrics of the music playing on the radio, words people may be saying or shouting around you, and for the little signs that occur everywhere all around you. They may contain answers to the powerful and empowering questions you've asked. You must have the willingness and the ability to hear the answers. Your listening is where you will find the information you can use to dig yourself out of the trenches which you have inadvertently dug yourself into over the years. This is where you can rise above your life and float on the clouds so that you can get a better perspective.

SURROUND YOURSELF WITH POSITIVE PEOPLE

If you want to learn how to be happy, do you ask someone who is not? It just doesn't make sense. Advice is free and everyone is happy to share opinions when asked. However, you must ask the right people the right questions in order to get the information you are truly seeking.

As we learned from Napoleon Hill in his book "Think & Grow Rich," our communities and the people who surround us are our biggest resource. They are also a major shaping factor for our growth and can affect us both positively and negatively. It's important to make sure that we take a look at the people we surround ourselves with most often as they influence us the most.

We've all heard the saying "You are the average of the five people you spend the most time with." Those people shape the way we feel as well as what we think and believe. Just being in a person's presence, you can feel the energy coming from them if they are angry or happy and it affects you, your physiology, and your emotional state.

If anyone's electromagnetic energy consistently brings you down, well then, that's where you're going to go—straight down. It's hard enough to manage our own emotions and lives, let alone try to manage someone else's. This is a losing game that nobody wins. You have to be able to not permit that type of contact or behavior into your life. Doing so allows those people the space to grow on their own.

A person's toxic energy does not have to be your emergency. You can hold your sacred ground. If there is a person that is cutting off your supply of nutrients, drinking your water, or blocking your sun, it's time to realize that you have the solution now.

They say if you want to be successful in something, hang out with people that have already achieved success in that area. If you are constantly surrounded with people that don't have their life figured out, chances are you will stay in the same spot with them. No amount of asking them for advice will help you get closer to your goals because they simply do not have the information. You must seek out the right people to ask those types of questions. When everyone is moving forward together, success takes care of itself.

Just because you have known someone who is prone to negativity your whole life, doesn't mean you have to keep them close to you. I'm not saying to delete them from your life, but it's a good idea to limit the time you spend with them as their thinking and energy will bring you down. People with positive energy will lift you up. How do you want to spend your time? Who do you want to influence you, your family, and your life? It's good to investigate the energy fields of those around you so you can bring yourself to the state and places you desire.

Relationships with those that bring you down should be limited. In this next exercise you can see how to rate your relationships to shift out of a community or set of people that may be inadvertently limiting your possibility of growth in your life. Pull out the weeds so that you can begin to elevate your current reality and create lasting results by feasting on your healthy garden harvest.

POSITIVE TRAITS EXERCISE:

Write a list of people that, when you're around them, make you feel safe or feel good about yourself. This list can be as long as you like, but it should at least be five people. It may not be the person who's the "life of the party" with a smile and a good word for everyone if their relationships are wide-ranging but shallow.

Look instead for someone who takes the time to see you and understand you and makes you feel good when you're around them. These tend to be the people in your life that you really look forward to seeing and spending time with. They have traits that bring you up and raise your vibration rather than bringing you down to their level or into their problems. Every one of us has problems, of course, but some people dedicate most of their time to wallowing in those problems instead of seeking and acting on solutions, and they end up bringing everyone down around them.

When you have your list of people that raise your energy, write all of their traits next to their name and then itemize the traits in importance to you that they each possess that make them that way. You may begin to notice that many of the people on your list have similar traits.

Once you've identified them, start trying each of them on and adopt for yourself any and all from your list that you see fit, choosing the ones that work for you. You can be confident of your ability to bring forth those traits because they're already in you, or you never would have been attracted to those people in the first place. We cannot be attracted to that which we do not possess inside us.

When choosing positive people to surround yourself with, I like to use the seven or above rule, with one being the lowest and ten the highest. Go through your entire friend roster and assign each person a number that correlates with how good you feel when you're around them and how much they contribute to your life in a positive way. People who make you feel good to be around and consistently enhance your life will be in the upper echelon of the scale somewhere around seven or above.

Conversely, if the people in your inner circle have scores of one to five it will lower your vibration, life force energy, possible opportunities, and overall happiness. A person that complains all the time, likes to fight, is aggressive or angry, or chooses extremely toxic behaviors, would have a very low number on the scale. Do yourself a favor and see less of them! How are you going to get more 8s, 9s, and 10s if you don't make room for them to come into your life? Create the space and allow nature to fill in the gaps. Trust nature.

PRUNE YOUR GARDEN

It's going to take a minute to recalibrate to where you want to go. If you have friends in your life that have been around for a long time but they just don't make the cut, it's important to take that time for yourself and make the space so that your nines and tens can come into your life. It's time to upgrade your life. I have a garden in my backyard and there was a time when I was growing 80% of my own food. Every planting season I'd have to pull out all the little sprouts that weren't performing as well as the other ones to allow space in my garden for the ones that were performing well. It's time to pull out all the weeds from your life so your garden will prosper.

In my backyard I have a massive orange tree that was getting out of control. I had to trim off several of these big, huge, beautiful branches with a ton of fruit on them. They weren't fruiting as fast or as well as the other branches, so we chopped them off to give the energy to the part of the tree that is doing better and performing at a higher rate. It's something we do in nature and there is no difference when it comes to our lives. We are nature.

The people you let go of who come back around in a way that feels good to you were meant to be there and the relationship is usually better than before. Some of those people will come back into your life, but you and they will be different people at that time. Maybe they needed you to kick them out to realize that they needed to be a different person, or take care of themselves and their needs so that when they come back to you they will be in a better place.

Your core five people will change according to your growth rate. You will grow and expand, that's what nature does. You will have different surrounding little shrubberies and bushes that evolve over the years right alongside you. By operating as nature does, you will have a continuing and revolving ever-changing circle of friends, but you can choose according to your vibration, because we are all electromagnetic.

My closest friends are the ones that I feel good to be around because it's safe to be myself with them. Just being in their presence makes me a better human and accelerates my personal growth. The positive qualities they possess have profoundly and positively changed my life.

I live in gratitude every day that I get to live into all these traits. I practiced them for so long that they stuck. You, too can try things on and if they fit, keep them. If they don't, move on to the next one. I am grateful for them in my life and for those whom I call my chosen family.

Remember, you cannot get the answer you are looking for from someone that doesn't have it. Ask questions from people that actually have the ability to give you the answer you want or you will get what that person has or does. It is as simple as that.

CHAPTER 6

ACKNOWLEDGMENT

Definition: //ac·knowl·edg·ment// /aknäljmnt/ ~Noun
1. Acceptance of the truth or existence of something.
2. The action of expressing or displaying gratitude or
appreciation for something. (www.OxfordDictionaries.com)

Acknowledgment comes in many forms, from appreciation to sharing and acceptance of all that is and for who people are. You can truly appreciate people more by acknowledging that everyone has their own truth and has a right to believe what they want, just as you do. This chapter gets into the nitty gritty of acknowledgment on every level so that you may have a deeper understanding of this key tool and ally for personal growth. Acknowledgment at its very core is pure acceptance.

THE BLESSING OF APPRECIATION

The simple act of genuine appreciation can heal the world. Humans must be needed or be of service or else we die inside. We need to be acknowledged for the things we do. Our love of service can turn into our life's purpose. Appreciation of our service encourages us to continue. It provides the feedback that all humans need and rewards us by letting us feel seen, so we have the energy to continue doing the helpful behavior.

We, as people, like to go out of the way for others, but if we keep doing so and never get a thank-you or any acknowledgment for it, we lose the desire to help and we may feel useless, disappointed and awful. When a person goes for a long time without being acknowledged or appreciated, their heart begins to close. Even Mother Teresa could have run out of steam if she were not acknowledged and thanked for her efforts. Appreciation creates encouragement and the energy to keep going.

Ammachi (the hugging saint) benefits from mutual appreciation when she gives her hugs. It gives her enough energy so she can go for over twelve hours without taking a break. Humans can run on appreciation and praise.

There have been studies all over the world, in multiple countries, where people were asked why they stayed in a job where they were paid much less instead of moving to a different, better-paying job. They responded that they'd rather be appreciated, acknowledged, and seen than be paid more money to be treated badly or disrespected. Studies show that people would rather take a 50% pay cut to be seen and appreciated rather than receive twice the amount of money at a place where they are not. What does that tell you? People are absolutely starved for appreciation! Start appreciating more in your life NOW!

Appreciation causes things to grow. When you appreciate something or someone for what they do, acknowledge it and them. The human race is starved for recognition. Letting someone know the impact they have on you or in this world is the most precious gift you can give. If everyone knew the impact they had on others all the time, they might act differently. You can acknowledge anyone for just about anything. It must be authentic and real, though. We can tell when someone isn't being authentic. You have the power to find at least one good thing about every person you meet or see and to acknowledge them for that quality. The people closest to you are the best people to start with.

And if someone acknowledges, appreciates, or compliments you, say thank you. Brushing it off and denying their gift is not only rude, it also sends a subconscious message to them that their opinion doesn't matter to you because your own insecurities are more important. If it's hard for you to find something to acknowledge in someone, you can at least acknowledge them for being the other half of whatever experience you are sharing with them. For instance, if someone thanks you for giving them advice, you can thank them and acknowledge them for asking for help, listening attentively, and allowing you to make a difference in their life. Share your gifts of acknowledgment and appreciation with compassion. Be clear and concise.

TYPES OF APPRECIATION

Appreciation is like turning an ice cream cone into two, because it's a treat for both people involved and creates positive energy in the world. Everyone benefits while raising the vibration in your bodies. You will for sure make someone's day and that always feels good! There are three types of appreciation and they are all equally important:

> **Acknowledge yourself.** Give yourself credit where credit is due for everything you have accomplished. This life isn't always a bowl of cherries and it's important to appreciate yourself for all you've accomplished.

> **Acknowledge others.** I know, it might seem way too simple, but it is so impactful and changes lives when done from your heart. Take special moments to point out to people, whether random strangers or dear friends, something awesome that you appreciate about them.

> **Appreciate and acknowledge everything that is happening in your life right now.** This one is probably the *most important one of all* to accept everything that happens in your life, just as it is. It wouldn't be happening if it weren't supposed to happen. Say yes to everything. Accept it and love it, because it is truly a gift for you, perhaps even more when you continue to dig into its meaning and the growth that comes from it.

APPRECIATION RELEASES DOPAMINE

Dopamine is a chemical neurotransmitter that is responsible for transmitting signals between the nerve cells of the brain. It has a powerful effect on many physical and cognitive functions including movement, motivation and memory. It's also responsible for the feelings of reward and pleasure, which is why it has been called the "feel good" chemical. Dopamine, Serotonin, Oxytocin, and Endorphins are the chemical quartet responsible for your happiness.

APPRECIATION TRAINING

It is easy to appreciate the things you love, but it becomes more challenging to appreciate someone or something when there's no benefit you can see at first glance. Looking deeper requires you to see beyond the first impressions of a situation or person. It trains you to find positive aspects in a moment even though you may have to look within yourself to find them. In life, there will always be situations or encounters where you have to be in close quarters with someone you do not like, who may trigger you, or who you do not resonate with. An appreciation practice will help you in those situations.

There is always at least one good thing that comes from everything in life and one positive quality you can find in any person you may meet. Even a raging alcoholic has good qualities deep inside. Even if it's just an article of clothing or a style that a person has—maybe they have great hair, a strong work ethic, or pretty eyes—just pick one thing to appreciate them for.

Hone in and focus on one simple thing to share with them and do not let yourself be distracted by any of your triggers or their shortcomings. I suggest catching the other person at a time when they are on their best behavior. You can simply acknowledge them for how they are in that moment, such as: "Wow, you have a great smile, I never noticed that before." Remember to acknowledge them for something you'd like to see more of which provides them with positive feedback, letting them know they are doing something worth appreciating.

A CURE FOR DEPRESSION

A depressed person is someone who has a major blockage in their energy source and mostly focuses on their problems, comparison of others, and their lack or limitations which is all about SELF. You cannot access your energy source by only thinking about yourSELF. This is the true ugly meaning of selfish. You must put your focus outside of yourself to tap into that energy. If you love life, then you will do whatever it takes to keep your heart open. It's the point of access to all your power and energy. You get there faster by taking a look at the positive aspects of your challenges instead of rehashing all the pain and trauma from the past. You most likely have already visited all the most depressing stops on Memory Lane often enough. Take a different road now!

It's actually the way I cured my depression. In grade school, I met a girl and we became best friends. Our parents met, got married, and we became sisters when I was eleven. It wasn't until after the marriage that she told me about the abuse from her biological father, which I soon found out about on my own. He was extremely emotionally and physically abusive to the both of us, but saved the sexual abuse for her. I already had been through court from being sexually abused when I was five years old by a "friend of the family" babysitter, and then again at seven from another family member. I was sexually spared from my step-dad; he knew I would tell if he ever touched me that way.

My depression continued to worsen as I moved into high school. Things were not looking very good for me, and I attempted to suicide twice on my own, and once more with my step-sister when things got *really bad*. I could not stand the thought of her going through that torture again, so I told on him. It went very badly for the both of us because she denied it and my mother thought we were trying to kill her by taking all her prescription drugs she needed to live.

That's when the emotional and physical abuse worsened. The day I was thrown across the room by my step-dad, my sister and I decided our lives were so bad that we must end them. We scoured the house for the deadliest things we could find.

My mother had Lupus and took some serious prescription drugs, so we grabbed the most dangerous-sounding pills and washed them down with all the liquor in the house. We knew we had limited time and wanted to say goodbye to all our friends and let them know what they would be inheriting of ours after we were gone. After our fifth phone call everything got really swirly. We began to hallucinate and had double vision, seeing flashing lights outside the house. Then in one moment we were soberly snapped to attention by banging on the walls and police calling out to us over a loudspeaker. One of our friends had called 911 and saved our lives.

Apparently, trying to end your life is against the law and they punished us to the fullest extent, at our parents' request. The judge gave us 500 hours of community service each, which we had to complete in six months. My mother was so pissed she didn't talk to or look at me for a month. We were grounded for two years which ended up being three in actuality because more time was added for any unsatisfactory behavior. We wanted to die even more than before. I don't know if you have ever been grounded, but it's worse than being quarantined, only in this unusual situation my step-dad came up with extra added bonus punishments.

He felt that the only way for us to atone for the horrible thing we had done was physical labor and continuous chores on top of our mandatory government-appointed community service. One of his favorites was to have us remove every single dish, utensil and piece of cookware from all cupboards and wash them by hand, dry them, and then put them away—and we had to do it several times a week. We were not allowed to see friends unless they did manual labor with us.

At my high school reunions there were so many wild stories brought up by friends remembering how we carried a wheelbarrow to harvest rocks from the fields so we could build a pond in our front yard, which went on for months. Or the time we had to devise a rope and pulley system to put a swamp cooler on our roof. We weren't allowed to see relatives during this time either except on holidays when it was unavoidable for him to keep us secluded. We were completely isolated, except at night, when we snuck out. Sneaking out kept our sanity and was the only way to see friends or do anything fun.

Since I couldn't see my friends, I started calling them instead. Every day I called one to three people to let them know how much I loved them, what they meant to me, what I learned from them, and how they made me feel. Turns out, when you are vulnerable enough to be in a state of appreciation and participate in the act of appreciation, there is no way you can be depressed in that moment.

One call turned into three or four and soon enough I did it every day, even teachers, store clerks, and strangers. I didn't know about the powerful effects of the hormone Oxytocin then, but I also had that on my side. I changed the chemicals in my brain and my body for the better by doing this one simple act every day.

Then I was able to start looking at the occurrences in my life and what I got from them. I received so many gifts from my childhood! I learned how to put sprinkler systems in the ground, how to install a swamp cooler on a roof, install tile and hardwood flooring, build a waterfall pond, paint a house, and clean like Mr. Clean. As an adult all these skills have helped me tremendously and I am very grateful for it all.

KILL 'EM WITH KINDNESS

Because my mom was a single parent and I was an only child for most of my life, I didn't have much supervision. My mom couldn't afford daycare very often, and I stayed home by myself a lot or with my mom's best friend. I pretty much did whatever I wanted to when no one was there to stop me. When I was bored, I would go to the old folks home in our neighborhood and listen to their stories. They became some of my closest friends because they were the only people in my life who understood me, and I genuinely listened to them.

There were so many different types of characters at the convalescent home. There were the Bingo ladies, the garden gnomes, the yellers, the scooters (my favorites) and of course, the grumpy old men. There was this one grumpy old man that yelled and screamed at everyone. He shouted very mean things to me each time I came to visit. The staff and my friends told me to ignore him, but he was very persistent in trying to get a rise out of me. There are some people that will stop at nothing to get you down to their ugly level. The rants that he directed toward me consisted of "Get outta here kid, no one wants you here!" "You're ugly!" "You look like a boy with that short hair!"—those were his favorites. I tried to ignore it at first, which didn't work. Then, I took it very personally and would cry all the way home.

A nurse told me that the gentleman was very sick and only had a short time left to live. I began to understand him so much more. I had empathy for him because no one was coming to visit him on his last days, not even his family. He must have felt so awful, abandoned, and lonely inside.

When a person is sick, they can act in ways that are out of character for them. I wanted to turn that grumpy old man's pain into something he could smile about. We have the ability to help others step into more of who they really are, by being relentlessly dedicated to love. We can choose not to respond to the person's bad behavior or actions while holding them accountable for their greatness.

Everyone has more great qualities than bad. You can turn the person that you despise into a friend, or at least into someone you can tolerate. I am not talking about abusive people here. There is no excuse to stay in *any* situation where you are being abused or are in danger.

His screaming was very loud and felt like abuse when I took his words personally. Verbal abuse in your personal life and work environment is not acceptable. I willingly chose to find a way to include him in the positive aspects of my visits. They were only words and he only had days to live, after all. This is how I killed him with kindness and flipped the convalescent home upside down in a good way.

When the grumpy old man yelled at me to get out, I would bring a newspaper for him to read. When he started throwing things and cursing at the top of his lungs, I would say, "Stop being so silly." and clean up the mess he made. I did not take it personally. I saw through that anger and hurt and reminded him of love and joy.

When you disarm the anger you get through to the real person instead of responding to their trauma. He would cause a scene and I would applaud and tell him how amazingly funny it was, give him an Academy Award for best actor, or tell him how it must have felt so good to do that. When he yelled something mean across the room, I yelled back louder, "I love you, too!" Everyone laughed. They started treating him in the same manner.

When everyone stopped taking him so seriously, he was able to laugh at himself. We acknowledged him as a clown, and treated his antics like a funny joke. Obviously, no one in their right mind could be that mad for something so insignificant. Sometimes people are just on autopilot and addicted to their feelings which gives them a charge of energy, until you transfer that energy in a positive direction.

When he made people happy instead of uncomfortable, he stopped yelling altogether. That made it possible to have regular conversations with him. It turned out he was a very interesting and even loving man. He got to spend the last few weeks of his life getting to know the other residents better through the act of laughter. Sometimes, all we need is one person to see through our pain so we can be reminded of who we really are—this takes vulnerability. I have been killing pain with kindness and healing with love ever since.

And the winner is.....Miss Vulnerability!

VULNERABILITY

Definition: // vul·ner·a·bil·ity// /vln()rb()l()ti/ ~ Noun
**1. The quality or state of being exposed to the possibility
of being attacked or harmed, either physically or
emotionally. (www.OxfordDictionaries.com)**

BE VULNERABLE

In order to truly acknowledge or appreciate life to its fullest you have to learn to be vulnerable. Sharing your feelings with another is extremely vulnerable. Learn to love it! Being vulnerable is a strength and your sharing with another has the ability to transform situations and people. Many people know they are loved, but it always feels good to share with a person how you feel about them.

And it can be vulnerable to openly appreciate someone. When you open yourself up to someone, it allows you to be seen, heard, and understood. It gives them the opportunity to let you know their experience in the moment. When you share something vulnerable, it makes the other person feel good because you trusted them with your deep, private, personal experiences.

ACKNOWLEDGMENT + VULNERABILITY = SUPERPOWER

Superheroes have superpowers and everyone on this planet can step into their superhero-self at any time. Ever wanted to be a superhero growing up? Well, I did! I used to play "She-Ra and the Princess of Greyskull" (sung to the theme song of the cartoon) in a friend's backyard. We'd climb on top of the black widow-riddled wood pile and claim our throne.

I had no idea then that you could actually positively affect people in real life just like a superhero. Superheroes would just be plain ol' people if they didn't have super powers and a super mission. But when any living person combines acknowledgment and vulnerability, they get super powers! The next several distinctions are things to consider when practicing the art of acknowledgment, appreciation, and vulnerability.

SHARING IS CARING

It's important to share responsibly. Share your story or perspective with someone in a loving way and without judgment. Humans need to share and receive feedback in order to grow. Whether sharing something personal or having to tell them something difficult, it is all about love, caring, and trust. Sharing allows you to be vulnerable and makes room for the possibility for everyone to understand each other.

It's important to know whom to share with and when to share. Avoid deep personal sharing with people that do not care about you or who are dishonest. People must prove themselves trustworthy first.

It is a human desire to be understood, trusted, seen, and heard. When you share with another, it shows you truly care and respect them. Trusting that someone you care deeply about is strong enough to handle the truth allows them to step into that strength.

Withholding information from your loved ones because you deem it might be "too much" for the recipient makes them weak, and can deteriorate the relationship and kill all possibility for growth. Loving, graceful full-disclosure is always best in the long run and feels better for all involved. It shows you respect, trust, and even believe in them to handle the situation. That level of trust provides the foundation for growth, even if initially they get upset.

STOP ALL TOXIC SHARING!

Toxic sharing includes gossip, complaining, and judgments of others. You must be a responsible sharer and avoid toxic sharing at all costs. Talking about your life experiences and feelings is great, but talking about other people and their lives is toxic. It is best to share only things of value pertaining to your own life with others and avoid sharing other people's intimate details to anyone.

Sharing stories about the personal or private affairs of others is gossip and must stop at once. If you or the other person sharing the story isn't part of the solution, then it's gossip! It's also none of your business. Participating in this type of idle talk with zero substance lowers the vibration for all that are within earshot. If the sharing isn't personal, it's toxic and not a good look for anyone.

I have a very deep respect for myself and others, therefore I have a strict NO gossip or complaining rule in my presence. I make a point to request changing the subject if I hear any toxic sharing. I consider this ear pollution. Nothing good can come from it and makes you look bad. It sends an unconscious message to others not to trust and avoid the person sharing the toxic trash because most likely they would do the same behind your back.

ACT NOW ~ NOT LATER

The moment you think of saying or doing something is the BEST time to act on it. You have all the energy from the universe, your guides, and even your own intuition on your side, which is why you are thinking about it right at that point in time. It is not an accident. When you ignore these signs from the universe you create suffering in your life and in others'.

Share when you feel it or are thinking it in that moment if you can. It's best to take action in the exact moment that a situation comes up so you can address it—unless you or the other is triggered. It may feel especially difficult when you must break unpleasant news to someone. It's uncomfortable to confront someone about their inappropriate behavior, but it is best to do it right away so the behavior doesn't continue.

For some reason, humans have an aversion to doing these types of things right away and they want to "find the right time" or "wait until later" which only prolongs the inevitable. Often the person waits so long to share that by the time they finally do, the relationship has been severed. Suffering keeps increasing and more time is wasted until action is taken. You could have used that time to be more productive or do something fun. There is no better or more perfect time than right now. Ask them when they would have twenty minutes of undisturbed time or however long you think you'd need. You want them in a good place to receive it well.

Not acting or choosing to ignore your feelings when something comes up sends negative messages to your subconscious. Disregarding your intuition in those moments makes it difficult for you to trust your "gut instinct" in the future. Peace comes faster the sooner you take the actions you know you need to, like ripping off a band-aid.

The more you wince at the thought of the pain, the more pain and suffering you experience and then you still have to remove the band-aid. You must communicate your feelings to the person you are having an issue with, no matter how much you wince at the thought of it. Why waste time feeling like shit? Just do it and skip feeling bad.

People will treat you the way you allow them to until you make a request. Otherwise, they have no idea you would like things to be different. It is best to get right to it. Do not avoid talking to them and be clear in your requests so you don't end up confusing them. It's important to bring all your compassion and love into each word when you're speaking to someone about changes or requests that you'd like.

What doesn't kill me, makes me stronger."
~ Friedrich Nietzsche ~

Trusting that someone can handle the truth is a sign of respect. Anything other than being plain and honest sends a message to their subconscious that they are weak. Respect yourself and them. You would want someone to come right out and tell you their truth, so give them the same courtesy. Stand up for their greatness and trust they are strong enough to handle the moment. Give them the opportunity to grow instead of deciding they are weak by avoiding telling them your truth. You owe them your heart-centered honest and compassionate feelings. Let them decide how to react and respond.

ACKNOWLEDGE *ALL* LIFE EXPERIENCES AS A BLESSING

It takes having a different perspective in order to change. You must acknowledge "what is so" and then continue to find all the positive things in your situation. Not paying attention to these small gifts cheats you and all the people you love out of so much goodness. You cannot change the past. Accept it and move on. Dwelling on it is suffering. The faster you acknowledge it and look for the gifts, the better your quality of life will be. See GIFT MINING BRAIN TRAINING in Chapter 8 for a full breakdown on how to identify the positive attributes from even the most horrid events.

Imagine how your life would change if you just accepted everything and saw it as a gift. It took me half of my life to realize that my mom's death was a blessing in disguise, a gift that would continue to keep giving and shaping me for the rest of my life. Up until then I was *Tripper Trapped* in victimhood. You will learn all about tripper traps in the next chapter, but it's something you keep getting tripped up on and trapped in a negative state of being.

I lived that past pain almost daily and I found solace in anyone that would listen to my stories of trauma and abuse. I continued to live life as a victim of the circumstances of my past. I relived the pain every time I repeated the story. I repeated the story to get the appreciation and recognition I never received when I was a kid. It was what I thought I needed. People felt sorry for me and I felt sorry for myself.

I would share with whomever listened and on one particular day, I met a really nice lady and I began as usual to tell her my life's story. At the end of it, she shook her head and said, "You poor thing." Something struck me in that moment. Maybe it was her choice of the word "poor" or the way she shook her head in disgust, then sadness, but I realized I didn't want anyone to ever feel sorry for me again.

I would *never* be a "poor thing." Instead, I decided to look at my experience as a gift and see what came from it and how I would go on from there. Everything changed. I stopped sharing my past with people in the way of being a victim and made lists of all the gifts I received from my shitty childhood. It's harder to do or change anything when you play the victim.

This was how I got my power back. Now when I share my past with others, I start with the strengths and gifts I received from what they may perceive as insurmountable loss. When you share your gifts in the face of adversity, people see your strength and growth. It allows them to see that possibility for themselves to no longer wear a veil of victimhood. They get to be stronger because you shared your transformation.

You can also listen when people share their personal stories of loss with you and look for what they may have gained from that experience and respond gently with an appreciation of it. If someone tells you they lost their job, you can give them support and then congratulate them for how they can finally start doing the very thing that lights them up—living their dream. It's important to see beyond the lack, limitation, and trauma.

TURN LEMONS INTO DELICIOUS LEMONADE

No matter how sour something may be, you can always add sweetener and water to make it taste good. You would have first had to taste the lemon on its own to know it was sour, which is the first lesson. Had you not learned that lesson, there would be no lemonade in your imminent future.

Accept the source right away and develop your number one recipe by adding new ingredients like mango, mint, or watermelon. There is always a lesson or something good that comes from any experience. Find the gift of appreciation in every challenging situation.

> **"A person's success in life can usually be measured by**
> **the number of uncomfortable conversations**
> **he or she is willing to have."**
> **~ Timothy Ferriss ~**

WITHHOLDS ARE DEADLY

Withholds are the opposite of sharing—and negative outcomes occur from this lack of acknowledgment or not sharing. This is where you avoid or ignore your feelings when it comes to sharing with someone. We lightly touched on this earlier but I want you to know the severity of it. Withholds are when we withhold a piece of information or a specific conversation from the person that it pertains to.

Not sharing is not caring. Whether it's with someone close to you or an acquaintance, the act of not sharing how you feel with another person is a withhold. The problem with not sharing something on your mind with that person for whatever reason—such as "it's not the right time"—holds a degenerative energy inside you which they can feel too. It can be very confusing for them; they may not be sure what's going on, but it feels off and icky. They might not know why you are avoiding them, or where the uncomfortable feeling may be coming from, but they will sense there's something wrong with the relationship and they may respond defensively, pull away from you, or double down on their difficult behavior.

Withholds are toxic! If the withhold has gone on too long, it can actually destroy a relationship. There is no need for this. It's the equivalent of sitting at the dinner table with that person while you are cutting their legs with a knife under the table. Both of you feel something is wrong, but by the look on your face, the other person can't tell. You must use your words. The other person doesn't have any idea why there is a pain in their leg when you're looking into their eyes and smiling. It's inauthentic to both you and to them.

Withholds are like sharing a bowl of soup with that person, only you put one drop of poop in the soup bowl because you are mad. Since you cannot take that one drop out, the entire bowl of soup has become toxic. You must share what you need to in order to have a fresh new bowl of soup for the both of you. Get comfortable with being uncomfortable. If you don't share something that is important to you, the chemicals your body will generate can negatively affect your thyroid, liver, kidneys, and heart. Meanwhile the other person is completely clueless as to why you are ignoring them (ghosting) or how they can help or support you.

GHOSTING
Definition: //ghost·ing// //ōstiNG// ~ Noun
1. Avoidance because of the inability to share or
handle emotions: one's own and another's.
(Dr. Sarah Larsen)
2. The practice of ending a personal relationship with someone
by suddenly and without explanation withdrawing from
all communication. (www.OxfordDictionaries.com)

Thanks to online dating, we now have the term "ghosting." This could be an indefinite, temporary, or permanent habit of avoidance. It could be unconscious or a conscious decision. Either way you slice it, it's damaging to you and the other person. It's pretending as if the other person doesn't exist while ignoring your own personal growth. If this has happened to you, you must know it is not your fault. It is the other person's weakness and inability to be deep or intimate. If you are the ghoster, it's time to take responsibility for your impact in the world.

I'll have you know that this was my former go-to solution and it started when I was a kid, because I have been in many situations where I was abused. Ghosting was my defense mechanism for getting out of danger and staying away from abusers. In college, you might say I was even proud of being able to "cut people off" that hurt me and never looked back.

It worked really well for me then and I even carried on its ripe old traditions into adulthood. When I wasn't treated well, I left the person's presence. I am not talking only physically, but emotionally too. I struggled with this up until my 30s, when I decided to examine it, take responsibility for it within myself, and then heal it.

I have a very dear friend of over ten years that I love so deeply I would do anything for. However, I cut her out of my life for two years and just let her back recently. Technically I ghosted her, which is a strange thing to do with a friendship that close, but I had been going through some serious emotional healing and needed the people in my immediate space to be extremely kind, compassionate, and gentle. She is a wonderful woman, but there was another side to her that I felt was a little too brash and mean at times.

There was a period when I was extremely sensitive where every time we had gotten together over the course of months we ended up fighting for no reason. I had just gone through my Kundalini rising or "Conscious Awakening" and every little thing magnified in my heart. Behaviors such as rolling her eyes at other's words and actions and saying bitchy things, especially when she didn't get her way, hurt me to the core and I felt I needed to protect myself and run for cover.

She is an absolutely outstanding person who is very loving and generous, and if I weren't in that activated state everything would have been fine. From what she has told me, her mother was horrible to her and other people. Abusive behavior is continually passed down until someone flips the script.

I had to heal that quality within myself before I could be present in the friendship again, and it took me two years to find all the tools to help me get there without judging or blaming her. I used the trigger technique to look at how I had within myself those difficult characteristics I saw in her, and healed them. I took ownership of all those qualities and started doing the work on myself.

In the past, I have also been known for being a very brash person that could say mean things. I wanted to heal that within myself. I had to cut out one of my best friends from my life in order to change my behavior. I needed time to heal from my deep childhood traumas and avoid any influence (triggered state) of going back to that behavior. I am so grateful to her for being so patient, loving, understanding, and present with me now. I love her dearly.

It's the analogy of being a recovering alcoholic and not hanging out at bars or with friends while they are drinking, until you have gone through all the 12 steps. You have to stay away from the behavior that triggers you until it is healed within you. Being mean is NEVER how I want to come across to anyone, including myself. This process took a lot longer than I thought!

I needed time to investigate how and where this behavior infiltrated my entire life. I used every tool in my toolbox. I am happy I did the work on myself to create a healthy interaction for the rest of our lives.

OOPS, MY BAD

Acknowledge your mistakes and come clean with everyone it affects. Everyone makes mistakes, even "perfect" people! Mistakes can be made all over the place, from super small and trivial to massively huge ones. It's important to take responsibility for your mistakes, apologize and do whatever you can to rectify the situation.

Whether they forgive you or not does not matter, you only need to do the right thing: let go of your attachment to the outcome. In one particular situation, I really screwed up badly. I did something to really disappoint someone I care about deeply. I have loved her as my soul family since the day I met her. We had worked side by side building our company together for years. We spent countless days turned into nights, sewing costumes, creating shows, acquiring new skills, rehearsing, recruiting, and building something we truly believed in. We built the company with our blood, sweat, and tears. It was one of my dreams to come true.

But one mistake and everything tumbled down in one fell swoop. I was kicked out of the company, which was everything to me. She told me that she hated me and never wanted to talk to me again. I was devastated. At first, I honored her request by staying away, paralyzed in regret. My identity, which was wrapped up in what we built, was gone. Who was I if I was not part of that anymore? I did not pray much until then. I prayed every night for answers. It was my calling to be a part of it all, and something had to be done. My staying away was not a solution that healed anyone.

I sent her several emails and text messages apologizing. I let her know that I loved her and that I was still there for her if she needed me. She ignored my emails and texts for a year, so I had no other recourse but to go to her in person. I told her all the same things to her face, and she said, "Get away from me. I hate you. I don't want to talk to you ever again. I never want to see your face." I stood there and took it all in, knowing she had every right and reason to be mad. I calmly responded, "I know you're upset. I'm sorry. There's nothing that I can do to make up for what I did. I can only begin again. I love you, and I'm here for you. We are family and we're going to be in each other's lives. I love you!"

I continued to do this every time I saw her at events and gatherings, as it was the only way I could ever see her in person. I continued to send love to her and focused on solutions all the while not attached to whether or not she actually forgave me. She eventually came around and did forgive me. Her forgiveness changed my life.

I would never make a mistake like that again. I am happy to say it's been almost twenty years since then that we have worked and traveled the world together. I love my soul sister so much! Anything you give your heart to will turn to fruit, eventually. Even if that fruit comes from a different tree.

CHAPTER 7

CHOOSE POWERFULLY

THE GREATEST GIFT WE HAVE IN LIFE IS CHOICE
The secret of change is to focus all of your energy, not
on fighting the old, but on building the new."
~ SOCRATES ~

"The best time to plant a tree is twenty years ago...
The second best time is today."
~ CHINESE PROVERB ~

Are you counting on someone else to make you happy? Are you counting on your partner or another close person in your life to make your life better? If so, good luck. The only one that can make your life the way you want it to be is YOU. You have the ability to create all the happiness that you want in your life but it's a choice. If you don't have the *exact* life you want, you don't really have time to watch TV, movies, or Netflix until you're in action on realizing your goals, dreams, and purpose!

Make the most powerful choice in every moment! Choosing powerfully means you have assessed the choices available to you, considered which ones align most with your purpose and goals, and made the choice that will result in the best outcome within every opportunity. Choose what's happening *now*. Choose what's right for you. Choose what works. Focus on what you want the outcome to be, make the choice to support the future you want, and then let things unfold. Choose happiness—it's a good choice, after all.

You have the power to choose. You have your own reasons for your actions, which then become your "why" for doing things. Whether you are conscious of it or not, you are constantly making meaning out of everything. Being aware of your choices and your "why" are where your power lies. This is how you choose your path. Approaching any fork in the road and choosing powerfully which way to go will allow you to create the experiences you desire, rather than being stuck with situations you don't want. The beautiful road called your life can go in the direction you consciously choose.

To help yourself choose powerfully and precisely, you must bring awareness to every moment of your life. You must be aware when you are in flight or fight mode so that you have the awareness to choose a positive outcome. Most situations are not actual life or death situations.

When we are self aware we can choose not to respond from our automatic response FOF mode and learn to consciously choose the right actions. Greater awareness will help you in every situation, every time. If you desire to feel joy, ask yourself what would give you that feeling of happiness in the situation and then choose that. Choosing powerfully allows you to create a more beautiful world for you and others to live in.

CRITICAL THINKING

Daniel Kahneman won the 2002 Nobel Memorial Prize for his research in Behavioral Economics with his discovery that most people make irrational and inconsistent decisions based on certain cognitive biases, not critical thinking. No matter how intelligent they are, most people make decisions using shortcuts and emotional states that make it easier to form quick—but not always well-thought-out—opinions.

Marketing companies have been studying human behavior for decades and have found how to significantly influence our economic choices. Studies have proven that humans can be made to make biased decisions using comparison, word-of-mouth, likability, expert opinion, scarcity, and reciprocity—all of which are called nudges.

If you're not using critical thinking to make decisions, then you are ruled by your emotions because of your brain's tendency to want simple answers. Most people make decisions based on those nudge principles above, which have been thoroughly investigated in order to understand human behavior and manipulate it for marketing purposes and business gains. This is what most decisions are based on unless one specifically uses critical thinking.

For those of us that have a really important decision to make, such as which car to buy, we want to use a critical thinking approach rather than a more emotional one because there is more at stake. You need to take into account the price of the car, how many miles per gallon it gets, where you'll park it, and more because you will have to deal with the major financial burdens if not. But for almost all other purchases, human behavior can be controlled through those nudges—as you know from experience if you've ever dealt with a persuasive car salesman. Having a system in place and practicing the proper way to make decisions until your critical thinking becomes second nature will protect you and your family.

There is so much that goes into critical thinking. The part of the brain that makes decisions is the frontal lobe. This region of the brain controls your ability to think, reasoning and self-control. Many factors affect your ability to make sound decisions, such as proper structural alignment of your body, ample sleep, and proper nourishment.

For example, having bad posture cuts off the proper flow of blood and oxygen throughout your body. People have improved poor circulation and many other health issues just by addressing their posture using the Feldenkrais Method. Posture is something I have to be consciously mindful of everyday.

Hunching over causes you not to have full blood flow to your frontal lobe and therefore not work at full capacity. You may experience some brain fog, maybe forget what you went into a room for, or have what we call "brain farts." The first step to making sound decisions is a good posture, a good night's sleep, and proper nourishment. Only then can you find the best possible outcome for yourself.

Since choice is the greatest gift in life we have, we must arm ourselves with the ability to make the most rational decision possible. Most of the time we think that we are living a rational life when we are not. Kahneman proved that humans make irrational choices consisting of factors motivated by what is in fashion and popular or by doing what everyone else is doing.

But when you know your own nature, you can make decisions based on what is in alignment with your life purpose and your specific goals. All of those biases come from the space of ego. How much ego gets in the way of our daily life?

Critical thinking is the fastest way to make decisions to get what you truly want, and part of living a life on the path of least resistance. I happily choose this path and hopefully you will too. Your life can be your personal Paradise; you can create anything by consciously choosing it. Every choice you make can inhibit or exhibit who you are in this world. All your choices got you to this moment and created what is happening right now— including reading this book. If you want something different, you can create an action plan that will lead you to your goals. You just have to plan it!

To create your plan, you will first want to gather information on the factors that will go into your decision. Say you're deciding which college to go to. You'll want to gather and organize all of the information for the colleges you like, as well as information for other options, such as not attending college and starting your own business instead. You'll have to consider all the factors for each option such as student debt, loan repayment, available jobs offered after graduation, and the like. If there is no job guarantee, is it better to get a small business loan and start your dream business?

Map out all possible scenarios and outcomes and the arguments for and against each option. Get creative and think each possible choice all the way through to the end. Consider the impact on your life from each choice, and then get the perspective of other people whom you trust.

I like to keep all the information gathered for each option on a separate page of paper. I then draw a line down the middle of the page to weigh the pros and cons of the decision I'm making. I usually sit quiet in a heart-brain coherence meditation for at least five minutes, with my hand on my heart, and ask which choice will bring the highest version of myself forward.

CHOOSE LOVE OVER FEAR

Fear is the anticipation of pain. Choices you make that stem from fear rather than love lead to malignant shame, overgrown guilt, and resentment. Comparison is the thief of joy, and will steal time that you will never get back. All these things can clog up the flow of the vital life force that's constantly trying to repair and heal us.

You don't have to buy into the fearful voices in your head. Take action despite fear. Take chances like you take vitamins. You can never remove your ego from the equation, but you can tame the beast. You can acquire techniques and practices that allow you to use your ego as a tool.

This greater awareness keeps ego from running (and ruining) your life. Love is the only real currency. It is a power best described as having the strength stronger than gravity because, even after death, when gravity isn't an issue, LOVE PREVAILS! The amazing Taj Mahal was built for love, and is proof that love can do anything. What has fear done for you lately?

We are constantly making choices. We choose what to listen to, what to read, and what to believe. Right now you're making the choice to read this book. Your limiting beliefs and programs are listening and making the choices if you aren't aware to powerfully choose.

I want you to have the freedom to listen to new information, even if all your upbringing tells you not to. Most everything you think about yourself and the world is something you heard from someone you trust. We then spend our entire lives either proving or disproving those ideas.

We still carry these belief systems with us until we break them down and then choose for ourselves what we want to believe. Most of the things you believe are based on experiences you had when you were younger. As we grow, we find ourselves choosing the action we decided was the best option back when we were little. Now as adults we still make choices based on the decisions we made as children.

The problem is we are not children anymore, yet we are still living our lives from that childhood mentality. Generally, when we make those decisions as a kid, we are responding to a need for self protection with very limited resources available to us, and we make those choices because they are the best coping mechanisms we have available to us at the time. Our resources and potential responses as adults are vastly greater, yet our beliefs lock us into the limited range of decisions available to a child. How often do you challenge your own beliefs now?

EPIGENETICS

Epigenetics is the study of biological mechanisms that switch genes on and off. The Human Genome Project brought to the forefront that we are not doomed to suffer the ailments encoded in our ancestors' genes inside of us. Our environment, thoughts, and beliefs shape our health. We have the ability to make different choices and limit our ancestors' genetic expressions by how we take care of our mental and physical health. We no longer need to take on the so-called "disease" that our parents or grandparents had.

It's up to us to create our reality, physically, mentally and emotionally. Because of the truths uncovered by Epigenetics, we can now choose all those positive traits we have always wanted like ordering from a catalog, or online from the number one monopoly company that starts with an "A." In this day and age, we truly can be anything we want to be. We can change our biology by changing our beliefs. Check out any of the books by Dr. Bruce Lipton or Dr. Joe Dispenza.

CHOOSE FORGIVENESS

Actively practice forgiveness—this includes forgiving yourself. Forgiveness is a sacred act. We would disintegrate if we didn't have anything sacred in our lives. Most of our suffering comes from a lack of forgiveness or the fear of not being loved.

The inability to forgive protects our heart and prevents us from experiencing love. Not forgiving someone doesn't hurt who you think it does. When you don't forgive, you hurt yourself more than the person who betrayed you. Love is fast and can heal the heart instantly when you present yourself with it. Forgiveness gets easier the more you practice it. Life is too short to hold a grudge.

The act of not forgiving holds the pain and trauma inside of your being and fills your cells with toxic energy. When you do not forgive, you keep that wound open, which causes scarring. Do not be committed to a scar.

Be willing to forgive anyone for anything—it's easier than you think. Forgiving yourself and others releases you from the past. Forgiveness does not mean you should forget! Forgiveness is for *you*, so *you* can have complete freedom. Forgiveness is a beautiful gift to give to yourself. Forgive and set yourself free.

Most often, the person you are holding a grudge against doesn't even know you have one, nor are they affected by your negative feelings, so they get off scot-free. You are the only person suffering in the grudge-holding process. If we sit in a prison of self-righteous resentment we cannot be free.

If you have done something wrong or are regretful for something it's time to clean it up as soon as possible. Communicate with love to all the people involved. Nobody thinks they are a bad person and everyone is doing the best they can under the given circumstances, including you.

When you let go of the past, your present moment becomes richer and fuller. Holding on to pain and hurt keeps you stuck. Free yourself and everyone in your life from all past hurts. You and they will now be free to move into new glorious experiences together.

The point of power is in the present moment. You can begin to change in this moment with forgiveness, for as you change your thinking, your life also changes. The past is over and done and has no power over you when you forgive. Release the need to blame anyone, including yourself. You can begin to be free in this moment. Today's thoughts create your future and you are in charge. Take your power back.

Even if we don't know exactly how to forgive, we can be willing to forgive. The Universe will respond to our willingness and help us find the way. This is a practice you'll get better at with time. It is not an easy fix-all solution.

Malcolm Gladwell's book *Outliers* says that if you want to be a professional at something, you must spend 10,000 hours doing it. If you want to be an Olympic athlete, you need a coach. If you want to lose weight and are inexperienced with nutrition, discipline, or exercise—you hire a trainer. I know you want to live a happier life because you're reading this book. Sign up for coaching or get someone to hold you accountable at <u>www.POLRLIVING.com</u>. You can also make this book your mentor, put in the time, and become a world champion at forgiveness!

Begin to surround yourself with people who already think like you do or see you for who you really are. Keep your heart open— RADICALLY! Do not cut out people from your heart even if they have hurt you. You do not need to keep them close to you, but you can continue to send them love. Chances are they need it more than you know.

CHALLENGE YOUR BELIEFS

I started questioning my beliefs when I found myself speaking matter-of-fact statements or repeating statements like "You can't always get what you want" or "You can't have it all." Now I know to question those types of blanket statements. Most people never question these colloquialisms because there is so much "agreement evidence" that it must be true. We hear those statements in song lyrics, read them in books, or get them as advice from friends.

Learn to question everything and believe nothing. People we love instill us with these beliefs thinking they will protect us, because they were true for them in their life. But as life evolves, those previous habits of thinking become an old paradigm.

My mother would tell me, "You can't always get what you want." She couldn't always provide what I needed in life and didn't want me to be disappointed, so she passed this belief down to me. Her thinking from an old era became my thinking. It was true for my grandmother as well. She went through the Depression and passed it down to my mother. I now know this is not *my* truth.

I am grateful to have distinctions on what's mine and what belongs to someone else. There's even a fun Rolling Stones song I used to love to sing out loud enforcing the same limiting belief: "You can't always get what you want." I carried that song like a torch until I questioned it. The best part about growing up is getting to make your own choices. You can choose different things to believe.

Choosing powerfully to create new beliefs that are in alignment with your goals and dreams gets you closer to all the things you want in this life. Now, when I hear these types of phrases come out of people's mouths, I kindly respond, "That's not a philosophy I subscribe to anymore." It keeps their limiting belief to themselves and allows them to see there might be another way to look at it.

OLD PARADIGM

In 1999, I quit my day job and committed to a path of following my dreams. I chose a different belief: "I can have it all." I wanted to make a living doing only that which I loved, which is a long list of things. People told me I'd never make it. "You have to choose only one thing and give it your all." You know the saying, "If you're a Jack-of-all-trades, you're a master of none." This was not my understanding. I saw examples of people being good at several things and even heard it called the new Renaissance.

Times change, and the status quo ain't what it used to be. It is safe to identify this one-track way of thinking as old paradigm thinking. Another popular limiting belief is, "You can't have both a career and a family, you have to choose one." Those were never my beliefs. I started to look for women that had both a successful career and a happy family.

I found them in droves. I knew in my heart that if I wanted it, I would be able to get it.

QUESTION EVERYTHING

Humans often assume there's only one solution to every problem, but there are so many different types of people on this planet and there are just as many different ways to do things. I suggest questioning everything that comes out of your mouth in the beginning. Question every thought. The layers are deep. The more you question, the deeper you can go.

FOCUS ON SOLUTIONS

In a game of soccer, what is the point of the game? You might say to score as many goals as possible, to win the game, or to have fun. In order to do any of those things, you must keep your eye on the ball at all times. What is the ball in your life?

What is the one single thing in your life that will always do the right thing for you? Your heart—because it always knows what's best for you! You align your spirit, body, and mind by acting on inspiration from your heart.

This is Divinity, your divine nature. Living in the space of your divine nature is the purest source of life. Getting into this state is easy when you focus on the things you want, not what you don't want. What do you spend a lot of time, energy, and life force thinking about? What takes up the majority of your focus?

DON'T JUST KEEP TREATING SYMPTOMS— LOOK FOR THE CAUSE

It's important to look for the root cause of any disorder or discomfort instead of just focusing on and breeding the symptoms. In western medicine it is customary to treat only the symptom and not investigate the reason for the issue. There are people out there that have dandruff and ask their doctor, "What are all these white flakes in my hair?" The doctor says, "You have dandruff. Here is medication." To "cure" your dandruff, you're given a special shampoo and an internal medication that helps reduce it to almost nothing.

You are now certified as a person that always has dandruff, instead of a person who may be sensitive to something in their diet or environment. Have you ever asked yourself what is causing the dandruff? An alkaline and Candida-free diet can change your entire life. There are great natural treatments for dandruff out there, but you have to find and remove the root cause of the issue.

Because Western medicine mostly treats the symptoms, it keeps you ill and often on medication for the rest of your life. When you dig down to the real root problem in searching for the solution to the dandruff, you can start with something small like switching all your soaps and detergents to biodegradable non-toxic kinds. You may want to try a Candida or an elimination diet to remove the excess yeast from your system before taking a medicine to mask the problem.

After living in Los Angeles for five years I came down with very strange symptoms that caused me some difficulty breathing. For no apparent reason my lungs would fill up with liquid and I wouldn't be able to get enough air. I was essentially drowning. Friends who had inhalers would offer them to me and they always worked, so I reported all of this to my doctor after several months of this going on. He didn't do any tests whatsoever but simply said, "Yup, you have asthma," put me immediately on steroids and gave me an inhaler.

I was using the emergency inhaler three to five times a day as well as taking the steroids twice a day for two years, never once questioning if I might be allergic to something. We put so much trust into a doctor's practice, but that's exactly what they are doing—*practicing*, ON YOU! The medicine wasn't really working, so I asked for an allergenic blood test, but Medi-Cal didn't cover it and I couldn't pay for it at that time.

I decided that I was going to heal my lungs with whatever healing modality came into my path, so I posted a message to my community. The first person that reached out to me was an acupuncturist, and he told me to cut out gluten and dairy. "NOOOO!!" Those were my favorite things. I thought there was no way I could do that, but I reminded myself of the promise I made and did it anyway.

Within two months, I stopped the steroids and only used the inhaler a couple of times each week. After six months of no dairy or gluten, I stopped the inhaler altogether and have now been free from its death grip for more than six years. Any time I have tried to eat gluten or dairy since sets me off again. I stay clear of them now because the quality of my life, not to mention my figure, have greatly improved!

CHOOSE WIN-WIN SITUATIONS

A sure-fire way to get positive results is by choosing Win-Win situations. Win-Win is a solution to a situation or a result that is beneficial for all parties involved. If one person is losing, everyone loses. When everyone is winning, life is great! It's always possible in every relationship to create win-win situations.

Begin the conversation with others involved by stating what you want and any solutions you can think of to reach your goal. Then let them come up with their own options and go from there. You can take the solutions and work backwards to discover what you can do as a group to find a solution that works for everybody. When everybody is winning or getting value out of the transaction or experience, it feels good. If anyone is in disagreement about the solution, ask what they need to feel supported. Listen to the answer and let them know if you can provide it or not to create the most powerful negotiation you can.

You may be having a hard time with someone close to you. Maybe you always seem to bicker about insignificant things. Usually, this is a sign that someone's needs aren't being met. It is easy to nip it in the bud and just get right to the solution when you bring your awareness to what will resolve things in that circumstance. When experiencing conflict in any situation or relationship, focus on all possible answers. You can come up with solutions together with all the people involved to create a situation that works for everyone. There is always a way.

Start with statements like, "I am committed to us working this out" then follow it up with questions such as "What are you seeking as an outcome?" "How can I help you?" or "What is it you need me to say or do for you to be complete?" You will want to use your own words and make them relevant to your current situation. Nothing else matters. Once you hear out what they want, you can let them know what you need as well. Drop all arguments and declare what you want and what you are committed to with love in your heart.

DUMP TRUCK

I use the metaphor of a dump truck to mean dumping all the choices, actions, and thoughts that leave you feeling inadequate, small, sick, unhealthy or any other way you may feel unfulfilled or out of balance. Then choose positive choices, actions and thoughts instead. You must DUMP TRUCK to take out all that trash in your head. Why would you waste your time, energy, life force, happiness, job, or relationship because of a feeling of inadequacy or insecurity?

Those thoughts and feelings become negative looping thought patterns and are a waste of time. This small-picture thinking does not serve a positive purpose. It only makes you feel bad. It ruins relationships and has never done anything good for anyone!

Spend your valuable time doing and thinking about things that make you feel adequate, happy, and safe. Take the actions necessary to enrich your life so you feel secure. Do not let those feelings of insecurity get in the way of your quality of life. Feelings aren't the truth. It's time to let go of those small thoughts and small habits that do not serve your highest good.

Free yourself from your own mental slavery. DUMP TRUCK any small thoughts, habits, or actions that don't support your goals and dreams. In a moment, you can decide never to let those things have power over you again. Just imagine a dump truck coming to your house for you to get rid of all the unusable things in your home and life. Put all those small thoughts, toxic behaviors, and negative loops into the dump truck and watch it drive away.

Let's put it into a business perspective as an example, so it's easier to remove you from the story of it. Someone sells you a box that you put $1 into, and a gold coin comes out. You buy it for a lot of money, because this is going to be really good for your business. But when you put a dollar in the second time, nothing comes out.

You call the guy immediately and he comes over to ensure it works. He puts in his own dollar and out comes a gold coin. He leaves, and you try it again, but nothing happens.

Over the phone he says you have to shake it a little and it'll come out. You put a dollar in again and nothing comes out. This time you're extremely irritated, you paid a lot of money for this. So, you call the guy again. "Hey, you told me that this box would drop out a gold coin if I put a dollar in it. I tried shaking it and nothing!" He says, "just keep trying." You hang up on him and continue to put dollar after dollar into it and nothing ever comes out.

You have lost your money, your time, and now you don't know what to do. Do you keep putting money in the box? No! The guy that sold you the box is your ego. The box is Small Picture Thinking. You must DUMP TRUCK the small picture thinking, adopt new thoughts and take new actions.

Another example: you move to a new town and you're looking for a new fishing hole. You find a spot you like and you cast your reel. After one full day without catching a thing, you go home. You really liked that spot for whatever reason, maybe there's a shady tree, so you decide to go back again. The next day is extremely hot, and again you do not catch any fish. You go into the water and look underneath. You see that there are no fish at all, in fact, there is no life at all. Would you continue to try fishing there?

No! You would find another place. It's time to find a different space for your mind or different actions for your body.

If you wouldn't continue to throw time and money away on things that don't work in your business, why would you continue to do this in your life? The moment you start thinking those negative thoughts about yourself, you can stop them dead in their tracks and replace them with new ones. If it does not serve humanity or mankind, it will not serve you. You were born to do great things. Live your biggest life by focusing on solutions, behaviors, and actions that bring you what's really important to you. DUMP TRUCK what's not working and move on. Doing this will allow you to release all the insecurities and small-picture thinking by transforming your trash into treasure.

NEUROPLASTICITY

NEUROPLASTICITY
Definition: //neu·ro·plas·tic·i·ty// //n(y)oorōplastisdē// ~Noun
1. The brain's ability to reorganize synaptic connections by forming new neural networks in response to learning or experiencing new things and following an injury. (www.OxfordDictionaries.com)

Evolution is the act of adapting to changes in our environment for our survival. Neuroplasticity is what allows the nerve cells or neurons in the brain to compensate for injury or disease and adjust their behaviors in response to new behaviors or situations. Science has finally discovered that the hippies were right about their "Positive Affirmations" all along.

You can rewire your brain and get free from the negative loops and negative self-talk by creating new thought patterns and habits. The more you think a certain thought, the more those particular synapses fire, and the more often you will think those thoughts. If you've been thinking a negative thought for a long time it may take a little longer to transform, but it is completely possible!

You are also susceptible to other people's bad habits or thinking just by being around them. Your brain wiring can even be influenced by TV or social media. Television programming can influence what you believe and how you react to situations. I go into further detail about this in the Spirit, Body, & Mind Chapter 11.

Media is a multi-billion-dollar business that creates programming for you to zone out to, and the media producers control the mainstream narrative. It's high time we define our own narrative. This is why it is crucial to rewrite your own programming. Once you understand how powerful media is in influencing your actions, you can choose a different path.

TAKE THE BILLBOARD CHALLENGE

The advertising world uses major psychological games and tricks to get inside of our heads. Have you seen all the billboards and ads around? Try this for yourself to see how powerful marketing actually is. This game is super fun to play on road trips or in cities. While you're driving, see if you can choose to NOT LOOK at the billboards! Just try it. You can't help but look because they were designed that way. I play this game as often as I can, although I have to be very diligent and aware enough to not look at them. The busy mind does whatever it wants to do unless you have trained your mind through meditation and other practices to do something different.

My friends and I have only been 100% successful at winning this game when we are completely immersed in some other activity or deep in conversation whilst on the road. The constant barrage of advertising leaves imprints on us which the ad agencies plan for, knowing the messages will make it more likely that we eventually buy. Take the billboard challenge and see how you fare. You score one point for every billboard you successfully avoid looking at and deduct two points for every billboard you accidentally see. The first person to twenty points wins.

CHOOSE YOUR WORDS CAREFULLY

I know it's hard to imagine that people think differently than we do because we only know what's in our own brains. Assumptions can get you into trouble and end up hurting you and those you love in the long run. It is easy to think that when you are affected by something that everyone else is also affected in that same way. However, it's just not true.

Everyone's experience is different and we shouldn't assume that our experience is the same as someone else's. When you talk about any opinion or situation, speak only for yourself. Let others decide if your experiences are similar to theirs. Do not assume for others. When you unconsciously speak for others by using words like "we" and "people" to describe your own issues or problems, it shuts down another person's ability to listen to you when it's not how they feel.

It is also extremely important to use non-confrontational words like "me" or "I" when explaining your problems and disagreements. Check out "Nonviolent Communication" by Marshall Rosenburg for other great communication techniques. Choosing your words carefully improves your communication skills and gives others the ability to hear you.

I have a very dear friend who was just starting out on her journey of being a life coach and she was having issues with people showing a lot of enthusiasm in the beginning but then not following through and signing up as a client. This left her royally disappointed *and* she took it personally. I told her that in order to help her clients she would have to get out of her own way and work on removing her attachments first. She was extremely attached to getting more clients and making more money but she hadn't done the work on herself. She knew she needed to move through her own issues so that she could be the coach that she knows she is, but she got very defensive when I explained my view of it.

She used the words "we" and "people" to describe her own personal issues and experience. It really threw me off because I was the only other person in the room and I don't subscribe to the philosophies she was claiming "we" held. She went into a diatribe about "People need to feel insecure in order to have the next evolution to raise their consciousness, otherwise we would all just feel like gods and that everything is perfect." I had to stop her before she continued and I responded with "I simply don't subscribe to that philosophy." She became emotionally triggered by my response and she had to take a moment before continuing.

I kept reminding her throughout her rant that whenever she tried to throw me into her negative loop by saying "we" I wasn't having it. She became angrier because I was not rising to her triggered state or becoming emotional about it either; she wanted someone to jump on the bandwagon with her.

After her ten minute time-out to collect herself and gather her thoughts, she came back in the room to get to the point and get things off her chest. It turns out she made up a story that I did not care about her from this little experience. I reminded her of all the obvious reasons I do care very deeply for her and how I have endlessly gone out of my way for her.

In this instance, I simply stood my ground and wouldn't allow her trauma to misrepresent me or my beliefs. She had to take ownership of her beliefs and not push them onto me. Later in the evening she came around and said she looked up to me because I had what she called "strength." I did not see it as a strength, I was just being very clear and taking a stand for what I believe. Being authentic in every communication creates clarity in life.

INTENTION + HEART-BASED ACTIONS = MAGNETISM

You don't have to be bad to get better! Yes, even at your best you can still do even better. There's always room for improvement. There is always the option to do it in the way in which you can have the most fun, too! If your obligations lead you to something you truly want and desire, you might as well have fun with them!

Humans have a funny way of only focusing on the immediate feeling or experience, which can cause suffering. Simply choose with your own awareness where to focus your mind, instead of letting your mind or ego run your life. If you are not consciously choosing to live your life from the experience of your heart and choosing actions that love would take, then your ego or emotions are running the show.

CHOOSE FUN INSTEAD

By *not* choosing to have fun doing necessary things to make your life happen, you send mixed messages to your subconscious. For example, when my house is clean, I like to have guests over or relax in my own home without stress. When my house is dirty, it stresses me out and I don't want any house guests. So instead of begrudgingly cleaning or doing chores because it doesn't feel good at that moment, choose the feeling you'd get after the task has been completed instead.

Try to make it fun or enjoy washing the dishes, sweeping, mopping, or doing laundry because you get to relax and walk around a clean house when it's done. Why would you fill your heart and spirit up with any feeling that doesn't make you feel good when you can be grateful and focus on the feeling you get after completing those tasks you dislike? Bring a joyful heart to all the things you do, especially the gross or disgusting things that positively impact your life. If you have to do something anyway, wouldn't you rather have fun doing it? This approach creates an overall sense of well being for you and those around you.

Most people choose to be unhappy about menial tasks that eventually help them in the long run. You get to choose to be different and focus on how the task at hand or new habit you're trying to create will make you feel, after doing it for an extended period of time. Now, add fun, joy, and happiness to the equation to improve your results.

You magnetize more things to you that you want in life when you are in a joyful state, and more people want to be around you when you're in that state. You have the choice to wash dishes feeling like crap, hating the whole experience, or you could put on music, wash dishes, and sing your way through. In my world, that is a no brainer. I take the playful route every time because it's waaaaay more fun! Making things fun or doing tasks in the most fun way you can do them, trains your Spirit, body, and mind to do the things that will make you grow and feel better in the long run and live a happier and healthier life.

PLAY = ACCESS TO POWER

As we go through life acquiring more responsibilities and dealing with stress or heartbreak, we can become hardened. Some people have become serious all the time just to manage all the things life throws at them. Staying in this state makes it hard to let loose. It is extremely important to have a sacred time for play just as you make time for other things. When you are happy and feeling good, everything comes into alignment and people are attracted to you. People prefer to be around happy people.

When kids are playing, anything is possible. They make stuff up, they pretend. When I was really young, around five or six, I liked playing house or grocery store.

My aunt had a treadmill that we would put to a use its manufacturers hadn't planned on: we'd pull all the food out of the cupboards, pretend to scan it and then send the food down the treadmill. The other person had to bag it before the next item came. It was so much fun! We'd start speeding up the pace and if anything dropped on the floor, you were out. My aunt would come home and never be the wiser, although there were a few times she wondered why the pasta boxes were wrinkled or some cans had dents in them. It's a very weird game looking back on it, but it was one of my favorites because I felt so alive and on-fire! To this day, I can still fast-pack a grocery bag perfectly without anything getting smashed.

Think back to the last time you were "on fire" and felt unstoppable, a time when you were feeling so good that anyone that might have bothered you before, didn't. Keep a list of when you accessed this state so you can revisit it anytime! This is what I call PLAY STATE where you have full access to power—it's a power move. It's like you're up for anything, rolling with the punches, saying yes, and taking things head on. When you are in this space, you have the ability to attract everything you want.

Being in a PLAY STATE allows you to look at something in a unique way, especially where you have been previously blocked or stopped. Try bringing play to those tough or challenging situations to see what opens up for you. Consider that when you are stopped, it may be your ego. Ego gets triggered all the time. When you are in your play state, your ego becomes your bitch!

There is nothing like the feeling of being in that flow state. When you're tapped into PLAY STATE, and everything is on the upswing, you feel sexy and everything you say is funny. When you are playful and having fun, everything goes your way. You are unstoppable! If you were a river and you came up against a rock, you wouldn't stop, you would go around it and even over it. You are nature and you can do that, too.

BE AUTHENTIC WITH YOUR WORDS

AUTHENTIC
Definition: //au·then·tic// /ôTHen(t)ik/ ~ Adjective
1. Real or genuine: not copied or false.: true and accurate.
2. Having an origin supported by unquestionable
evidence. (www.Merriam-Webster.com)

Unconscious words keep us unable to be authentic when we speak, until we have an awareness around it. For instance, a conversation starting with "I don't mean to interrupt you but...," when indeed it is the VERY thing you meant to do. You had to interrupt them because you wanted to speak to them. How do you expect someone to listen to anything you have to say when you start it off with a bald-faced lie?

I'm being harsh, but we must bring awareness around this unconsciousness vernacular so we can better align with who we really are, what we want to communicate, and what we want to achieve. Instead, you can say something like, "I apologize for interrupting you," or "Pardon the interruption." Consciously choosing authentic words does wonders for the soul and all your relationships.

"Your beliefs become your thoughts. Your thoughts become your words. Your words become your actions. Your actions become your habits. Your habits become your values. Your values become your destiny." ~ Mahatma Gandhi, Indian political and spiritual leader (1869 - 1948) ~

SPELL CHECK

Our words are casting spells which is why it's so important to check what spells you may be casting into your future consciously or unconsciously. We live in a world shaped by beliefs. What are you manifesting? Those beliefs are spread by words. In the early 1900s if you were fat and pale, you were considered rich, and if you were thin and dark-skinned, you were poor. Now, being fat is considered worse than being poor. Being skinny and tan is in. We are all products of the time, place, family, financial reality, and skin color we are born into. We were born into those specific programs by the sheer birthing process itself.

In our first moments out of the womb most of us are screaming and crying. It's not until we get older that we start to develop goals and desires, and to empower ourselves. Some of us even search for tools that help us expedite self-empowerment and self-improvement, such as you choosing this book to read.

You must talk about your visions and the situations that you want to bring into your life, more than you talk about your problems. Whatever you talk about, you breathe your life force into it. Your words are casting spells. They are like prayers being sent into the universe to be fulfilled.

SPELL CHECK is a fun game for when you catch and stop yourself or someone else in a negative thought pattern. When you hear yourself doing this, shout out (or think in your head) "SPELL CHECK" and rewire your programming to rewrite your destiny. For instance, your friend gets fired or dumped and they may say "This always happens to me." which casts that spell into their future.

Just because it happened in the past, doesn't mean it will happen again. That's when you say "SPELL CHECK". It's a fun game to play with friends to call each other out. We are here to help each other after all. The more aware you are of all the spells you've been casting, the easier it is to create a new improved future.

You can join the P.O.L.R. LIVING Community online to meet and be with other like-minded individuals. Meet new people to play these games with https://www.polrliving.com/ and join our Facebook and Telegram Groups.

"Community is much more than belonging to something.
It's doing something together that makes belonging matter."
~ Brian Solis ~

HOLD PEOPLE ACCOUNTABLE FOR THEIR GREATNESS

If you don't, no one will. Perhaps all someone is waiting for is to be called upon to be a hero. By bringing it to their attention in a loving way when someone is playing small, we can offer them the ability to choose powerfully. They can either step into their greatness or not.

It's not about judging them, making them do anything, or being attached to an outcome—it's calling into their awareness how they're showing up so they have a choice in the matter. Maybe right now they just can't and that's OK. Share from your heart and compassionately help them notice if they are playing a small game.

This process may be bumpy at first, but we all have things to contribute to others. The stronger your intuition gets, the more effective you will be at identifying these things as they come up. We are all born for greatness, we wouldn't be here otherwise. Holding others accountable for their greatness allows us to step into our higher selves.

I have now had the honor of being the "Orange Color Team Captain" at the Dirtybird Campout Music Festival since the festival began. This role has forever changed my life for the better. Dirtybird is very different from most music festivals because it's set up like a kids camp with games and camp counselors.

There are four colors you might get when you sign up for the games, either a green, purple, red or orange. You get your official Dirtybird bandanna as a free souvenir gift that you wear throughout the festival indicating which team you're on. As Orange Captain, I was responsible for enrolling people into playing the games, coaching them, and creating memorable lasting experiences for the participants of the festival and my Orange teammates.

Coaching the games at this festival is where I learned how to turn someone into a leader in 30 seconds. Because how you do one thing is how you do everything, if I saw someone hesitate on the field during a game, I'd call them out right away. They in turn would have the opportunity either to stand in their greatness or fumble.

I was able to help them see that how they played the game is how they live their life. It is easier to first see yourself in a game rather than your own life. Practicing new ways of being through the medium of games helps you in your regular life. Choosing to play each of the games in this book with others solidifies new growth and opportunities. Besides, games are more fun!

TRIPPER TRAPS

A tripper trap is anything that trips you up and keeps you trapped in negative thought patterns and behaviors. It can be a series of thoughts causing a downward spiral chain reaction that keeps you in a negative thought loop and unable to get free from the triggered ego. Until you identify its existence you are trapped. Stay clear of them and know when you are in one.

You may be a victim of the tripper trap if you are consistently triggered, confused, anxious, upset or angry. It doesn't matter what happens to you, it matters what you do about it. You can turn any moment into a movement. You'll be able to choose powerfully to eradicate all Tripper Traps from your life once you learn to identify what they are.

TRIPPER TRAP: COMPETITION

We live on an abundant planet but we've been programmed to believe that there isn't enough for everyone. This philosophy has been shoved into our heads since birth. We are programmed to think that we need competition to have progress.

Games are the only real place for competition. The reason we play against eachother for the win is because it's fun to pretend and get all amped up while you are playing. Having only one winner makes the stakes higher and is the entire concept of the game—to win. A "game" means it's not real, which makes it fun to play these various roles. After the game is complete the participants relax and go back to being friends again because the competition only has its place in the game.

When you take that competition out of the game and continue to be upset by your losses or gloat over your wins, it creates weird interactions with others and is unpleasant to be around because it isn't real. Nature doesn't compete—organisms work together in systems. You cannot compare apples to oranges and that competitive thinking leads to scarcity mentality. When we are in that state, fear rules all.

Success or failure for corporations depends on competition and creating scarcity so that consumers will buy. Business competition can lead to new technology and new inventions that improve our lives, but human competition can be detrimental to our health. Competition has become a poisoned pool that we've been given no other option other than to swim in, but when things switch from competition to collaboration it creates equilibrium.

Only out of unity will you contain infinite diversity. We can diversify into an infinite amount of fractal diversity as long as we create from the infinite center—the ONE. The moment we have dismissed this unifying center there is dissonance which separates us from the ONE and is very destructive. From the microcosm to the macrocosm, everything is working together. The Hopi say, "It's written in history that we are the answer to our own problems and that we are the ones to create solutions in our future." Competition is not a solution, it's a problem.

TRIPPER TRAP: WORRY

Worry is a state of mind where we allow ourselves to dwell on problems or imaginary circumstances instead of focusing on solutions. This condition causes anxiety and triggers us into a fight or flight mode. We can't create a positive solution while worrying. It is important to stand in the possibility that everything is working out in the best-case scenario until you receive new information that tells you differently.

The energy that we use to focus on all of the worrisome negative possibilities only causes them to come into creation, as well as make us and everyone around us feel bad. There is no need to feel bad before you know for certain something bad has happened. Until you actually know the hard facts, it's all just guesswork and assumptions based on your perception from past experiences.

Everything is colored by perception, so if the view from which you are looking is not a hopeful one, then you are giving power and energy to manifesting those possible negative outcomes into your future. Worrying will drain your life force of energy and vitality and make you unpleasant to be around.

TRIPPER TRAP: TIME SUCKS

Time sucks are anything and everything that distract you from what you say you want to be doing in your life, and includes procrastination. What are you doing daily that keeps you distracted and further away from your goals? We can distract ourselves through every waking minute until we choose not to. How much time do you spend on your phone or social media? How much time do you spend watching TV, movies or media?

If you aren't living the exact life you desire, you certainly do not have time to watch TV or surf the web. If you are spending too many precious minutes and hours on these time sucks, I suggest doing a media fast until you have a regular routine and are making progress with your goals. Maybe you're a people pleaser and have a hard time saying no. It's important that you do not commit to other things until your basic needs are met. Practice saying "No." If it's not a HELL YES, then it's a HELL NO!

TRIPPER TRAP: SELF-SABOTAGE

Self-sabotage includes any and all behaviors that create problems in your life or interfere with your dreams and goals. These behaviors zap your life essence and leave you feeling exhausted and depleted by cutting off access to the energy you need to create your wonderful life. These are things you know are bad for you, yet you continue to do them, such as flying off the handle, procrastination, lethargy, over-indulgence, lack of self-control, anxiety, depression, cynicism, self-medicating with drugs or alcohol, eating disorders, and all forms of self-injury such as cutting.

TRIPPER TRAP: CONFUSION & INDECISION

You can tie up a lot of time in the famous tripper trap of confusion. You may ask yourself "Should I do this? Should I do that?" That's when you know ego is running the show. The ego creates confusion to gain power. Your heart knows what it wants. Love is always the right answer. Set it straight once and for all.

Most confusion occurs from either not having enough information to make a powerful choice, or engaging in a classic battle between the ego and the heart. Your heart wants it more than anything, but your mind tells you not to do it. You might stay in a dead-end stressful job you loathe because you are desperate for money and can't see a way out. Years pass, you have no energy for yourself because you have given everything to build someone else's company and you begin to feel dead inside, not to mention the effect on your family and friends.

Years of ignoring yourself affects other areas of your life until you choose to take different actions to support your heart and soul's purpose. Confusion is your mind's way of protecting you and there are feelings underneath that are usually present, either fear or anger. You can use curiosity or play to find out why you are scared/upset/angry/frustrated. Investigate *why* you are feeling that way instead of giving in to all the things that make you feel more frustrated or fearful.

ERADICATE CONFUSION & INDECISION

Consider that there are no mistakes and everything happens for a reason. Investigate all of the benefits or results that can come from any decision you're called to make. Often we focus on what we don't want or have and don't honor ourselves or God by investigating what benefits came from the thing that happened that we've been resisting. If you've already made a decision and taken action, when the results show up you might as well enjoy the ride.

Choosing to focus on the things that didn't happen will only cause you more suffering, creating a deeper rut for old programming. Continual practice in focusing on the things that you want and the opportunities that arise from every decision and situation, no matter how small, is crucial in elevating yourself. Focusing on what you don't want just leaves you miserable and sitting in a big pile of feces.

During that time you're lowering the vibration of all of your cells. Your cells are batteries. You can charge them up with love by focusing on all the opportunities that arise. Focusing on disappointment and losses creates sickness and disease. Bruce Lipton said it best: "Your biography becomes your biology."

PLAN FOR SUCCESS

You are either consciously planning for your success or unconsciously planning for your failure. Plan and prepare for the future now. Plan your perfect life. What you do with your time defines who you are. It affects your future and applies to every aspect of your life. It might feel easier to put things off and say you'll do them later, but what you'll find is, later never comes. This is part of choosing powerfully!

Planning for your success is what will bring you success. Take actions that support your goals. Many people spend more time staring into the fridge than planning for their future. Whatever your goals are, you can schedule all the time you need to complete each task. If you find yourself running late all the time, it's because you aren't planning enough time for yourself. Recognize you need way more time to get ready and plan accordingly. Traffic is never an excuse for being late, especially if you live in a big city. Traffic is expected. Be exceptional.

I plan for my success in many areas of my life so that I get to experience more joy and peace on a daily basis. Before I get ready for bed each night, I look at my calendar for the next day to see what's on my agenda. I lay out the proper clothes and pack food if necessary. I ask myself what would make my life even better so I can pack those things in my backpack too.

Often, I have to bring my food to gigs because I am allergic to both gluten and dairy and am also a vegan. Planning my food ensures I am well nourished throughout my day so that I don't have any blood sugar dips or brain fogginess. In my car, I always have a toothbrush and food snacks in case I get home later than anticipated. Anticipating spontaneity is a plan for success that elevates my well-being so I can do whatever and whenever I like, should the opportunity arise.

If I have a project or deadline, I write out all the steps and plan for when each task has to be completed so I am never rushed or stressed in my work. You can literally plan for everything, even for extemporaneous experiences. All it takes is a little thought followed by an action as opposed to stressing out yourself and everyone else around you. When you rush you will not do your best work. Create a plan for success anywhere and everywhere you can to improve the quality of your life.

TAKE RESPONSIBILITY - FOR EVERYTHING

Taking responsibility is owning up to what you do or how you acted in every situation that wasn't your highest self. When you take responsibility for your cause in every exchange, you begin functioning at higher levels of service. Call yourself out!

Stop old patterns and create new neural pathways. Take responsibility to heal the situation at hand. It is food for your soul and for those that you interact with when you do.

Be sure to take responsibility in a way that does not blame the other person. You are responsible for how you feel and respond in every situation. Within every miscommunication or interaction there is some responsibility you can take for how things occurred. You cannot change another person or expect them to behave in a certain way. You can only control yourself, your behavior, and what you made it mean. So be consistent.

HAPPINESS IS A CHOICE

You have the choice and ability to learn through joy or pain. You can choose to learn things through happiness, wisdom, nobility, grace, or intellect rather than fear or pain. We all learn the lessons anyhow, so we may as well have fun instead. It's the *how* you do things that make your journey either pleasant or miserable—it's your choice.

In nature there is no such thing as a drainbow. Nature doesn't sit around and talk about how nature sucks. When you act out of accordance with nature, even nature doesn't want to be around that. What makes you think people are any different?

There are studies all around the world on how plants are affected by the way they're spoken to and by what music is played in their environment. Positive upbeat words and music make for a healthier, robust fruiting plant. Negative sounds and soundtracks, such as people yelling or complaining, actually make plants grow slower, wilt, and even die. Nature chooses happiness and so can you!

The secret to being happy in the future is to practice being happy now! Practice makes perfect. I was lucky enough to have the *best* algebra/philosophy teacher in high school—Mr. Lippman. He was one of those teachers that always pushed you up against yourself to expand what you thought was possible. He taught us to think outside the box. I now permanently live in this space.

My teacher demonstrated that happiness is a choice in a test for us all to see when he stood in front of the classroom and asked for a volunteer. I emphatically threw my hand up and was usually the first person to do that in all my classes. He whispered some instructions in my ear and told me to go outside until he signaled me to come in. He proceeded to talk to the class about perception and happiness, and how you can find the best possible outcome from every situation. In other words, you can choose your experience in every moment, creating exactly what you want, for the good of all.

After he finished explaining he signaled me to come back in. I walked into the room and followed his instructions exactly—taking the scissors he gave me to cut off one of his pant legs. The class gasped. They freaked out and he acted surprised, which shocked me.

He asked the class how they would feel if this happened to them. They responded with "I'd kill her" or "I'd slap her into Timbuktu" or they would scream, yell, cry, or call for help. Then he calmly responded, "What just happened? Someone just cut one of my expensive pant legs off and I can choose any myriad of ways to react. The action is in the past, and I can't change it, but I can choose how to react in this moment. It's June, it's hot. I love the way these pants fit me and now I can cut off the other leg to make a pair of shorts. I'll have my wife hem them when I get home."

Most people would be caught up in the flight or fight reaction ego space and respond accordingly with fear, anger, sadness, etc. When you are a Master of your emotions you can choose to see the positives and create your own happiness. Focus on the big picture and all possible solutions available to you.

On that memorable day, my teacher cut off the other pant leg and continued to teach the rest of the day. This was an invaluable lesson I never forgot that has since impacted my life greatly. There is always more than one way of looking at a situation. Why not choose the option that makes you the happiest and gives you the most power?

CHAPTER 8

CELEBRATIONS AND PRESENTS GALORE

This chapter is by far the most fun! We will go on a deep dive exploration where you will learn many ways to discover all the gifts and treasures in this world for you to enjoy. Did you ever wish for unlimited wishes or presents as a child? I know I did.

Maybe you've wished for a genie to give you three wishes and you'd use one of them to wish for an infinity of wishes? Well, this is very close to granting that. With practice you will get virtually endless presents by looking in the right places, doing all the exercises, and playing all the games lined up for you.

Celebration is the marking of one's appreciation by engaging in enjoyable acts. Celebrate all the wins in your life as well as the challenging times. Celebrate the things going on in your life right now that are working, especially if you want more of it in your life.

Celebration is acknowledging something you like and bringing joy and gratitude to it. Celebrate the things you're grateful for. Especially celebrate the challenges that made you stronger or wiser! You wouldn't be the person you are today had you not gone through everything you have thus far and that, my friend, is a gift to be grateful for!

Even some experience you may have initially thought a failure, but then found a gift or golden nugget within it after time passed, deserves to be celebrated. Every challenging situation has a gift in it, and usually the more difficult the experience, the more gifts you get from it. Perhaps a distant relative dies and the whole family experiences a loss, but then you are gifted a house in their will.

Maybe you get sick from something you ate in a restaurant and it was absolutely miserable for you, but because you got sick, the restaurant cleaned up its act and another diner who is deathly allergic to the thing that got you sick from avoided the danger and lived thanks to you. I have seen all types of seemingly random occurrences happen that were actually linked in a hidden chain of blessings.

Those things can be easily overlooked by the untrained eye until you change your perspective. This chapter will help you develop this new sensibility. It's totally possible for you to train your mind to find the gifts in all situations and celebrate those gifts. You will always be able to find them amidst present challenges, which then bypasses suffering.

Choosing where to put your focus is key. Focusing on the events of the past, things that NO ONE can change, creates unnecessary suffering. You can eliminate it all together by focusing on all the possible gifts that came from that situation.

I warn you now that the ego does not like this—it might be extremely challenging at first. However, with practice and persistence, all things can be mastered eventually. It takes 21 days to form a good habit, and one day to break a bad one. This is where you begin practicing any of the tools in this chapter for 21 days. You can choose more than one. They go hand in hand and complement each other really well.

It is disrespectful to the creator to ignore the gifts and the lessons from life when nature has so much to give to us. When you look a gift horse in the mouth, how can you expect the gifts to keep coming? You must acknowledge gifts from any place that they may come from. The sooner you recognize and receive the gifts, the faster your growth and healing occurs.

IMPROV FOR EVERYONE

Take an Improv class. I highly recommend it for anyone wanting to get practice in thinking and acting fast on your feet. Improv is also great for those that want to learn to go with the flow, as well as practice moving through your FOF in a playful way. It is real-world training in the form of a fun game with challenging rules. Improv can and will set you free if you choose it.

When you are in a state of play, you do things differently than you normally would and almost always surprise yourself. When you are playing a game you focus on finding solutions right away or you're out of the game. Improv teaches you to take big silly risks while being in a safe space. Plus, it's full of life lessons which you can take with you.

Even the first rule of Improv is so valuable: "Always say yes and agree to whatever the other actors have said and then contribute your idea in return." It's called "Yes, and...." It's your gift to the others on the stage, to the audience, and to the scene. Being in the habit of accepting things as they are by saying YES will free you up so that you can then contribute your part in the scene.

Take an Improv clowning character class and see what you're made of. Practice new methods of being in this play state with a community of like-minded individuals. Learn how to explore your weirdness, get over social anxiety, or face your fear of public speaking. No matter what it is, your play state will shine through and set you free!

CLOWNS ARE ALWAYS RIGHT

I do not say this lightly, though it is in fact a funny saying that came out of my deep dive into clowning. The history of the clown dates back to 200,000 B.C. The clown archetype crosses multiple cultures and is as sacred as a shaman. In the Lakota culture, the jester archetype is called "Heyoka," one of the many names throughout the ages for this funny guy the clown represents the sacred and the profane.

A shaman generally lives in isolation and only helps people that come to her/him while the clown is on the front lines among us all for all of us to have heart healing. Shamanism for all, if you will. Shamans treat seekers while clowns educate and heal the masses by exposing the truth—we need them both. Clowns are truth sayers and truth seekers and like to push people's buttons in a way that challenges people to participate in a playful way.

The fool was the only commoner the king would take advice from because the fool always told the brutal truth and had nothing to lose. The fool would mock the king right in front of him, and in a way where everyone in the room would laugh, including the king. It was healing for everyone. Laughter is the best medicine. What is something you could laugh at yourself for? Where in life could you have more fun?

I have been the class clown my entire life and it has always steered me in the right direction. I got through my childhood making myself and others laugh at everything I could find a joke in. It was more fun to laugh than to cry.

After college, I ran away with a circus and became a professional clown, which I still am to this day. We often toured in countries where we did not speak the local language. Sacred clowning crosses all borders. I was able to make people laugh no matter what language they spoke because I delivered truth in a funny way without using words, just my heart.

Clowning around is also the fastest route that I have found to disengage someone's ego so there can be a real and pure connection. I put myself on the line and purposely make myself look like an idiot to make others not worry about looking bad. I enjoy being able to relax an anxious or judgmental person.

Clowning is all about bringing fun and play with the right intention to provide an experience of transformation and healing for another, even if it's just to laugh. The clown will always act the biggest fool so that others may be free to be a little foolish, to play and try something new. I am always down to be the bigger fool so people can be at peace and ease in my presence.

The most important thing I learned in all my years of clowning is that being in a playful state is the fastest way to make a connection to another

Soul. It is a craft of getting past another's fears or blocks and into their psyche to tickle their intellect, such that they trust and play along. When that light turns on there's a shift from them being in their head to dropping into their heart.

They can feel it too, getting into it even more which usually makes them laugh. Laughter is my favorite song. I highly recommend taking a clown class if you feel called. It's a great way to stretch your boundaries and elevate your life at the same time. If you are ever in Sedona, AZ you can take one of the clown or Improv classes I teach: https://www.jesselynn.net/.

THE EARLY BIRD GETS TO PARTY MORE

Moonlight Rollerway is a skating rink in southern California. My favorite thing to do there is, obviously, roller skate, but I like to get there way early so that I can beat the line and have time on the empty rink. When I am working out new routines with skate partners we need a lot of space to work and generally no one gets there early.

As with most things in life, if you can just beat the line you will have an edge on everyone else. That's why I get up at five a.m. every day when I'm working on a project. I want that time to work by myself. I'm the first one in the office or the first one on that skate floor. I can get a lot of work done while everyone else is still sleeping. When you show up early, you give yourself the space and time to take care of your needs and get ahead of the curve. You can't try out new tricks when you show up with everybody else, because there's no room on the dance floor. Showing up early is a gift that keeps giving. Where in your life can you create that gift for yourself? It's time to celebrate!

CELEBRATE
Definition: //cel·e·brate// /'sel, brāt/ ~Verb
1. Acknowledgment of a significant event or happy day
with a social gathering or enjoyable activity. 2. Perform
a religious ceremony publicly and duly, in particular
officiate at. (www.OxfordDictionaries.com)

CELEBRATE THE SMALL STUFF

Kool and the Gang sang it best: "Ceeeeeeeelebrate good times, come on!" We all love a party where we can celebrate freely, though granted, everyone celebrates in different ways. Celebration is the honoring of something special. A big change doesn't happen overnight. There is substance to the power of gratitude. Celebration is filled with gratitude, which is why it's so juicy. Celebrate whenever you can, especially the small stuff.

Celebration brings awareness, intention, and meaning to something specific, which your subconscious sees as reward and then sends more of the same to you. It brings you more of what you are grateful for because gratitude is the absolute highest vibration. Being thankful for things brings you closer to them.

You must be aware of all those things you want to bring closer to you so you can celebrate where you are already receiving those things in even the smallest of ways, to be thankful for them. If you want a big change in an area of your life it's important to celebrate where you are already experiencing those positive things in another area and celebrate them. Celebrating the small wins along the way is the most valuable way to begin your transformation. You must enjoy the journey or you won't appreciate the destination when you finally arrive.

Celebration starts from the inside and moves out from there. Therefore, we must assess, identify, and track all our personal successes first. For some it may be hard to identify successes and for others it will be easy. The more practice you have, the easier it gets and the more you'll begin to notice other accomplishments to write down. This is going to be an ongoing list you can continue to add to, and is a great reference to look back on periodically—especially when you're down or blue. Collect them all in your journal.

COLLECT YOUR ENDLESS GIFTS

Whether or not you grew up with a custom of receiving presents, everyone loves gifts. Life is full of them, like an eternal Christmas, Hanukkah, Kwanzaa, etc. filled with never-ending gifts! Everything in life has something to offer or give to us, even the bad things.

There are reasons *why* things happen. The positive reasons *why* are the gifts. Find more reasons and you will discover more gifts. Collect your gifts so you have more to give to others, especially the people you care about.

The more you look, the more you find!

ENDLESS GIFTS BRAIN TRAINING

Train yourself to find as many positive things as you can from every situation presented to you. You deserve it, and wouldn't you love to open more presents? Make it a practice to find the gift in everything. Not only is it a fun game, but its effects will leave you with a rich and deeply fulfilled life as you become aware of all the wondrous things right in front of you at every given moment.

I say this with confidence because I have done the work and seen the results. I suffered for many years until I trained myself to do this. When I started looking for all the gifts in every situation, it healed my soul. It laid the foundation for what would soon play a major role in every area of my life, including writing this book.

GIFT MINING

Practice mining for gifts. In each moment you can ask "why?" to find the answers yourself. Why did you follow your instinct to go to that place? Find people to play this game with because it's more fun with friends. With practice, you will eventually go right to the answers without all the suffering in between. You can also sign up for coaching, group coaching, seminars, and workshops to personally go through your own process with me at www.POLRLIVING.com.

In order to find the gifts, you must ask the question, "What is there to learn from this situation?" Exhaust all possibilities and then continue looking for more. For example, you twist an ankle simply by walking down the street. It happened to be in front of a lot of people and now you're embarrassed. You can't put any weight on it and your foot swells up. A friend has to drive you home. You realize that you can no longer play in your soccer match this weekend which you were really looking forward to.

Most people would see this as a negative event and say they're having a bad day. It's really easy to get sympathy from people in a situation like this. Somehow we think it will make us feel better if they feel bad too. I'm not sure why it is a customary go-to for us humans to choose *everyone* feeling like shit instead of everyone choosing to focus on the good things in stressful times like that. How much difference would it make in your life if you were to start playing a game to find the good things?

Here's the game: find as many good things as you can from all situations— start with small things and get creative! Those good things could be lessons or something you learned from that circumstance that springs forth. When you shift your focus to the positive you can roll through life like Super Mario Kart and collect all those coins.

Let's use the previous story and consider that spraining your ankle has many lessons and gifts attached, otherwise it wouldn't have happened. What might some of the lessons be? Here are some I came up with for this set of circumstances. You may find different ones, as each set of circumstances are completely different for each person. The point is to start thinking in this way and practice, practice, practice. What lessons/ gifts can we find in this situation? I challenge you to find ten in each circumstance. Can you find any more than the ones below? Train your mind to ALWAYS look for more!

GIFTS FROM YOUR BUM ANKLE—LESSONS LEARNED

Lesson #1: Slow down. Take the time to do things properly and in a safe way—always a great reminder.

Lesson #2: Pay Attention. Sometimes we aren't paying enough attention. Many of us still text and drive, even though it's against the law. I call this the "Paying Attention Tax" that comes from moving too fast and doing too many things at once. Be aware of your surroundings.

Lesson #3: Ask for help. Oftentimes really headstrong and independent people injure themselves in a way where they are forced to ask for help. Allow yourself to be vulnerable enough to ask for help without having to be injured. Asking for help doesn't make you weak. Being asked for help is a sign of respect and honor. It tells the other person that they are a capable person and you trust them. In asking for help you allow people in your life to be there for you. It feels good to be of service, useful, and to help a friend. When you don't ask for help you cheat others out of the gift of giving.

Lesson #4: Confirmation that people care about you and have your back when you need it. This is a very valuable gift!

<u>Lesson #5:</u> You get to finally spend time with a friend you haven't connected with in a while because you both were way too busy.

<u>Lesson #6:</u> You get to be waited on and pampered for a bit. I suggest you soak this one up and enjoy every minute of it!

<u>Lesson #7:</u> You get to finally catch up on rest while you're recovering.

<u>Lesson #8:</u> You get to spend some quality time with your kids or spouse instead of going to that game.

<u>Lesson #9:</u> You get time to read! Instead of going out for drinks after the soccer game and being too tired or hungover the next day. Now you get to indulge in relaxing literature—escape to another world or learn something new.

<u>Lesson #10:</u> Suddenly everything is put into perspective. We remember what is important to us. We often become stuck in the same old routines and don't know what we are missing until something like this happens.

Whatever the situation is, there's always more than one lesson or gift if you keep searching. Collect as many gifts as you can to win the game called *Your Life* because your life *is* a gift and should be celebrated! Some people go their entire lives ignoring parts of themselves until they have a heart attack or get cancer. It takes a life-shattering event from the universe to get some people to WAKE UP in order for change to occur.

Why does it take almost dying to finally allow oneself to live in a different way? My suggestion is to start living exactly how you want to right now, so you don't waste any more time here on earth. Honor yourself, your goals, and your dreams right now.

We have a very limited time on this planet, let's not continue to waste it. The universe is conspiring for you to live your truth for the highest good. Practice mining for gifts in every challenging situation or trauma.

LOOK EVERYWHERE FOR GIFTS

As kids we naturally did this, especially around holidays but for some reason we stopped doing this as adults. It's time to start looking again. No matter how seemingly small or big something may be, there is ALWAYS a gift to be found, even in the most horrible of tragedies.

Take the Covid-19 pandemic as an example. If it never happened—this country *and the world* would still be asleep and doing nothing. It has forced the entire world to really take a look at our own personal lives, corporate systems, and everything in between. The pandemic has given us time to go within, take time for ourselves to see what is of real value and evaluate where we have been spending our time.

I am grateful we have been shown how broken many of our systems are so we can restructure, realign and re-invent our future! More people are aware now than ever and taking actions they never would have before. In a sense the pandemic has brought our divided globe together by causing us to wake up. When we band together, we get a stronger voice and therefore the power to make a difference. We are better together—Unification!

CHECKS & BALANCES

The reason I liked science and math in school was because I could check my work. I could do the equation backwards to see if I was correct or incorrect. I never doubted my answers. When I was lazy in school and didn't check my work, it left room for errors. The same thing is true in life. There are ways to see if you are in alignment with your higher purpose. There are ways to become much more fulfilled in any area of your life. Anything you want is possible with structure, the right tools, and perseverance.

We can determine for ourselves what works or doesn't simply by listening to our intuition. Your intuition gets stronger when you not only listen to it, but also act on our deeper understanding of nature. When you reference nature it helps put things into perspective, allowing you to get out of your own way.

When you apply these principles and practices to your life, your true soul's purpose can be fulfilled. The truth will be evident to you when you go through your own set of checks and balances. Using tools in this book will help you develop a stronger habit of listening to and connecting with your intuition. You will never steer yourself wrong once you gain that perspective.

Growing up in poverty, I didn't get many gifts. My mother was a proud woman and she didn't want anyone to know we struggled financially, especially me! She had me believing that I was "a bad girl" because she put coal in my stocking every year, which I found out later it was to cover-up her not being able to buy me any gifts.

Her financial embarrassment became my low self-esteem. When I realized that my mother did that—especially after learning that Santa was a lie, things *really* shifted for me. It shattered my trust with her and I became leery of holidays.

I love presents and I always have! I love both receiving and giving gifts and have manifested a partner that heals this deep childhood wound—he brings me gifts everyday. He is the most kind and generous man I have ever met and everyday with him is like Christmas. I thank God everyday for bringing us together.

The only time I remember getting a Christmas present from my mom was when she put my name on a tree at our local store, and someone bought me an item I desperately needed, a pair of shoes. I remember them like it was yesterday: they were light purple (which I hated) and they had two Velcro tabs that secured them to my feet. I had to wear them for a couple of years, even though my feet grew three sizes bigger and eventually my toes stuck out of holes that wore through the top. They were my only pair of shoes for several years. I was made fun of for this my entire middle school career. Kids thought I had Velcro because I was handicapped and couldn't tie my own shoelaces. It was terribly embarrassing.

Growing up without gifts and knowing how good it feels to give, as an adult I give little gifts to myself all the time. I was able to look back and check the situation and then restore balance in my life. You can, too! The gifts are your checks and balances.

This book is filled with many presents and is my gift to you. I hope you like it! I did not have time to wrap it, I apologize. That would be wasteful anyhow, because you would just throw the paper away. This book is filled with games. Play to win, or not at all, so long as you do it powerfully. This is my intellectual and soul arm wrestling challenge for you. I'm fairly certain you're a fun person who wants more fun in life, which is why this will be as easy as you allow or create it to be.

REPLACE BAD HABITS WITH GIFTS

Take a look at your bad habits and investigate the payoff you get from them so you can replace them with gifts. Ask yourself, what's the pull to keep doing it? Then replace it with a good habit. You'll get double the gifts and double the fun.

For instance, I started smoking at age eight and I continued until around 24. On days my mother didn't have a babysitter, I went to the arcade inside the casino where she dealt cards and tried to stay out of trouble. She checked on me during her breaks, but I didn't have any supervision throughout the day.

I liked to sit outside the front of the casinos and watch all the various people coming in. There were famous people arriving in limos, cabs filled with tourists, families, and cracked-out gambling addicts. People would get out of their vehicles and light up a brand-new cigarette, take a few puffs and put it out right before walking into the casino.

I collected all those cigarettes and smoked them myself or took them home to share with my friends. I was addicted at a really young age. All through school and college I tried to quit, which only ever lasted a month or so.

It wasn't until college that I quit for good. I was sitting at the park smoking away and this old man came and sat on the bench oddly too close to me. He turned to me and said, "Why don't you find something better to do with your time?" I hated anyone telling me what to do (even though now I probably would have done the same thing) so I told him off.

I felt bad about that knee jerk reaction for years, but it got me thinking. I began to explore all the reasons why I smoked and all the benefits I got from doing it. Continuing to do something that you know is awful and even tell others is bad is not only extremely toxic for your health, your spirit, body and mind suffer too.

For example, people told me that "smoking is bad for your health" and I'd say "I know" but would do it anyway. In my investigation I realized that I only got high the first few times I smoked and I never liked the smell of cigarettes either. I don't know anyone who does. There is always a reason we start doing something which is the place to look first.

It's important to find the gifts in the toxic behavior and replace your bad habit with a good one. For me, it was taking that time for myself away from people to think and get clear. Back in that day, in the corporate world, they allowed you to take smoke breaks during work hours. If you did not smoke, you worked more time than a smoker. For an eight-hour regular day of work, we would get two fifteen minute breaks, unless you were a smoker. Smoking cigarettes got you at least two more 10-15 minute breaks on top of that, if not more. I would get an extra hour of paid break time throughout the course of the day, all because I smoked.

I replaced the bad habit with a new one instead. I still went on my "smoke break" but instead, I inhaled essential oils, stretched, napped, did homework, or yoga. Doing something positive will still give you all the benefits of the bad habit but will not harm you. You can find alternative habits to feed your spirit, body, and mind to create powerful lasting results. I have been smoke-free ever since.

"The time has come to turn your heart into a temple of fire.
Your essence is *gold* hidden in dust.
To reveal its splendor you need to burn in the fire of love."
-RUMI-

BECOME A GOLD DIGGER

Humans have been obsessed with gold for eons. It's not that hard to see why. Gold is beautiful, especially the 24 karat or rose variety. Now you get to learn how to dig for gold.

Not all gold diggers are bad. Supposedly, you cannot make gold, but you certainly can find it if you're looking hard enough. Your life experience is where your gold is hidden. Everything you have gone through is for you to use to your advantage to live the best life possible. To find all your golden nuggets you must dig like never before.

MINE FOR GOLD

It is through the deepest traumas of our lives where we find the GOLD. In our lives, we have many things that are unpleasant, difficult, and downright painful at the time. It's in those troubled times we must mine for gold.

The gifts you mine automatically help others because they helped you. I refer to this as "gift mining." Seek those golden nuggets. They are more valuable than actual gold! Take all the pain and trauma and distill them down until you have gold. Do this for all things that brought you pain, suffering, sadness, and anything uncomfortable. These gifts could never come to you if you didn't go through those experiences.

Horrible things happen to many of us, and it is easy to continue to suffer from tragic experiences without the proper tools to help you see the bigger picture. I am talking about removing the years of suffering after a tragic event because of limiting habits and beliefs that form after a trauma which stay with you through your whole life until you release them. I say feel your emotions deeply, express them, and allow them to come out of your body.

Emotions are energy in motion. They need to move through you to be released. You can shake, run, jump up and down—anything that gets your body moving vigorously will do the trick. Laughing out loud, having a good cry, or screaming in a pillow works too. Play the GOLD GATHERER GAME at www.POLRLIVING.com to gather all the precious gold from your deepest traumas. You can play it with your whole family, which is extremely healing.

INCREASING PROSPERITY

When I first started doing Oracle work as a full time profession I wanted paying clients just like my colleagues were getting. I wasn't exactly grateful for the small amount of money that people gave me, because it didn't look like what I wanted it to look like. It wasn't the large sums of money my friends received for dispensing an even smaller amount of information or transformation than I provided.

In order to increase your prosperity you must first be grateful for what you have. I wasn't, I was only focusing on what others had. Once I stopped comparing myself to others and got clear on what I wanted, I stopped pushing it away from me. I sought to be financially compensated for all my gifts and talents. I realized I was already getting that, even if it was in small amounts. I began to celebrate every time I received money which only led to more of it coming into my life.

The real issue was my limiting beliefs around money. I was tired of missing out on experiences because I didn't have the money. My entire childhood, I sat by watching all the other kids go to summer camps, field trips, take school photos, and play after-school games that my mom couldn't afford. I felt absolutely stuck in every way as I moved into adulthood. This childhood belief carried over and the poverty consciousness was negatively affecting my adult life. I knew I needed to do everything in my power to lift the blocks and remove the veils that hide that light from me.

MAKE LIFE A RITUAL

Everything changed for me in 2015 when I created a ritual that allowed me to transform and expand my barometer for financial success. Money had been one of my biggest hurdles, as it is for many. I was able to finally break free from the poverty consciousness I was raised and programmed with by performing the FINANCIAL CELEBRITUAL (see below) each time money came into or left my hands. I celebrated every penny I found on the ground, thanking the universe for rewarding me for following my dreams. I celebrated every time I paid my bills or bought anything, including food, clothing, or trinkets. What a wonderful gift to be able to pay for services I need and enjoy!

I shared these rituals with close friends and it worked for them too, so I started telling my clients about it. It was 100% successful for them and may even work for you. One of the reasons Tony Robbins is so successful is that his work helps people create new neurological pathways by activating the spirit, body, and mind. I didn't realize this was why my ritual worked so well. Supporting the people doing those things is good for all. I have different rituals for different things.

CELEBRITUALS

Celebrituals are celebration rituals that you create for special things in your life. Create your own or use one of mine! You can celebrate anything. It's great to get yourself into the habit of celebrating.

Celebritual = physical action + vocal engagement
+ feeling gratitude *(all at the exact same time).*

The physical action must include both the right and left side of your body (and therefore brain) to be activated and stimulated. You can clap, jump, throw both arms into the air, dance, etc. Vocal engagement is using your voice to activate and resonate from deep inside you, telling all your cells to pay attention. The vocalization can be powerful grunts, sounds or words. My favorite things to say are "Yes" and "Thank you."

While those simple actions will take you far, to transform harder challenges I use this entire sequence:

"Yes, thank you, more, please?!?"

Yes = the acknowledgment of the gift.

Thank you = gratitude for the gift and is the highest vibration.

More please = the "Ask and you shall receive."

You must be able to ask for what you want in order to get it. Most people can't read minds so you must let people know the things you want in life. They may be able to help you get them faster than you doing it on your own!

Celebrate the fact that you have air to breathe and have the ability to see, walk, or talk. Celebrate winning first place at something you've trained your whole life for, or maybe beginning a new project you've always wanted to do. Celebrating the wins with the practices below brings your energy and attention with a physical movement, which brings your spirit, body and mind into alignment. This is how one can experience perfect harmony and therefore transformation.

These Celebrituals create and strengthen new neurological pathways in your brain (neuroplasticity) which tells the universe and your subconscious you want more of it in your life. The reward system is the same method you'd use to train an animal. It is also the way to train yourself into transformation when you are stuck. You are just like a wild lion or bear at first before training. With a little energy toward practice and rewards, very soon you will jump through your own ring of fire that used to stop you dead in your tracks!

FINANCIAL CELEBRITUAL

This is a ritual to perform every time you receive money as well as for manifesting or bringing in a certain amount of money. Create your own or use the one I have been using for years. You'll want to make it easy and fun, but most of all—consistent.

Create a sacred and private space to complete this. Stand as tall as you can, elongating the spine to allow proper blood flow and oxygen to get to your frontal lobe and entire body, while facing north. Inhale as deep as you can and reach your hands high above your head. Pull the gratitude energy from the universe down into the crown of your head and through your body as your hands push it down and out to the sides while saying out loud, "**Yes, thank you, more please!**"

Do this three times facing north, east, south and west. Imagine the amount of money you just received, and fill your body with gratitude the entire time you do this. I perform my Celebritual under my copper pyramid on my special rug in my living room that my dear friend Carey Thompson made with his psychedelic sacred geometry art, which makes it fun. He is an artist that intentionally creates from his heart. I highly recommend checking him out at @careythompson_galactivation. Whatever you do, make this practice really fun for yourself. The more fun it is, the faster the results occur.

DOUBLE CELEBRITUAL

This celebration ritual is done anytime you want to positively reinforce anything you may be talking about at that moment or for declaring what you want to bring in (manifest) with another person. I really enjoy doing this with others and have found this one to be the most fun. I love watching people get excited.

You and the other person stand across from each other. Lift the crown of your head to the sky, elongating the spine as you deeply inhale. You basically play a mini game of patty cakes.

First, use your right hand to high five while saying "YES," then the left hand, same thing. You finish with a "high ten" with both hands at the same time saying "YES" for a total of three yeses. Breathe in deep before each yes.

The yes should be *powerful*. Your stance should be strong. Feel deep gratitude during the entire process. You can do this anytime you or others are speaking about something you resonate with or desire so you can acknowledge and celebrate it. Taking the time to set it on a cellular level acknowledges and rewards both of you. Doing it with another person will only magnify the celebration.

GROUP CELEBRITUAL

This is for three or more people. The more the merrier! For example, when going for a night out with friends, we all focus on finding rock star parking. We visualize it, embody the gratitude we feel in finding it, and then let it go. Of course, we find one right in front.

Stand in a circle facing each other. Deep inhale with legs shoulder width apart, and put your hands out to the sides, giving both the person to your right and left a "high five" at the same time. As you do, say "YES." Repeat it three times with a deep inhale before each out loud "yes." It sends messages to the Universe and your subconscious and reinforces positive outcomes in a group setting.

Utilizing the tips and tricks to help you celebrate more often will make your life more fun. That is my goal. We only get this one life to live, so let's live it up. I celebrate you for reading this book and taking the time to elevate your own life! Yes, thank you, more please! YES, YES, YES!!!

CHAPTER 9

DISCOVERING AND CHANGING UNDERLYING BELIEFS

IF YOU APPROVE OF YOURSELF YOU DON'T NEED APPROVAL FROM OTHERS.

CHOOSE TO STOP SUFFERING

When will you realize you are made of pure love and choose to stop suffering? When you see the value of each aspect of yourself you will see it in others as well. Begin to take advantage of who you have the opportunity to be in this lifetime and stop eliminating parts of yourself or burying them deep within your consciousness. Stop hanging onto the past or resisting what is happening right now because that is suffering. You cannot remove pain from your life, but you have the choice not to suffer.

DNA = MEMORY BANK

Many scientific studies have tried to find where memories live and have discovered they are in fact not stored in the brain. Memories are stored in your DNA. So something your ancestors may have gone through may carry over to you without your knowledge.

There are people I know who have very irrational fears, like a fear of dogs or water, only to find out that their indigenous tribe was wiped out by a flood or was attacked by rabid dogs. If you have a crazy block and cannot identify where it came from, you can do ancestral clearing and healing. For any debilitating fear where you have no real explanation or reason for it, I highly recommend doing a past life regression to assist you through this.

There are many qualified practitioners that can help. Things that cannot be explained in this lifetime may stem from a past life.

I didn't believe in past lives until last year when I had an experience with Shaman Durek. He was the "Soul Share" guest on the conscious-elevating talk show OPTIMYSTIC that I am a part of. We had so many amazing guests on the show, see for yourself www.Optimystic.tv. Everyone working on the show wears many hats in order to get this passion project off the ground. I wear many different beautiful hats, namely Supervising Producer, Make-up, Hair, Stylist, Choreographer, Oracle, and sometimes Co-Director. The taping had finished and the after-party was in full force. We were in the kitchen, which is where everyone typically ends up during parties.

I asked him a question, though I cannot remember exactly what it was. It had something to do with removing the blocks around finishing my book and fear of singing in front of people. He began to do his magical work on me. He started moving energy throughout my body and magnifying it in certain places, causing me to shake. We were in a room full of people, all of them staring at me. As he began telling me the reason why I was blocked and where it came from, I was instantly back in my past life reliving it all.

The feeling was so strange, very familiar yet foreign. It's like you're with your friends and they say "Hey, do remember that party we went to?" and you have no idea what they are talking about, but then they add more information: "Yeah, we went and got smoothies beforehand" and it still doesn't ring a bell so they add more details to jog your brain. "You were sitting on the swing and that guy came up to you and scared you into throwing your drink at him" and then everything floods back into your mind and you even remember what you were wearing, whose house it was and what it smelled like, just like it was yesterday. Well, that's what it felt like, only it was my past life.

I was burned at the stake because I was speaking up and sharing plant knowledge and medicine with my community to protect and heal them, I was deemed a witch. It's no wonder I have been blocked with the completion of my book, because in my past life I was hunted down and killed for sharing information and knowledge. I have also had recurring nightmares of being chased by people wanting to kill me as well as an unexplained fear of burning to death.

CLEAR ANCESTRAL BLOCKAGES

It was such a relief to me because I had been praying almost every night for the blocks to be removed to finish this book. Now having this new awareness I could easily move past it. Previously, I couldn't figure out why I had the block or where it came from, so I had been making myself wrong and feeling bad all that time.

In your prayer or meditation you can ask for guidance. I use this prayer/ mantra from Dr. Hew Len: "Divine creator, universe and energy force, if I or any of my family ancestors have offended any other ancestors' families or relatives with their thoughts, deeds, or actions from the beginning of our creation until the present, I ask your forgiveness. Let this cleanse, purify, release, and cut all the negative memories, blocked energies, and vibrations, and transmute these unwanted energies to pure light." I also add "In Jesus's name" and "So it is".

REMOVE WORRY FROM YOUR THOUGHTS

We touched on this earlier but worry really can be completely removed altogether. Unless you like to suffer, struggle, or waste time and energy— then keep worrying! Did you know according to the bible that worrying is a sin?

Worrying is focusing on your fears and what you don't want. Worrying is an inherent mistrust of the Universe, God, Energy, Source, and Light. Worrying will take you down!

You're reading this book because you want a better life, so get your head in the game. You have got to be able to roll with things with ease and grace in order for you to be able to handle more prosperity in your life. If you were running a race, the race isn't the hard part, it's getting up every morning and continuing to do the training no matter what is going on in your life.

Your head can take you out of the game while consistency will keep you on point. You must pass the test to get more abundance in your life. Make it a goal to be mentally calm and composed. You can choose it and move through it. Get out of the state of worry the moment you recognize you're doing it! Worrying ages you. Worrying cuts you off from access to your own divine self, leaving you unable to make sound decisions.

The lyrics to Bobby McFerrin's "Don't Worry Be Happy" says it best, "Don't worry be happy now. When you worry, you make it double. Don't bring everyone down. Don't worry whatever it is, it will soon pass. I'm not worried." I suggest putting this song on while you read the rest of this chapter.

Worry comes from our ancestors, as well as all the fear porn propaganda we get inundated with on a daily basis. It's almost as if the powers that be want to keep us in a state of worry so we are more easily manipulated. I come from a long lineage of people who worried. I used to worry all the time until I realized I wanted to use my time for better things.

Worrying causes stress and sends you into FOF while your body secretes cortisol into your bloodstream. Cortisol breaks down your cells, ages you, causes inflammation, sickness, and disease. Worry and stress can kill you and it all stems from the cellular breakdown from cortisol. Change your thoughts to change your life.

Our consciousness was not designed to inhibit us. Nature does not worry. When we do as nature does, the ego becomes a tool again and not the amateur running the show. Nature doesn't have an ego and is mighty powerful. The Dalai Lama taught me that worrying is pointless! "If there's a problem, then there's a solution. If there is no solution, it's not a problem."

If you have a problem, you don't need to worry because there will always be a solution. If there is no solution, then accept it the way it is, because it is just part of life. Worrying doesn't help *any* situation or anyone! Worrying has never done any good, it only hurts you and brings everyone around you down. If you have real concerns that need troubleshooting and back-up plans laid out, that is very different.

If you are a person that is constantly stressed out no matter what you do, consider making a change in your physiology through cardiovascular exercise. Sometimes a person who has a bunch of pent-up energy and isn't getting it out through physical movement will turn into a worrier and stress addict, which results in deteriorating health. One hour of a cardio workout daily will change your outlook as well as your body. You will burn off that extra energy in a useful and productive way instead of letting it fester and damage your health. Transform your worrisome thoughts to solution-based thoughts. Consider what thoughts would make you happy or what would solve the problem in this situation? Focus on the thing that would make you *most* happy overall.

RELEASE AND LET GO OF JUDGMENTS

Judgment is not for you. Do not cast it upon others or yourself. Judgment is for you to create discernment around a situation for your own protection and safety in the future. All negative events are blessings from the past that bring you presents in your future even as soon as you're ready to open them by focusing on what there is to be gained. Save the judging for the judges. Guilt, shame and fear are passed down to us and we add them to our collection. That is not a worthy collection. We then take these judgments over time and turn them into core beliefs from which we operate as if it's reality.

There is a difference between judgment and discernment. Judgment is the final decision or label making something wrong for anyone or everyone, whereas discernment is your ability to recognize when something may be alright for others but not right for you, in order to protect yourself. For example, you can discern what type of people are safe to share your feelings with, as opposed to judging those people you deem "unsafe to share your feelings with" with a label or name. Once you label something with your personal judgment it is very hard to change that attitude and mentality and it makes it virtually impossible for any growth in that area.

"AN ADDICT NEEDS SHAME LIKE A MAN DYING OF THIRST NEEDS SALT WATER."
~ Terrence Reel ~

Judgments cast guilt and shame upon another. Guilt = Action is bad. Shame = Self is bad. Shame is a gremlin that dies when exposed to light. The term comes from the "Gremlins" movie from the 80s. Those evil creatures would multiply if they got wet but would die in the sunlight. It's a bad habit to judge and blame someone else when feeling uncomfortable and coping with shadows. It is better to choose discomfort over judgment and resentment. You are responsible for the energy you bring.

Judgments can appear instantly and are everywhere. I like to say, "Cool isn't as cool as Cool thinks he is!" Being "Cool" is an emotional straight jacket that restricts growth. Cool is dangerous. It's a cover-up for the shame of being goofy or dorky. Once you begin to understand how often we judge people and things, you can disassociate yourself from them and begin breaking them down. I love being a-dork-able because I get to call the shots. Be proud of all your idiosyncrasies because that's what makes you the best you possible.

The problem with our society at large is we judge someone for the rest of their life by one thing they did in the past. If a person gets caught for something illegal, they're stamped a "criminal" for the rest of their life, and it is a bleak future for them. The penal system spits out the reformed person into society in such a way that the "mark" of having been to jail disallows them to work in any normal job from then on. The institution pretends to rehabilitate and adorns them with a scarlet letter while receiving $30,000-$150,000 of taxpayer dollars per inmate. A teacher gets paid less than that!

I am not advocating breaking the law, but it is important to note that we all have done things we regret or have made mistakes in the past or acted in ways that do not reflect who we really are. When we judge another, we disallow them to ever change. There are challenging experiences in life that people go through where they don't feel like themselves and can act out in various ways. Especially when a person's health isn't great, it makes it hard for them to be fully present.

One of my family members is *still* mad at me for things I did when I was a child. I was a messed up kid and did whatever I wanted because I was abused, I had a skewed version of self and was unable to interact with people well. It certainly doesn't make it right, but holding the space for people to grow actually allows them to blossom into someone who would never again hurt others the way they did in the past.

ALLOW PEOPLE TO GROW

Every seven years the human body replaces and renews every single cell, making you an entirely different person that you were seven years previously. Every day we are different people as we grow, evolve, love and learn. The person you were last year is not the same person you are now. This is the same for all people because it's just a fact of nature. The same way a tree last year was completely different than it is this year.

In my garden, I grow many things and now my fruit trees are finally producing fruit! I have had many of them for years and they have grown and changed every day, just as people do. I can see how even the leaves change direction according to the path of the sun throughout the year, the same way people change according to how they are getting their nutrients, information, and emotional support.

It's much harder to track it in people unless you have the tools and systems set up to become conscious of them. A person constantly working on developing a relationship with their inner self will see vast results. Consistent inner personal work makes you more able to listen to your higher self as well as others.

LISTEN
Definition: //lis·ten// /ˈlis()n/ ~Verb
1. To pay attention to someone or something in order to hear what is being said. 2. Make an effort to hear what someone said and understand it. 3. To give one's attention with the ear to sound.
4. Be alert and ready to hear something.
(www.OxfordDictionaries.com)

LISTEN TO EVERYTHING

The reason why we have two ears and one mouth is because we are supposed to listen twice as often as we speak. We listen with more than just our ears; our eyes listen for body language and our heart listens to tone. You will need to pay close attention to all verbal and nonverbal communication. Listening is the most important interpersonal skill and requires active consciousness to do it well. It must be nurtured and developed to practice it properly.

Most people take the act of listening for granted, thinking it's something that just happens. More often than not we talk *at* each other bidirectionally where each person is trying to be heard but not really listening. The English language is designed for negotiating.

We are programmed to speak from our head, which has us talking "at" each other. You never know what you'll learn when you're listening to everything. Listen closely in all communications so you can receive and understand the other person carefully. Misunderstandings can easily happen when we listen ineffectively, which is why it's a good idea to repeat back what you heard so the other person can confirm you understand. You will need the ability to H.E.A.R. to effectively listen.

H.E.A.R. ~ 5 STEPS FOR BETTER LISTENING

1. HALT SPEAKING & LISTEN TO THE ENTIRE STORY. We can only think about one thing at a time, so when we are talking we cannot listen. Our listening is the greatest gift we can give to another. Allow a person to finish their thoughts and do not interrupt them. Do not try to talk over them even if you think you know what they are about to say. Give them a safe space to speak. Listen for any and all nonverbal communication. Only when you have heard the entire story will you have full understanding to respond appropriately. Misunderstandings cause major suffering.

2. EMPATHIZE & BE OPEN-MINDED. Look at things from their perspective and let go of any and all preconceived notions. Avoid judging them and release any personal prejudice. Put yourself in their shoes and try to see it from their side.

3. ALL EYES ON THEM. Focus entirely on them. Remove any distractions—turn off your phone, TV, etc. Clear your mind from all your busy thoughts so you can concentrate solely on what they have to say. This is NOT the time to be formulating your rebuttal. Eye contact is essential and respectful.

4. RELAX & BE PATIENT. Everyone has their own pace at which they speak, and that must be honored. Allow the other to say what they have to say at the pace in which they deliver it without getting triggered as they may be very emotional. You may want to try the Ho'Oponopono Technique when emotions are high.

HO'OPONOPONO
Hawaiian definition: //ho·opo·no·pon·o// //hopōnōpōno// ~Verb
1. To correct, put in the right order, make tidy, neat,
arranged, cared for, attended to, administered.
2. To put to rights; shape, revise, adjust, amend, regulate, rectify,
tidy up, make orderly, administer, superintend, supervise, manage,
edit, reorganize, work carefully and neatly; to make ready.
3. Mental cleansing—where families and relationships were set
right through prayer, discussion, confession, repentance, and
mutual restitution and forgiveness. (www.WeheWehe.org)

HO'OPONOPONO TECHNIQUE

I became aware of this technique through a Yoga Galactica Spaceshift Kundalini yoga class I took in Los Angeles. If you get a chance to take one of their classes, do it—www.YogaGalactica.com. The instructors Kamala and Siri would sing the phrases below during the breath work, so I didn't know it was called anything or where it came from until I read Zero Limits by Joe Vitale. Joe got to meet and work with Dr. Ihaleakala Hew Len, the man that simplified this technique for the western world. This technique has been used in Polynesian cultures for centuries, and I am grateful we have it with us now.

This technique should be practiced often and for anything and everything. There is so much pain in the world—that we have a lot to clear and heal. It comprises four simple steps, which are Repentance, Forgiveness, Gratitude, and Love. These forces combined have great power and are amazingly effective. You can do it alone, with a friend, or with the person that you need specific clearing with. I have done it every which way whether the person is reachable or has left this dimension.

You can speak these words aloud or say them quietly in your head. Generally, when I am in a group setting, saying it out loud is extremely powerful! Hearing another person say those words has brought me to tears.

I also like to do it silently in my car while driving alone. When you are doing it with a friend, substitute them for that person you need healing with, and vice versa. Like anything, the more you practice the stronger it gets.

Each session is somewhere in between five to twenty minutes for each person you need to clear with. You must be authentic and come from the heart. Be willing to let go, forgive, and be forgiven, as we all make mistakes. You can give it up to the Universe or let God take care of it so you can let it go and move on.

Repeat these steps in this order:

Step 1: Repentance – "I'M SORRY." Take responsibility for how the relationship got to be at this point. You may be feeling distressed, regretful, or sorrowful for something you have either done to yourself or another. Something in your consciousness has caused these feelings, so you can own up to it and clear it—especially in times you have forsaken yourself.

Step 2: Ask for forgiveness – "PLEASE FORGIVE ME." This is your opportunity to repent and ask for forgiveness. You are worthy of forgiveness, so allow yourself to be forgiven.

Step 3: Gratitude – "THANK YOU." This is the opportunity to presence yourself with humility and gratitude. Thank the person you are working with, yourself, everyone, and everything—whatever you do, just keep saying it. Remember, gratitude is the highest vibration!

Step 4: Love – "I LOVE YOU." Place your hand on your heart and speak those words with all the love in your soul. Be intentional. Say it to yourself, another, the person you need to get-right with, all your problems and all earth's creatures.

IDENTIFY LIMITING BELIEFS & REMOVE SUBCONSCIOUS BLOCKS

The reason New Year's resolutions don't always work is because they don't address the obstacle that is stopping you in the first place. They say, "The road to hell is paved with good intentions." You can set all the good intentions and plans you desire, but unless you identify and restructure your limiting beliefs or destructive repetitive actions, you will undoubtedly travel the same road. You must create structure for continued growth and stability in the area you desire to change. Transformation only takes seconds: changing your perception changes your reality. When you remove the veil of limiting beliefs, the subconscious block is removed and then transformation can occur.

If you aren't experiencing your highest joy in every area of your life, there may be subconscious blocks that are holding you back. Who we are is shaped by our upbringing, the people in our lives, the environment and countries where certain beliefs and practices have been programmed into us and stored in our behaviors. Your limiting beliefs affect your thoughts and how you see the world around you which affects how you emotionally respond to those thoughts.

There are things we say or do because it is a habit or we picked it up from someone else and made our own. We do this so easily and for such a long time that now we cannot even distinguish its origin. It just becomes part of our being as if we have always done it that way. We are so easily influenced that it's frightening. Everything becomes absorbed into the tiny little sponges we call brains. Once absorbed, it may become a limiting belief that runs our lives and keeps us from things we want. Most of our limiting beliefs are subconscious, and until we identify what they are we will continue to be a victim of ourselves.

It's important to recognize that beliefs are *not* real. Continue questioning everything because your beliefs can be deceiving. Things that may have even been true for you in the past can change in the future. You may have even made poor decisions and then created a belief about the world that stays in place until you uncover it. There's a huge difference between the person you were when you were a kid and how you are now as an adult, and therefore your beliefs need to change with you. Your past experiences do not represent your life today and must be challenged.

Memories create what the subconscious mind experiences and can keep you from having things in your life if you aren't aware of it. Take money, for example. There may be lots of memories around money that prevent you from having it now in your current state.

You must tap into your heart to remove or bypass the blocks that you may have around money to bring prosperity into your life. When you operate and live from your heart space, the negative memories of the past are not the ones running the show. Painful memories never stop replaying in your mind and your experiences until you take the opportunity to heal them.

You will need diligence and willpower to recognize and notice your thoughts as they occur so you can change them right away. This is a full-time job, and it will never end! Daily meditation is a great way to practice noticing your thought and letting them go.

Growing up in poverty I saw how many people with massive amounts of money were unhappy. Sometimes they treated others horribly and were extremely wasteful, and I didn't want to be anything like that. I thought people with that much money were bad, mean and miserable. It's no wonder it took me so long to break that barrier with money because I never wanted to be mean or miserable, I was unconsciously pushing money away from me. All the praying, visualizing and meditating I did wasn't working until I identified the limiting belief, broke it down, removed and replaced it.

What are your limiting beliefs surrounding money? Examine why you hold onto any of your current negative beliefs. Maybe your mother told you that rich people are greedy. Maybe you knew someone or saw a TV special that highlighted rich people that swindled their way to wealth. You may have held onto the belief that rich people are selfish or duplicitous. It's easy to talk yourself out of wealth when you believe these things. You may simply believe that you just can't make enough money without a college degree. Whatever your current limiting belief is, you can switch it with an alternative belief.

Alternative beliefs could be, "Rich people have more opportunities and resources to help others" or "I could do more for others if I had money." What is at the root of the belief? Once you discover what it is, you can change it. You may learn in your discovery that you got the belief from your own mother, although your mom has never been wealthy. Neither has anyone in her family and none of her friends are rich either. You can conclude that she's probably not a good source of information on the topic and seek out an expert's opinion. It's important to remember that we are not living in our parents' time, so the things that may have been relevant and true for them are simply not true for us.

CREATE NEW HABITS FOR SUCCESS

Did you know it is easier to prevent rather than cure disease? Yet most people wait until they are diagnosed with cancer, an auto-immune disease, diabetes, heart attack, or stroke before they start making positive changes for their health. This forces them to either get surgery or endure painful medical treatments and often turns into a lifetime of taking prescription drugs. This modern American mentality is literally killing us, destroying our quality of life, and taking many much too early. Create new habits for success in any area of your life you desire and *start now*.

Habits and beliefs are part of what determine your health and longevity. Creating new habits in your life can and will set you free from suffering now and in the future. If anything in your life isn't working, it's because you do not have a system for success in place. Creating empowering habits allows you to transform any area of your life into exactly what you were born to live into. Create strong, fun, and powerful habits to set yourself up for success. Health is simple. It's not a complicated thing. You are meant for vibrant health. It's your beautiful, human birthright. Here are five examples of habits that can have an immediate impact on what your health looks and feels like:

1) **Plan for your success in health.** Make a commitment to healthy nourishment. Fast food is killing society. It is time to opt out of the fast food industry once and for all. Go grocery shopping at the beginning of the week to get all the ingredients you need to make your meals. It's pretty easy to plan out and prepare your meals for the whole week.

In the winter season I have a crock pot going at all times and anyone visiting can be nourished as well. You can freeze meals in separate containers so you can take them to work. I use mason jars so I can just grab and go. Pack snacks in your car for times when you are stuck without food. I always have to have something in my car to snack on, or I can get *hangry* (hungry + angry)!

2) **Move your body!** When you stop moving, your body starts degenerating. If you don't use it, you lose it! New Year's resolutions are filled with broken promises around exercise. Make it a habit to stretch each time you get up to go to the bathroom. You can make it part of your daily routine to take a walk around the block either before you leave for work or after, and maybe grab a friend or neighbor to go with you. You could even make it a family thing you all do together, which brings you all closer.

Chances are, whoever you get to go with you has been saying the same thing you have and needs it too. Do something active for twenty minutes each day and *start today*. I like to send videos of my workouts to my accountabili-buddy to hold myself accountable. I will go further into this technique/concept later in this chapter.

3) The supernatural power of fasting. Educate yourself and clear it with your health professional first before going gung-ho into a fast. Read the Complete Guide to Fasting by Dr. Jason Fung and then grab a fasting buddy to make it easier and more fun. The benefits are mind-blowing.

Giving your body a chance to heal, rejuvenate and repair on a deep, cellular level drops excess weight off you. Our bodies encapsulate the toxins we either put in or are exposed to with fat, so they won't be absorbed into our organs or hurt us. Some people get lumps where their body has built up an excess of fat in one area to protect them.

I had one on my back once, and it was very painful. I thought it was cancer, but the doctor said that it's perfectly normal. When we fast, it allows our body to release those toxins in a safe way. Start with intermittent fasting and then try one day to see how you feel. Work your way up to more days or just jump in and go for it. Speak to your doctor to make sure you can do it first. You'll want to drink only distilled or pure spring water for any fast and do colonics or enemas in tandem to help remove all those stored toxins safely and efficiently.

4) Forge strong physical social connections. Humans are physical and social beings. We need touch, connection and deep long-lasting friendships. The communication we get through social media, messaging, or texting does not count. We have to feel another person's circuitry and the vibration of their voice to fulfill our human needs. It is essential for us to have connection and pets are lovely for this. My sweet little pup Cellphone is my saving grace.

BIG PICTURE THINKING

There are many ways to look at any given situation from various vantage points and through different lenses. Big picture thinking is looking at every situation from the best vantage point that gives you the most options to choose from. In this place of possibility, no excuse or setback can deter us from that path.

In order to have big picture thinking, you must widen your scope with further investigation. If you have been stopped by something in getting something you really want, chances are you're not thinking big picture. If you find yourself stressed daily by little things, big picture thinking will help you.

Being in the entertainment industry for as long as I have been, I have seen many actors upon first arriving to an audition be extremely rude to the receptionist when they check in. Later, the same actor is on another audition or at an agent's office and that same receptionist is now the film producer or agent and she remembers their rudeness. If they were thinking **big picture** they might have gotten the job. I cannot tell you how often people in the entertainment industry burn bridges like that.

In life, we meet people at a certain time when they may be playing a certain role that does not last forever because all people change. They may not be at their best in certain moments, but judging them or treating anyone badly in those moments is small picture thinking. It is important to remember that we might run into the same people at some point further on in the future, and if you don't have big picture thinking you might cut off your chances from something you really want down the line. Also, it's just good practice to be a nice person.

Maybe you really hate doing this one specific thing at work every day, but doing it allows you to keep food on your table and a roof over your head, so focusing on the big picture can get you through challenging times. Small picture thinking is like walking around with horse blinders on where you can only see what's directly right in front of you, but nothing to either side. This leaves you blind and with limited options instead of being aware of the truth of where you are and the scope of possibilities at your disposal when you use big picture thinking.

Big picture thinking is thinking about your beautiful future ten steps ahead and choosing actions that are the highest good for all involved. Ask yourself if there is another way to look at it because there almost always is. Being able to change your focus at a moment's notice allows you to see more possibilities.

PLAY THE LONG GAME

Play the long game, not the narrow focused short game, and you will always win. Chess is a great game to practice playing your long game. In planning moves ahead, you can prevent one of your pieces from getting captured. It's not reacting to impulses or being reactionary. It's not getting caught up in the little things which can and will distract you, because they also cause you major stress. Playing the long game is playing for keeps till the very end. This requires perseverance, trust and expanding your focus.

Say you want to get a car or a house, but you must get a job first to qualify for the loan. You get the perfect resume together and go on many interviews and no bites. Though you feel discouraged you revamp your resume and continue to hit the pavement, but still nothing.

It's at this point where most people freak out, or worse yet they quit and make a negative decision about themselves: "Maybe they were right, I am a loser." This is where narrow-minded focus becomes toxic. For one, it's not true—it's a test to see how bad you want it, and two, it doesn't feel good, plus it drains your energy and motivation. Sometimes you talk yourself out of the dream car you wanted even though you can totally get it.

Playing the long game keeps your eyes on the prize, allowing you to see the big picture and think outside the box. Big picture thinking allows you the ability to see if something isn't working so you can re-approach it from a different angle. From this view, you still want that car so you might make a list of people you know with money to ask for a personal loan.

I once saw someone do a creative Kickstarter for the best Mac N' Cheese recipe that raised over $20,000! Even when it feels like you have run out of all options, continuing to play the long game means thinking even bigger to find a creative solution. What you eventually come up with is usually a much better idea than your first one and probably easier and a more direct method to handle the situation.

TAKE TIME TO DO IT RIGHT THE FIRST TIME

You ALWAYS have time to do it right the second time, so you may as well save yourself the headache, money, and time to do it right the first time! It's funny how people trick themselves into thinking they don't have enough time to do something so they choose the half-assed or ramshackle way to do it, which causes a misfire. Then they have to do it all over again, which takes double the time, energy, and effort than just doing it right the first time. With big picture thinking you always have time to do things the right way the very first time.

You may find yourself stressed out about not having enough time in the day to do all the things you want to do. Time slips away from you, which pushes that vacation to next year, but you really need it now. You have a full-time job, three kids, and a spouse, and are in the middle of remodeling your home. You work late because you're on a deadline, need the money, and can't be home when the contractor arrives, so you ask one of your kids to let them in. The contractor finishes the job, but you come home to find the wrong wall taken out. Stressed and feeling rushed on your deadlines, you completely forgot to explain to your kids what was supposed to be done. Take time right from the start to give all the proper information to ensure positive results.

I was painting my bedroom and for some awful reason I thought it would be better to just go and paint and skip priming the walls first. I wasn't doing the job for anyone else or I would have certainly done it right the first time. Because I went right to doing the color without a primer, there were places on the wall where the paint didn't stick due to some waxy residue. I even knew better because I paint sets for film and television—I was just being lazy.

Instead of just starting all over again right then, I tried to paint over those spots, but paint dripped all the way down the walls and dried. Instead of doing it right the first *or* second time, I then had to sand the entire wall to remove all the paint drips, prime the wall and then paint it again. I ended up not sleeping in my bedroom for three weeks until it was completed when it could have easily been a week long project. It's interesting how often these types of things happen until we catch them.

SAVE THE DRAMA FOR ACTORS & PERFORMERS

Even if you are a professional actor, it is time to let all that personal drama fall to the wayside. Being reactionary is never cute. It causes unnecessary suffering and rarely gives you positive results. A person who stresses or freaks out all the time over every little thing is unpleasant to be around. Their suffering is caused by their own hand by simply not taking the time to gather more information about the situation or focus on the bigger picture. As a result, everything is blown up way out of proportion because their mind can only focus on the worst-case scenarios they are reactively expecting to occur.

When your focus is narrow there are less options, and small things suck your life force energy away from you and anyone that might be near you. It's like driving a car by only looking two feet in front of you, causing you so much stress you constantly overreact or pull all your hair out. Broadening your view allows you to see the turns ahead so that every move isn't an emergency. You must stop focusing on the freak-outs so you can focus hocus pocus on solutions. Emancipate yourself from the headaches of small personal dramas and save the drama for the movie you'll watch later.

It's important to notice who in your life is constantly bringing major drama into not only their life but yours as well. You are not obligated to manage their drama. I love the following quote that was written on my English teacher's wall in high school: "YOUR LACK OF PREPAREDNESS IS NOT MY EMERGENCY!"

People who often fail to plan well push their drama onto you, making you think and feel that it's now your problem. It's a wonderful gift to be aware of when this happens so you can let that person know that you will do your best to help, but you will not drop everything to do so. I plan weeks ahead of time to make sure that I do not inflict an emergency on others, so I simply will not sacrifice my personal well-being for someone who just doesn't think ahead or plan well.

PLAN FOR YOUR FUTURE

What is the plan for after your death? Plan for your future and your children's future, if you have them. The only thing that is 100% inevitable in life is death.

Create a will that either delegates your stuff to specific people or a person that you trust to make all those decisions for you. Set aside money for funeral costs, as you wouldn't want your loved ones to be stuck with that. If you don't have the money now you can start an account or fund to save up and by the time you pass on, it won't be thrown onto the shoulders of the ones you care the most about.

The last thing you want after death is to be a financial burden for those you leave behind. You would also want the people you love to have the beautiful belongings you worked so hard for, or you can donate them to a good cause or charity. Otherwise, everything will be tied up in bureaucracy or sold by your creditors trying to recoup what you owe them. This radical planning for your family's future will emancipate them from that suffering long after you have left this dimension.

RADICAL
Definition: //Rad·i·cal// //radk()l// ~Noun~
1. A group of atoms behaving as a unit in a number of compounds.
2. A person that advocates thorough complete
political or social change. ~ Adjective ~
3. (especially of change or action) relating to or affecting the
fundamental nature of something; far reaching or thorough.
4. Representing or reporting an extreme or progressive
section of something. (www.OxfordDictionaries.com)

PRACTICE RADICAL ACCEPTANCE

Keeping your heart **radically** open expands your heart's capacity to love and therefore your capacity to be happy. Choose radical acceptance in every moment. Accept everything as it is and exactly how it comes to you in that moment. Your happiness depends on it.

Radically accept everyone as they are right now for who they are. Continuing to get mad at someone for not being or acting a certain way is like getting mad at a pine tree for not producing as much shade as a willow tree. You have to stop nagging or getting upset with those people because they won't do what you expect or want them to.

They are simply a pine tree (themselves). They will never be anything else but a pine. They will never give you the shade (the thing you want) of a willow tree no matter how much you shame, guilt, nag, or ask them. Accept them for who they are and move your picnic blanket to sit under a different tree that has all the shade you desire. Maybe you'd prefer one with fruit that you can pick and eat. Because after all "NATURE'S NEAT!"

GETTING UP OFF THE MAT

I grew up in a small town, and because I didn't have the best home life, I sought out as many after-school programs to participate in as I could. One of the many things I did was join the boy's wrestling team.

We didn't have a girl's team as there were no other girls who wanted to participate. I was given an emphatic "no" when I said I wanted to join the team. I told them I would take it up with the school board if they wouldn't let me. They said they didn't have women's outfits and it would be very difficult without separate dressing rooms. I kept pushing for it and had to take it up with my principal and the school board. I did my research and brought a list of other schools that had women's teams along with places where I could get my own proper wrestling outfit. They had to accept me but said it would be on a trial basis.

I went through a lot of pain doing this, not only for myself but with my family. One of my aunts called to say, "You know, you're the talk of the whole town, don't you? They're saying the only reason you want to be on the boy's team is to get in those positions with boys." Are you kidding me? It was the opportunity to use my skills and precision to kick their butts! I was mortified and angered by this statement.

I came to realize it was just her judgment against me and was just concerned about my future and my reputation. I was teased beyond belief and harassed by many people in my school. I won my first several matches and then quit. I just wanted to prove I could do it. I learned so much in the process, including one of the most important lessons: to get up off the mat when your back is pinned against the floor!

No one wins all the time, not even winners. Winners know that, and that's why they win and how they survive their defeats. A winner is someone who falls down a hundred times and gets up a hundred and one times. Losers and champions both get knocked down. The only things that separates them is that the champion keeps getting back up—*no matter what*. The winner wins using focus and dedication, not wielding some crazy superpower. Sure, talent and genetics can play a role in some endeavors. Michael Phelps has a body built for swimming. But without focus and dedication, even he would not be a winner. When you are down or out, you must access the parts of yourself that give you the strength to get back up. Who do you have to be, or what do you need to focus on for that to happen?

In wrestling I got thrown onto my back many times during a match where it would appear that I was going to lose. In actuality I was just in a very challenging situation which is just part of the game. It's in those moments you can make a powerful choice. The ups and the downs are what make life so exciting. It's in the downs that we get to express courage, confidence and strategy. Whenever you are failing or losing it's your opportunity to turn yourself into your own hero and create another possibility.

Even if you lose, who cares? What did you really lose? You lost that one thing in that one moment in time. The real question is, "What did you gain?" For every one loss you experience there are numerous wins that come out of that. Losses make you stronger.

Being upset about a loss makes you weak. What's worse is getting upset about being upset. It's unnecessary suffering that—takes away your power and drains your life force. There is no use complaining or whining about it, so put your ego in check. Just because you lost doesn't mean you will lose every time—your past doesn't dictate your future unless you allow yourself to be stuck there.

Honestly evaluate your performance so you can learn and grow from it. Perhaps you need to lift weights to get stronger. Maybe you need to do more cardio to increase stamina. Whatever it may be, focus on the future actions necessary to improve your game or performance. Your can-do attitude will take you far.

EMOTIONS ARE YOUR TOOLS

When humans are healthy, happy, and free, they uplift, support, build, and protect others. Humans are happiest doing the things they love. Doing everything in your power to keep yourself healthy, happy, and free is critical. I believe we owe it to ourselves to do whatever it takes to keep ourselves in this state. You have always been able to change your life in every moment.

Use your tools, don't *be* a tool! Your emotional guidance system is a sacred tool to help you. No matter what state any part of your life is in, it can always get better. You can always have more happiness in your life!

Your emotions are a wonderful built-in checks and balances system once you learn how to use them. Your emotions and feelings are one of your greatest tools. Your thinking creates your feelings, which create your actions or inaction. Your emotions are vibrations in your body for you to look at and see where balance can be restored.

Emotions are a record of your past. You must respect them. You must honor them. You must release them. Emotions guide you to the next step. It's a flawless system for you to use as a tool, but not be ruled by them. The problem with most people is that they let their emotions run their lives. They have become emotional addicts that behave just like junkies on heroin, only worse.

Enslavement to one's emotions is called *emotional entrapment*. This is the state where one is constantly experiencing the same negative emotions over and over again, even when the situations and people involved have changed. Once you become aware that you are in a negative emotional loop, you can get out.

It is important to slow yourself down. Start by slowing down your breath—take five counts for each inhale and exhale for two full minutes before proceeding. Try going for a walk outside until you can get a different perspective.

These negative emotions can also affect your health, so it's best to stop them at once. Which emotions do you have memorized? Which emotions do you practice most often? What emotions are easy for you to resort to? What emotions are hard or difficult for you to experience? What's your emotional go-to? Answer these questions in your journal and then use the EMOTIONAL TOOLBOX EXERCISE on the www.POLRLIVING.com website to free yourself from your personal emotional entrapment.

WEIGHING YOUR OPTIONS

Put more weight on the good things, the things you want to bring more of into your life. Try to see the things you don't like or don't want as a pathway to a different way of seeing something that you hadn't noticed before that could provide you with peace, growth, and discovery. Think carefully about all possibilities or choices in any given situation. The more time and thought you give to something, the better chances you will have to make the best decisions. With whatever choice or option being evaluated, you can create a list of pros and cons. Use the WEIGHING YOUR OPTIONS EXERCISE on the www.POLRLIVING.com website for an easy helpful formula for making important decisions so that your ego is not choosing for you.

EGO
Definition: //e·go// //ēō// ~ Noun
1. A person's sense of self-esteem or self-importance.
(www.OxfordDictionaries.com)
2. The idea or opinion that you have of yourself, especially the level of your ability and intelligence and your importance as a person. (www.UrbanDictionary.com)

CHECK YOUR EGO AT THE DOOR

You can check your ego like you can check in your coat. You simply take it off and hand it to the coat check person. You will always come back for your ego because it is not only a possession like your coat, it is a part of you and your nature forever.

We obviously need our ego for our basic human survival. It provides a sense of identity and our boundaries in life. It's important, however, to ensure that the ego serves our highest interests rather than enslaving us with fear and the need to control everything.

An unchecked ego keeps you in fear. Fear keeps you small and weak, which keeps your dreams just out of reach. Our sense of purpose is sapped by the feeling that we are not worthy or deserving of love. If you are having a hard time trusting your own inner guidance system, your ego is running the show.

A life driven by ego is toxic and unhealthy. I like to make fun of and laugh at my ego as often as I can. I talk to it and have even given it a name as if it's another person. I chose Shirley because she is very *sure* of herself. It's a silly name to emasculate my ego.

You can name yours whatever you like. Naming it and identifying its behaviors keeps it separate from you, because after all *it is not you*—in the same way you are not your elbow! Most people identify their ego as themselves even though both have very different agendas. Learn what its voice sounds like and the tone in which it speaks. Accept it as your friend and learn its behaviors.

When you catch your ego in the act of doing something dumb, laugh at it! I keep a list in my journal titled "Shirley's Shortcomings" to keep her identity separate from mine. It's easier that way to distinguish the behaviors between us or see when she's in charge. I keep a running log of all the dumb ideas, thoughts, behaviors, and actions of my ego.

I remind myself that listening to my heart has gotten me all the accomplishments I have achieved so far. If my ego was calling the shots, I'd have no friends and would most likely be homeless. The ego means well but will stop at nothing to be right. Ego doesn't always make the right choices for my future and certainly doesn't pay my bills! It's time to remind the ego that you are back and you mean business. So go ahead and check your ego at the door.

GET AN ACCOUNTABILI-BUDDY

An accountabili-buddy is a buddy, friend, or partner who will hold you accountable to the goals and promises you make to keep you both moving forward to achieving your dreams. We each have goals we want to achieve but the little tasks along the way often get ignored or overlooked because no one is checking in on us. We can make promises to ourselves all day long and never make good on them because no one will ever know if we did them or not.

Sometimes we mean well but come up with excuses why we just can't do it right now. We can excuse letting ourselves down but we would never intentionally let another person down. That's why your accountabili-buddy will hold you to a higher standard than you hold yourself. This person is your checks and balances partner who will help you grow and rise.

Your partner will keep you moving forward on your goals and you will do the same for them. You can have an accountabili-buddy for just about anything. It not only makes it more fun to track progress, it's great to bounce ideas off someone else to get feedback. The best part about it is that it makes it really hard to back out on the things you said you would do when that person is checking up on you.

You can use an accountabili-buddy to set goals, to practice asking big questions, for inspiration and motivation, and to help keep you progressing towards your personal goals. It really makes completing challenging or hard things fun and achievable. To keep your momentum forward and your motivation up, find an accountabili-buddy. You will be assigned one as part of the monthly **Legacy Life Coaching Program** or you can find your own here <u>www.POLRLIVING.com</u>.

Have a buddy to practice asking big questions, such as asking for a raise. It's important to have confidence, speak clearly, and ask appropriately. Having that practice with your buddy instills confidence when you go in for the ask. You can practice your tone, volume, and overall demeanor for when you will be in front of the person that has the ability to change the quality of your life. Practice makes perfect. That's how you learned to walk, talk, and everything else you do confidently. You can practice asking different buddies the same question until it gets to be second nature. Use the Path of Least Resistance Accountabili-buddy Protocol for the best and most efficient way to hold someone accountable.

I have different accountabili-buddies for different things. The area where I have had the hardest time staying motivated is working out. My main goal in physical health was to be doing at least one form of exercise every day. On my own I'll seem to have inspiration and take action for a short period of time and then it all falls away when I work on major projects like writing this book. I tend to write for ten+ hours a day and after that I do not have the time nor energy to work out.

My favorite daily workout at the very least consists of twenty push-ups, 50 sit-ups, 50 leg lifts on each leg & 100 jumping jacks. You'd be surprised at how doing just these few things can make you feel and look, yet it is sometimes the absolute hardest thing for me to stick with despite how great it makes me feel. An accountabili-buddy is invaluable and makes all the difference in the world.

Find the buddies that have the same goals in mind to create accountability with. You can have different accountabili-buddies for each area or goal or keep the same one for all. Create daily and weekly goals with them, check in on them throughout the completion of the tasks at hand and put it on your calendar so you can start crossing off the items on your list. Join the Accountabili-buddy System on the www.POLRLIVING.com website to find a buddy with your same interest or in the same city you live. Join our FB and Instagram community to connect with other like-minded individuals.

EMANCIPATE YOURSELF FROM SUFFERING

Incorporating the techniques in this chapter will alleviate you from suffering. Learning how to identify and then change your underlying beliefs emancipates you from your past and gives you freedom to choose new things in your beautiful future. It is my greatest wish for peace for all beings in all dimensions, planes, timelines and galaxies. May you soon emancipate yourself from suffering with ease and grace, in Jesus's name, and so it is, Amen.

CHAPTER 10

THE INTEGRITY WAGON

INTEGRITY
Definition: //in·teg·ri·ty// //integrdē // ~ Noun
1. A firm adherence to a code of especially moral
or artistic values; incorruptibility.
2. An unimpaired condition: soundness.
3. The quality or state of being complete or undivided:
completeness. (www.Merriam-Webster.com)

Get on the integrity wagon! The reason I say "get on it" is because you'll constantly fall off of it. It happens to all of us. We are human, after all, and failure is par for the course.

You'll be on a roll with practicing perfectly every day, then life will give you a jolt and you'll fall off the integrity wagon and have to jump back on again. Living in integrity means you do exactly what you say you will no matter how much you may not "feel" like it. This means that your word is solid gold and incorruptible.

Honoring your word as law allows people to trust and rely on you, offering you more opportunities. Someone who says one thing and does another is not in integrity. People like that are not offered much because no one can rely on them.

Being on the "integrity wagon" means getting into complete alignment with all the parts of yourself, your purpose, nature, and the universe. When you take actions that support your intentions, goals, and dreams it creates great inner strength. Have integrity in all areas of your life or you will feel something is off or even experience negative results from it.

We all fall out of integrity in one area or more because we are human after all. Until we investigate and see where we are out of alignment we will continue to shoot ourselves in the foot. You will have to scan through each area of your life to find areas where you may be out of integrity. Obvious examples of where people are out of integrity are:

- A yogi or meditation teacher who curses in traffic or yells at people.
- A raw food chef who is a chain smoker.
- A parent who isn't taking actions to live a sustainable life (recycling, conserving water, using renewable energy) by protecting the environment to ensure their children will have a secure future.

No one is perfect. Things happen in life where we may fall out of integrity. It's easy to restore integrity when you fall out of it by cleaning up your communication about agreements or commitments you previously made with someone. In a person's lifetime they will be "in" and "out" of integrity hundreds to thousands of times. Integrity is not something you just have, it is something that most of us strive for in all areas of our lives. It's more than just being honest, it's not breaking your promises to people.

Having integrity with another person is different than having integrity with yourself, which is where many of us fail. When any part of us is out of alignment with the rest, it causes an imbalance. This chapter dives deep into all the levels of integrity so you have the power to restore it in all the areas of your life to align your spirit, body, and mind.

The integrity wagon is one of the best rides you'll ever go on. The payoff is huge and people in your life will take notice. It's like you're standing in line for a ride you really want to go on when you realize how hungry you are. The ride itself is only two minutes long and you are several people from the front. You see a food stand right across the way and your stomach is growling, so you make the choice to leave and go to the end of the food line while your friend keeps your place for the ride. You rush back as fast as you can, but you miss going on the ride with your friend. The ride in the story is the INTEGRITY WAGON. Your friend is your commitment to what you say you want in your life, and what you're willing to do to get it. The food stand is the stuff you fill your time with that isn't as important as your word or the goals you want to achieve which makes the ride called "life" so much fun.

It wasn't until I participated in Landmark Education that I truly knew what integrity meant. We're all aware of the basic principles like do not lie, cheat, or steal, but at Landmark I gained the realization that being out of integrity with ourselves and in our own lives is like lying, cheating, and stealing from ourselves. Once I created a deep and profound relationship to integrity it transformed me, leveled up my life, improved every relationship, and skyrocketed my game.

GET INTO INTEGRITY WITH YOURSELF

Before we can get into integrity with others we must first be in integrity with ourselves and all areas of our life. Many of us were told seemingly harmless lies as a kid which then carried into adulthood. Something that seems as benign as lying about the existence of Santa Claus or the Tooth Fairy leads us into us lying as an adult. We even have a fancy adult name, "white lie," to make it socially acceptable, as if the color white makes it OK somehow.

It's easy to fall into the canned responses to make your life more comfortable. "No, honey, you look great," or "Yeah, we should get together sometime" when in actuality you weren't even paying attention, or you really wanted to get away from that person, so you said whatever you could for a fast getaway. Then we lie to ourselves again and say it was the "polite" thing to do, so now lying has become a defense mechanism. There are other ways to respond respectfully without lying. The little white lies can spin out of control.

If you aren't constantly putting yourself in check, you may find yourself lying about other things. One thing that's worse than a liar is a person who lies to themself. There are so-called "honest" people running around who would never lie to another person but lie to themselves constantly and wonder why their virtuous "honesty" is never rewarded. Getting in integrity is easier when you are honest with where you are at. It's perfectly acceptable to be exactly where you are right now, reading this book.

Begin to notice if the words you are saying—to others and to yourself—*exactly* represent what you actually mean. You can call yourself out on all the things that are inauthentic to who you are, no matter how small or weird they may be. Own up to it or call yourself out when you are out of integrity, when your words don't match what you mean. Doing this before anyone else does gives both you and the other person freedom to decide what works best for them.

This year, I fell off the integrity wagon pretty hard and almost broke every bone in my body, metaphorically of course. To put things in context for you, I was at the Eclipse Festival in Oregon during the solar eclipse of August 21, 2017 when I got the download from Source to write this book. I was channeling pretty hard and writing as fast as I could for hours, to the point where my friends were concerned for me and wondered why I didn't want to leave camp. I had to get it all down on paper (consisting of multiple ripped-up paper bags which was all I could find) while the inspiration was moving through me. But when I came back home from the festival I didn't take any further actions on the book even though I got strong messages on two other new moon occasions.

Upon getting the initial message, I realized and established that writing this book would probably be the most important thing I have ever done in my life. I felt it throughout every cell in my body, and every time I talked about it with close friends the hair would stand up on both of our arms and legs. In my knowing and continuing to not do anything about it, I was out of integrity with myself, source and spirit and it began to negatively affect me. That's what being out of integrity does to you. I was letting life get in the way and a year passed by.

I had let things in my life go. I stopped taking time every day to write and work on my book. Then I felt really horrible about it, which only made things worse.

I started making excuses, which sent negative messages to my subconscious that I couldn't write a book, I'm a fraud, and I shouldn't take myself seriously. I found myself trying to talk myself out of finishing it. "I don't know how to write a book. What if it's shit? Who would read it anyway? It's going to be a lot of work." Even when I filled my head with nonsense to validate the time spent *not* writing this book, there was still a constant nagging in my head prompting me to finish it. Knowing this was the most important thing I will have ever done and then choosing to not stop everything to create it was me lying to and out of integrity with myself on the deepest level.

I couldn't stand not doing anything about it anymore. In order to restore integrity with myself I had to make some rash moves. I had to force myself to sit my butt down and write. In order to do that I could not be around any distractions or people. I rushed off to the Agua Inn in Nuevo Arenal, Costa Rica, a warm and remote place to lock myself in solitude to write the lion's share of this very book.

That is one example of how to clean up the mess around integrity so that you can get back on that train. To clean this one up, I first had to forgive myself for the betrayal of myself, move past the small thoughts and replace them with more accurate ones. Then I immediately put a plan in motion to be in action on my book until completion: I scheduled out writing days and times to fit it in my current working and traveling schedule. As long as you are taking action on your dreams and goals daily you are in integrity. Enjoy that ride!

If I didn't plan it all the way through, you wouldn't be reading these words now. I had to get in integrity despite all of the other things that I had to do to pay my bills. I was tired of getting in my own way. You might feel the same way about something. Being out of integrity with yourself begins to negatively affect your confidence and happiness over time. Imagine people who go their whole lives never following their dreams and how that must feel! At least you are doing something about it now by reading this book—it's never too late!

It had been a constant negative feeling until I pulled out all the stops to make it happen. I seriously had to use every tool in this book, which is why I know the tools work! I say do whatever it takes to honor yourself and your dreams or consider living an unhappy or less-than-desirable life.

Getting in integrity with yourself will set you free. In doing everything I had to in order to get this book to you, I know that anything is possible. It's that level of authenticity and commitment that makes magical things happen. If you'd like to see where in your life you are out of integrity, do the INTEGRITY EXERCISE or join the INTEGRITY TEAM to meet a community of like-minded individuals at www.POLRLIVING.com.

TIE UP ALL LOOSE ENDS

You wouldn't go running with your shoes untied, would ya? So, don't go doing it in your life. A loose end is something that you started that is not yet complete. Unfinished ends are the perfect place to start in your journey to success. The amount of energy it takes to actually start something is intense. If it's then left hanging in limbo, the energy is transferred to static and frenetic energy in the spirit, body, and mind.

Those unfinished projects are still taking up your mental energy until you finish them. Every cell in your body wants you to have completion. Tying up your loose ends enriches you with feelings of self-worth, accomplishment, purpose, and joy.

Write a list of all your loose ends and unfinished projects in your journal. Be sure to include *anything* that is not yet complete in your life. This can include closure in relationships, home projects, personal or work tasks, and any communication that needs to be addressed or cleared. Create a plan of action to complete one each week. You may want to check off one a month if you have a busier schedule. Over the course of a year you can free up your mind and focus much more clearly. You'll be amazed at what opens up for you in the process. All loose ends will be completed as part of the www.POLRLIVING.com monthly *Legacy Life Coaching Program* and you will have accountabil-abuddies to help you.

GET IN INTEGRITY WITH OTHERS

Practice radical honesty with all the people in your life, especially those that may be affected by your behavior. Consider the possibility that you can have everything that you want in a relationship. I have seen many people living in the old paradigms of relationships where they hide personal desires from their partners from the very beginning, in fear of not being accepted, and then betray their partner. For instance, knowing you may want to explore an open relationship and keeping it from your partner is not only deceitful but it makes it almost impossible for you ever to obtain what you really want.

You must be willing to communicate your needs and desires to those you trust and speak from the heart with conviction. It does not mean that they will respond with a "hell yes!" or affirm right away. Things take time. Or they may never want what you want, but being honest with them is a sign that you respect them and allow them to make their own decisions.

When you and someone else are experiencing a lack of unity, you can trace it back to the source to see that somebody—possibly both people— were out of integrity. Someone who is out of integrity or energetically lacking in truth creates a rift in the relationship. Both people feel it. Often you'll find that the perpetrator will start to emotionally leave the partnership or physically avoid their partner out of guilt.

Continuing with a lack of integrity within one's soul can cause a person to cheat and hurt all people involved, and sends negative messages to the universe and your subconscious that you don't deserve exactly what you want and that it's not possible. For example, you may be a person that wants your feet rubbed daily, or maybe work comes first for you, but you must request and clearly state your needs before entering a partnership. Why would you enter a partnership with a person that doesn't accept you as you are or want the same things as you?

Being honest with your partner from the beginning allows for the possibility for both of you to have *exactly* what you want. There are others that want the exact same things as you do. As Missy Elliot says, "Get your freak on." In order to find a person with your same desires, you'll have to be transparent. Be honest and let *them* decide if they want to accept you for all of you. The sooner you do so in dating, the faster you attract those that will accept and love you for who you are. Anything less is manipulation and fear-based.

I have many friends in the polyamorous world and I assure you, if you want this in life—it's possible. Whatever your deepest desires are, you can have them and can find someone else with the same kinks as you! You must be honest about your idiosyncrasies in order to attract those that desire the same. For those of you wanting to dive deeper into learning how to communicate your kinks and desires in the polyamory world, I suggest reading "The Ethical Slut" and "Opening Up - A Guide to Creating and Sustaining Open Relationships".

I have witnessed friends go from cheating on their partners to getting exactly what they want and feeling fulfilled in their relationships. The more enlightened we are and humanity is, the more transparent everything becomes. Let's start now and set our relationships, career, and future on the right course from the beginning.

AGREEMENTS

The entire world is made up of agreements. They are everywhere. There are four different kinds, that can also be combined: spoken, written, unspoken, and unwritten.

We are constantly agreeing to things. Every single app you download or computer program you install, you have agreed to their list of terms and conditions, often without reading them in full. You also inadvertently agree by simply not speaking out against what's going on around you. It is your responsibility to make clear agreements declaring where you do and do not agree in each situation.

SPOKEN & WRITTEN AGREEMENTS

All agreements have the ability to elevate you and your consciousness and expand your heart by following through on your word. Whether you honor your agreements or not will make the difference in whether people believe in and show up for you. If you are a person who does not honor simple agreements (such as the time you said you'd be somewhere), it sends negative messages out.

Your spirit, body, and mind, as well as any person you had that agreement with, will understand that you're not trustworthy or reliable. For simple dishonoring, you can restore your integrity by connecting with the person that you had an agreement with to recommit to a different one.

The moment you realize you are not going to fulfill your previous agreement you must energetically be responsible to clean that up right away. Let that person know what you are now available to commit to. For example: if you have a meeting with someone and you know you are going to be late or something else has come up, you need to call them and renegotiate a new meeting day or time.

UNSPOKEN & UNWRITTEN AGREEMENTS

Unspoken agreements run your life if you do not outwardly speak up about them. The unspoken and unwritten agreements affect the consciousness of the people involved in them. There are unspoken agreements at any place you visit, whether it's a church, school, a different country, or even your friend's home. It's important to investigate what all those agreements are before you go there so that you know what you're signing up for.

Not honoring the agreements can negatively affect all the relationships around you if others notice you are not following those rules or set of agreements. You can at any time speak up about any unspoken agreement you do not agree with, but until you have that conversation, you are committed to an unspoken agreement. In Thailand it is unacceptable to show the bottoms of your feet or raise them above people's heads. You wouldn't know that because it's not written anywhere and not spoken, unless you offend someone by doing it which is how I found out.

Money is an unspoken and written agreement. The paper that the U.S. Treasury prints money on does not actually have a value in itself. Money used to be backed by gold as a standard but now it's just numbers on a screen, willy-nilly. Money only has value because it's an unspoken agreement that it's worth a certain amount. Value is a construct. Values can change just like everything in this world, especially with money. In the beginning, crypto-currency didn't have much value, but now it's gaining momentum because more people agree that blockchain is valuable.

Now there is talk of eliminating money altogether so that it may be traced and every purchase will be documented and taxed accordingly. People can band together to declare any unspoken agreement into nonexistence by agreeing to something new. If everyone was to declare and boycott the current economic system, big banks and corporations—life as we know it would change.

I have attended the Burning Man Festival 21 times. The first time I went, there was a drive-by shooting art gallery with real vehicles and real guns—no people or animals were hurt in this game. By attending the festival, you agree to the ten principles that have been declared as well as any additional written statements on the website, on the back of the ticket, and in the booklet.

The ten core principles of the festival that you agree to by attending are: Radical Inclusion, Gifting, Decommodification, Radical Self-Reliance, Radical Self-Expression, Communal Effort, Civic Responsibility, Leave No Trace, Participation, and Immediacy. On the back of the ticket you agree and are aware that you could possibly die by attending. I am grateful I made it out alive 21 times. I know a handful of people who have not been so lucky. Can you imagine if we lived in a country with those ten core principles? I'd be the first to sign up to this world of impeccability.

BE IMPECCABLE

IMPECCABLE
Definition: //Im·pec·ca·ble// //impekb()l// ~ Adjective
1. In accordance with the highest standards of propriety; faultless.
2. Not liable to sin. (www.OxfordDictionaries.com)

IMPECCABILITY

Impeccability includes having impeccable behavior. If you want to be successful or have a good life, it is imperative to have a good work ethic and high standards and to take the actions necessary to complete the tasks needed to accomplish your goals. That is not saying you have to be perfect with zero flaws; rather, it speaks about your specific actions and ethics. You can be impeccable and still make mistakes. Being impeccable is knowing you did everything in your power to be your best.

IMPECCABLE APPEARANCE

Take pride in how you present yourself to the world. This doesn't mean you have to be fashionable, it means dressing in accordance with the highest standard for whatever event or space you occupy. I agree with the saying, "It is better to be overdressed than under-dressed." If you're chilling out at your house, sweatpants and a tank top are great, but I don't advise you wear them to a job interview.

Before going out, the time you take to "get dressed-up & ready" *ensures* that you are going to have a good time. You may as well do this anytime you leave your house just because you can and besides, it's way more fun! Preparing yourself for any occasion before you leave your house arms you with the ability to say "yes" to possibilities that may come up in the spur of the moment. As an actress, I always dressed the part. I never left my house unprepared to meet people in the industry. You never know when you'll meet the person that will change your life.

IMPECCABLE WORD

This is one of the FOUR AGREEMENTS by Don Miguel Ruiz. Speak with integrity and from your heart. Say only what you mean and in the direction of truth and light. Take full ownership by holding others accountable to be impeccable with their word in all the spaces you occupy. Actively remove any negative conversations in your head or in your physical space such as gossip, complaining or excuses. Be impeccable and unreasonable with your sacred words.

IMPECCABLE PERFORMANCE

Work on your craft, project, or business every day for at least five minutes. Doing so creates new patterns from which to pull from when inspiration is lacking. Soon enough, that five minutes will turn into twenty, and so on. Keeping this rhythm of daily practice can turn your twenty minutes into an hour each day. Before you know it, you will have done 10,000 hours, making yourself an expert at something.

You must train yourself to do things even when you aren't "feeling it" and creating this daily habit will pull you through those tough times. Take classes and read books to expand your current level of expertise in that field. We start dying when we stop learning and there is always more you can learn, even in the field in which you may be an expert.

IMPECCABLE BUSINESS

Maintain specific and high standards to practice excellence so your project or business will have a strong foundation from which to grow. If you have to hire other people for services along the way, it's crucial to use the best people in that field or consult the top experts. Get the best people for your team to grow your business.

GET A COACH

To jumpstart your impeccable performance you can hire a coach. A coach is someone who will hold you accountable to your goals in business and life and get you there faster than you could manage on your own. If you want to be successful in anything it's wise to get a coach to help you get there.

If you want to be an Olympian or be the best in your field, you will definitely need a coach. Someone who knows how to help you and has done it for themselves and others, and that you get along with. Even athletes have coaches to help them focus, strategize, eliminate bad habits and steer them in the right direction, while also cheering them on. Having a coach on your team is invaluable for success.

GET A MENTOR

Another way to improve your performance is with a mentor. Find a mentor or someone more established than you to learn from. It's important to do your research on a potential mentor to see who they are. Get to know them and see if they can help you. You'll also want to research the things they like to see what you can provide for them when approaching them instead of merely asking for a handout.

Chances are other people want things from them too, so offer something to contribute to their life. It feels refreshing for people when energy is exchanged, which is why your research on them is super important. Start the communication by providing how you can be of service to them before you go right to asking them for something.

TRACK YOUR SUCCESSES & GOALS

To be impeccable with your career you need to track your success and goals. By tracking everything you will see where you have progressed or where you need to focus more attention and then take action. Tracking helps you stay organized and on course. If you don't track your progress, it's very likely that you won't challenge yourself in the areas you need to or be able to make changes if you veer off course. It helps you to stay connected to the importance of your goals and dreams.

People are more active than they ever have been with all those fancy electronic trackers counting daily steps, heart rate, and sleep patterns. I know people who will go outside and walk at the very end of the day, even if they are exhausted, if they haven't reached their 10,000 steps. I initially had the goal of 10,000 words for my book, which I have far surpassed. Granted, I didn't know what I was doing when I first started this journey. I simply just set goals for myself.

If I didn't track it I would have missed out on the opportunity of seeing my progression, which became fuel to keep me going. It's one thing to think you are making progress and another to see actual proof that it's working.

I track all the hours I spend on writing and every process along the way. Tracking your actions and your goals ensures they will happen and how you can do things better. Tracking is a powerful tool to help you reach your health, wellness, and financial goals too.

Keep two ongoing spreadsheets, one to track all your time spent on the project and what the task was, and the other on all of your goals. They will be separate lists that you can keep adding to as you go. Being able to look back on these lists at any low point in your life can help cheer you up.

A goal list is fun and satisfying to keep. You can cross off items as you achieve them. I also like to take each goal on my list and work backwards to see what needs to be done to achieve it faster. It's like reverse-engineering your dreams and goals. Getting the goals out of your head and onto paper makes them easier to attain.

SEE A PENNY—PICK IT UP—ALL DAY LONG YOU'LL HAVE GOOD LUCK!

Are you out of integrity concerning money? There are people who have an ongoing conversation around not having enough money, but when they see a penny on the ground, they ignore it. We are not born with money in our pockets but value can be found everywhere. It's important to acknowledge value everywhere in order to attain more of it.

If you are seeking value, then it's value you'll find. It depends on how you're looking at things and where you're looking for them. Some people find money and pick it up because it's free money. They find it because they are looking on the ground and choose to pick it up. Some people don't look at the ground and therefore don't find free money.

Worse yet, some people see the money on the ground and still don't pick it up. Ignoring free money sends messages to your subconscious and the universe that you do not value it, which keeps you further away from having it. (Unless you are a person who intentionally leaves it for another person to pick up as a gift.) The universe will test you, so be sure to use the key of gratitude.

It's important to respect what the universe lays out for you. I know some who pick up coins from the ground and then give them to homeless people. They are still respecting the universe's offering and doing a good deed on top of it, doubling the action and therefore increasing the intrinsic value of the money. Money is energy. There are others that might feel insecure and don't want someone to see them picking up a penny because it might make them look bad. Those people may be looking for larger sums of money but ignore the free gifts that are right in front of them. It sends out a beacon that you disregard money if you refuse it when it's right in front of you.

It's not the amount of money, it's the respect, honor, and integrity from which you operate that should be the basis for your actions every day. It is out of integrity if you really want money and you don't pick a penny up off the ground when you see it. It is inauthentic to your values and is intentionally going against nature. Nature will always prevail. It's these little inconsistencies where people do not look and still blame the world for being hard, or repeat to themselves whatever other beliefs stop them from having all the things they want.

I believe money comes to me with ease and grace, especially when I need it. I have my own silly ritual when I find coins on the ground that I created from the spirit of my inner child. I see the coin, I get excited, I pick it up and in my head or out loud, depending on if it's a crowded place or not, I say "thank you, thank you, thank you" while skipping away with a smile on my face. I perform the same ritual when I find bills, which actually happens pretty often.

Getting in integrity with what you say you want AND the actions you take allows you to live in accordance with the laws of nature. When you live in integrity and perfect harmony with nature, you will get the full value of life and have the most fun. After all, free money is the best!

TRANSPARENCY

Transparency provides freedom. It creates clarity for anyone working together in any way, which makes everyone more productive and increases trust. When everything is out on the table, it shows others you have nothing to hide.

Being boldly transparent allows trust for all parties involved and you'll know if you have to draw the line in the sand to make a sound decision. You'll also be able to quickly and efficiently respond to problems or controversy if it arises. Being transparent establishes open communication channels so that everyone clearly understands you and the tasks that need to be performed.

Being transparent in business allows customers to be far more forgiving of mistakes and allows them to contribute feedback that could take the quality of your product or business to the next level. It's easier to fully invest in yourself when you make transparency a priority.

Whether it's personal or political opinions, product reviews, innermost thoughts, or even a photo of today's food item, people are living their lives completely out in the open online. This expectation for transparency has extended beyond personal interactions. It has now become a reality in business with all the distrust of shady corporations.

OUT OF INTEGRITY WITH TIME

Time management is a necessary tool in order to create success in any area of your life. To get ahead you must manage your time. For instance, you are really out of integrity if you are always late. If you're not actively planning to be on time, you are inadvertently and unconsciously planning to be late. Anything is possible if you make a plan for it. Improperly managing time is where most people fail. You can be a good person and still fail at time management.

Humans have an intense desire to succeed and make people happy.

Mastering time management will change your life for the better, causing everyone in your life to be happier. I remember being on the set of "Man on the Moon" with my hero Jim Carrey and one of the principal actors, who was supposed to wrestle Jim in the next scene, was four minutes late to the set. Jim is a method actor, so when the other actor showed up he was in full character and not his "normal self."

Jim played Andy Kauffman in the movie and boy, did he let her have it! Jim was on set six hours before his call time preparing for this big day because that's what professionals do. If that was me, I would've made sure I was there at least one hour earlier than my call time because I don't like to be rushed or stressed. I will even sacrifice sleep to honor my commitments, or renegotiate if possible.

This particular actor was consistently ten to fifteen minutes late, which she thought of as being on time. This was out of integrity for the world she was in. I would have done *anything* to play a role with Jim. Unfortunately, her being out of integrity with time got her fired.

The director calmly announced over the loudspeaker in front of thousands of people, because we were doing the stadium shots, "If you're fifteen minutes early, you're on time. If you're on time, you're late. If you're late, you're fired. Goodbye." He said all this with a deadpan tone and it was very clear that he was not triggered by her action but simply did not accept that kind of behavior.

In analyzing his words I started to see that the inability to plan for success by being on time disrespects another person's time. Leaving people hanging is rude. Have you ever gotten excited and put your hand up to do a high five and not gotten one back from the other side? Yeah, well, it sucks! Being late inadvertently sends a message to the other person that you don't respect them or their time and that whatever you had going on is way more important than your commitment to being there at the agreed time.

There are some friends I advise to be somewhere three hours ahead of time for important things so they get there right on time. Making commitments with others to be somewhere at a specific time when you know you are out of integrity with time is being out of integrity with your word as well. It is better to give an estimate such as, "Let's meet between 1:00 and 1:30." Plan to arrive at 1:00 so if you are a little late at least you're not out of integrity nor wasting their time. You'll also notice a shift in the way you communicate to others. You can be in integrity with being late if you communicate that while you're making plans with them.

Being late can be a symptom of not getting enough attention. Kids may act up in class because they want attention. They end up receiving it from the principal and most likely their parents, but it's all the wrong kind of attention. As we move into adulthood we still hang on to some of those childish ways without realizing it. Being late may be a symptom of attention-seeking. You may think, "I'm just always late," but consider whether there's more to it than that.

I had two aunts that were consistently late and everyone just accepted it. Sometimes we would be angry or frustrated, but we couldn't fire them because they were family. Every time they'd show up late everyone was so happy because the kids could finally start opening presents or the family could finally eat dinner. They were rewarded by both kids and adults cheering at their arrival.

When they arrived late, the attention in the room was all on them and it made them feel good. Plus, they got to tell the crazy story of why they were late, which delayed the dinner even longer. On those rare occasions they were on time, it was a very different scene. No one jumped with joy and the kids would barely greet them. They never changed their behavior because they got attention and all the focus was on them when they arrived late. There were many Thanksgiving dinners we had to push late into the night and we even had to open Christmas presents the next day waiting on them.

Being late sends a message to the subconscious of the person you are meeting to not take you seriously. How can anyone count on you to do the things you say you will when you can't even meet at a time you agreed upon? Being late may cause people to lose respect or stop listening to you.

While I was attending American Academy of Dramatic Arts, their policy was that traffic could never be used as an excuse for being late. The idea is that we all know that Los Angeles *always* has traffic so you had *better plan accordingly*. I have been living in Los Angeles since 1995 and have taken this golden advice seriously, and it has never steered me wrong.

TARDINESS TIPS

If you have trouble being somewhere on time, consider using time frames instead of exact timing. It allows people to plan other things in that time instead of rushing and then just waiting for you. If it's important to you to get better about being on time, write out all your actions and tasks for the following day and overestimate the time you think you need to complete each task. Tally up the time you've planned for so you can set your alarm and rock your tomorrow!

When applying for a new job, you can negotiate and come to an agreement on your work schedule before you get hired. I have friends that have negotiated work agreements and contracts to be able to come in whenever they want or make their own hours. Let the future employer know in advance that you are a person who works twice as hard and will even stay late to get the job done but who may not always be on time.

Acknowledging and being forthright with your weakness gives both you and them the freedom to choose if the arrangement will work right from the start. That simple act of vulnerability speaks volumes in integrity. It begins this new relationship with respect and trust because of your transparency.

CHAPTER 11

SPIRIT, BODY, & MIND

THE HOLY TRINITY TEMPLE

I call the spirit, body, and mind combined our Holy Trinity Temple. Restoring balance between all three is necessary in order for our temple to function properly. Building a house on top of an unstable foundation would create a horrible and unsafe place to live. Aligning your Holy Trinity Temple creates a strong foundation to build upon. Many of us run around as if these three things are not all connected, which in itself creates a shaky foundation. Making any changes to your life without a strong foundation leads to disappointment, failure, and collapse.

When the spirit, body, and mind are in integrity with each other you can have perfect health. Spirit, body, & mind medicine is a holistic approach to optimal health. When your Holy Trinity Temple is out of alignment, it creates sickness, disease and even the possibility of death. It is essential to address every aspect of your health, not just the physical. This is the longest chapter in the book because all these aspects of self are tied together and cyclical. Look at the whole picture including your mental, physical and emotional health as well as your spiritual well-being. Honor all parts of yourself to maximize wellness.

Take it on as a duty to honor yourself and your creator by restoring the alignment of your Holy Trinity Temple and to do it with grace, compassion, and love. Honoring the nature within you creates healing for you and the world. Your commitment to heal yourself helps others do the same. There is enough light for everyone to shine brightly. Use the natural cycles of this planet—waxing & and waning, ebb & flow—as a guide, so you know which action to take and when to jump in. The full moon is great for releasing, the new moon is a good time for new beginnings.

If things in your life are hard, it's usually one of three things: you're either pushing past a growth point, you just don't have the right tools to take you to the next phase, or there is something out of alignment in one of the Trinities. Honoring every interaction with authenticity and truth will keep you aligned with your purpose and provide you with answers to guide you to your next move. By using your feelings and emotions as a guidance system you will know what to do next.

Building a house with a rock is hard but not completely undoable. However, using a hammer is easier and a nail gun is most preferable. It may be hard at first to learn how to handle a nail gun, but once you push past the growth spurt you may be unable to imagine how you ever managed with just rocks. There are many different tools to use for expanding your Holy Trinity Temple. Knowing that "All roads lead to Rome" and "We all end up in the same place in the end," it doesn't matter how you get there as long as you're exerting your energy to support your positive intentions.

Your path gives you guidance to offer someone else the gift of your wisdom to aid them on their path. In my own experience, friends dispense the exact same lesson or message to me that I've given to them sometime in the past. The message always comes right when I need it. Often, I didn't even remember that I gave them that advice, because spirit was just flowing through me. Many of our soul's wounds are the same and we can learn together and find the strength to heal.

MIND, BODY & SPIRIT ARE ALL CONNECTED

The mind is connected to the body, which is connected to the spirit. They work together and enhance one another. Many clients come to me wanting a breakthrough in one area of their life, say, their finances. We focus on the other two sides of the pyramid rather than the area of the mind where financial beliefs live. We end up focusing on the body and spirit because they are easier to approach at first and make a greater impact. Once the body and spirit transform, the mind is now in a different space.

Blocks with money have a lot to do with your own value system and core beliefs. Often those core beliefs and value systems are deeply embedded, controlling your unconscious programming. You can raise your barometer for financial success by making your body pure and healthy, living in alignment with your soul's purpose, and taking on meditation practices to enrich your spirit.

GET INTO ACTION

Take positive actions now. Do not wait until you feel like it—that time may never come. There is always something you can do right away. Create immediacy in your life as if your growth depends on it, because it does. Be in action with each thing you say you want in your life, otherwise you're supporting the behaviors that keep you small and weak. Start with something small for each area until you can reach the bigger tasks. The small stuff is the juice that feeds you later in unshakable ways and creates the foundation for your new life. Now, go!

Surround yourself with people that encourage and support, giving you the motivation to work hard. Action is what separates an interest from a hobby. Drive is what separates a hobby from a passion. Obsession is what separates a passion from a profession! Take your hobby and turn it into your passion. Turn your passion into an obsession. Take your obsession and turn it into a livelihood.

If you are having a hard time getting into action around something that you say you want, it's probably because you need to identify the root of your inaction. The inaction stems from your thoughts and you can change anything in your life by first changing your thoughts. Your thoughts drive all of your feelings and your feelings drive your actions, reactions, and inaction. You cannot change anything unless you understand your own self. Look at your feelings first, which will lead back to your thoughts and beliefs that may be contributing to your lack of action. This will not happen overnight, this is a practice.

INVESTIGATE YOUR THOUGHTS

Take an area in your life where you have not been in action, see what the feelings are and what thoughts create those feelings. For instance, I had been very stagnant around writing this book even though I *knew* it would be the most important thing I had ever done. I would schedule it on my calendar and when it came time to do it, I just didn't. I always thought, "I'll do it later." Doing it later came from a place of fear. That fear created anxiety in my body and felt awful. Then I made myself wrong for feeling bad and also wrong for not writing.

By stepping into that anxious feeling I was able to identify several thoughts that were holding me back, which were "I'm not worthy. I'm a fraud. No one listens to me. It doesn't matter. Who am I to write a book?" All of those thoughts were the cause of my inaction and keeping me small. By committing to those small thoughts I was unable to be in action around finishing my book. I didn't even know that those thoughts were there until I investigated where my Holy Trinity was out of alignment, then got into action in each of those areas.

BE PRESENT

One of the greatest gifts you can give to someone, including yourself, is your presence. Being present allows you the space in which to identify anything that may be out of whack or off-kilter. Being present is showing up for the people you care about, fully ready to react peacefully in any situation. I'll even go further and say that how fully you show up for people with your gift of presence, love, and honesty will come back to you in powerful ways. With whatever task you do it's crucial to be present so you can fully show up and not just halfway pay attention, floating around in an unconscious flesh-suit.

Being present in each moment allows you to catch mistakes right when they happen, call people out, and hold them accountable immediately so they can have the opportunity to grow. This presence is a deep listening that allows you to be aware of what is happening within you and around you, and to be able to react wisely to any situation, which helps others around you also act wisely. This listening will provide you with more opportunities in life because even at the bank or post office you can overhear something useful.

Friendships, partnerships, and collaborations may happen when you're aware and present to those around you. Practicing active listening improves all communication. It is the key to healthy relationships and will help strengthen your intuition, which is essentially communication with one's own self. When you practice or have direct communication with your higher self your choices and your life become much easier.

PRACTICE SELF LOVE AND SELF CARE

Self-love and self-care is a full time job that, when applied to your Holy Trinity Temple, creates patterns that help you through the toughest of times. It's like the sayings: "What you give is what you get" or "Whatever you give, you receive tenfold." Show up for yourself in this way and you will have a good life because you take care of your needs. No one else can give this to you; you are responsible for your own happiness.

The power comes from doing it yourself, coupled with the ability to know your own needs. One of my self-care practices I do every night is to massage and stimulate my scalp. Massages are proven to heal and regenerate. Even after a really hard day, this simple practice seems to wash it all away and put me into a deep, relaxed state where I begin my meditation every night before I go to bed. Take on self care practices as if they are a sacred ritual—your life is *most* sacred.

SACRED
Definition: //sa·cred// //sakrd// ~Adjective
1. Connected with God or the gods. 2. Holy and
deserving veneration (great respect & reverence).
3. Considered too important to be changed. 4. Dedicated or set
apart for the service or worship. (www.OxfordDictionaries.com)

KEEP YOUR SPIRIT, BODY, & MIND SACRED

Keeping your Holy Trinity Temple sacred connects you directly to source with a heightened awareness of respect, reverence, and honor. This sacred state has a high vibration and can uplift those around you. Imagine if everything was sacred. You would treat things very differently and have a different perception of them. Everything we think about ourselves and the world exists because of a story that we've created or adopted. Create a new sacred empowerment story.

If you keep things sacred, you trust and respect that every single thing has its own life. So getting upset at something like a stain on your shirt is going to bum you out and lower your vibration. Consider instead that maybe your shirt wanted the best life possible and it wanted to be a different color. It got a stain on it so that you would have to dye it later in order to enjoy it or give it to someone else who would.

Most people just think it's ruined or broken and then throw it away. This disposability is a sign of our times. We often don't fix the broken or make things to last. As soon as they don't look brand new, we toss them. We do that to people as well. We just throw people away. Look at all the homeless in every major city. If we treated every single thing as sacred then we know that all people are sacred. Start valuing all forms of life because everything does in fact have a life of its own and deserves respect.

CREATE SACRED RITUALS FOR IMPORTANT GOALS

Create a sacred ritual for the important things in your life to provide a strong foundation for growth. Keep your life sacred by implementing these rituals for each of your important goals. A ritual is a series of actions you create that keeps your priority sacred to you in your own way.

I have rituals for many things. I find them fun to practice and it really helps me set the tone for what I'm about to do. You'd be surprised at how many small rituals you already have for seemingly unimportant things, like making a wish on a shooting star, knocking on wood, or touching the roof of your car when you go through a yellow light. Some people have the ritual of drinking coffee in the morning or doing yoga right when they wake up.

We all have our own little rituals and practices. In the car, whenever I go over cattle guards I lift up my feet. On a roller coaster and on airplane take-offs, I throw my arms up in the air. These little rituals make life more fun and meaningful. Creating a ritual around something that may be difficult will help you get through the rough parts and make your goals easier to accomplish.

When I first started writing this book, it was really difficult for me to sit down in one spot for any longer than an hour and my focus was horrible. As soon as I came up with my writing ritual I had more energy, power, and clarity around what I wanted to say and how to express it. You can create a ritual for just about anything, especially where you have trouble getting motivated.

> My ritual for writing is:
> Make tea
> Set intention for my day
> Light incense & candle
> Make breakfast
> Listen to binaural beats/Solfeggio frequencies on headphones
> Then off I go.

Creating a ritual around important things sets the tone, energy, and space for what you're about to create. Rituals inform the spirit, body, and mind that whatever you are about to do is important so they can fall into alignment. Rituals are a declaration of what you want and proof you are diligent about making it happen. My writing ritual sets the space in which ideas come easily so I can write them down. It narrows my focus and commits me to sitting down in the chair to write these very words.

~ YOUR SPIRIT ~

Spirit is the part of you where your emotions and character come from and is the very essence of your soul. Your spirit is a non-physical entity that even after death, may live on, especially in the hearts of those you loved and who loved you. The Hebrew faith interprets spirit as a mysterious power we encounter by feeling it through breath and wind, but can never see. It can be your guiding light and the reasons for taking certain actions when you listen to the messages it sends you.

GET QUIET & GO WITHIN

Have you ever experienced anxiety, fear, sadness, or pain? Take some time to go within and ask yourself why you're feeling those things and where they're coming from. If you're feeling lost or seeking all the answers outside of yourself, it is now time to turn your seeking within.

No one else can answer these questions for you because you alone are the only person who has lived your life. Therefore, you are the only person who can tell you what you need to do next in your life. Take the time to meditate and go within in order to get to the heart and the truth of the matter. All the answers are inside of you if you can sit quiet long enough to hear them. Meditation is a great way to discover what the next steps in your life will be or if that person you have feelings for is the right person for you. Until you take the time to listen to yourself you will never truly know.

TRUST MESSAGES FROM YOUR DIVINE SPIRIT

It is imperative to listen to the helping messages your spirit gives you. They come in many forms: a sudden impulse to call a friend or business contact, a flash of excitement that leads you to say yes to that big job that seems scary, a feeling of comfort, or perhaps discomfort, in the presence of someone you've just met. Spirit is constantly trying to communicate to us, but when we do not pay attention the messages get quieter and the mind becomes much louder. Let the spirit's whisper be louder than the mind's yell. Trust yourself and follow your hunches to see if you are on the right track.

I was driving my friend on my scooter on our way to a film screening. As we drove by Pep Boys Auto Parts Store in Hollywood, I suddenly felt the calling to take a shortcut through their lot to avoid the light at the corner. I turned into the parking lot and down a little hill only to realize that there was no other exit but the one I came in.

It was after hours and no one was there but a couple of parked cars, so we drove around in a circle to exit when I saw a bunch of twenty and fifty dollar bills strewn on the ground as if they just blew in from the heavens. Just like that, were $400 richer. You should have seen the dance we did. I'm sure the parking lot cameras caught it all on surveillance footage.

It wasn't the shortcut I intended but it was something better. This is a great example of being rewarded for following my intuition by receiving more than I asked for or could even think to ask for. I didn't need to figure it out, all I needed to do was simply act on my intuitive hit. How many times have you been driving down the street and thought about checking out a specific store or place? The more you listen to your higher self, the stronger your intuition gets.

TRUTH-BUMPS FEEL GOOD

I call goosebumps *truth-bumps* because I find it to be a more accurate word to describe what's really happening. Hair is the connection to electrical information and our other senses. There have been numerous occasions where indigenous people were used as trackers and hunters for finding specific locations deep in the deserts, jungles, and forests. In specific instances where the indigenous person was forced to cut their hair, they were no longer able to find their way, causing a complete inability for tracking or sense of direction. They were no longer receiving that electrical information which cut them off from their strongest sense.

Anytime you experience truth-bumps for reasons other than being cold, it is because your body is letting you know to pay attention to what is happening. It generally means truth. Truth bumps are your spirit's way of speaking to you through your body.

They usually happen when you or someone else talks about something that rings true and all your hairs stand up. It is usually something that hits your heartstrings and connects all spirits together. It could be incredibly heartwarming or hit some chord deep inside you.

Start writing down the times you experience this and what was being said at that time. Keep a journal of the times your spirit told you to listen and you paid attention. The more you pay attention to your spirit, the louder the whisper will grow.

STRENGTHEN YOUR INTUITION

Consciousness allows us to access our intuition so that we can grow from everything. Nature uses all the resources available. Use your intuition to bring yourself to the next level by utilizing all the resources that are available to you.

I noticed in my family that intuition was never fully ripened because my grandparents did not believe in acknowledging their children or giving them compliments for a job well done. They didn't want accolades to give their kids a "big head." So instead, my mother and her sisters grew up not trusting themselves and denying essential truths about themselves. Things that needed to be communicated fully and authentically were not. Whenever I showed signs of intuition my mom shut me down because she was part of the old generation and the old way of thinking.

Now I teach classes, workshops, hold summits, and coach my clients on how to increase their intuition. I believe it's important for everyone to have strong intuition in their life so they can be powerful and make sound decisions. It is imperative to distinguish true intuitive messages from ego-driven faux messages to stay on the right path. You can learn how to interpret the messages and increase your healing and psychic abilities with practice and coaching.

If you ever need help in developing your intuition or any other aspect of self-growth, I'm only a coaching phone call away. Check out all the classes offered at our www.MagicalMysterySchools.com either online or if you happen to be in Sedona, AZ come on down! You can also sign up for the www.INTUITIONACCELERATORSUMMIT.com for in-depth interviews with the leading experts on intuition.

KEEP YOUR ENERGY SACRED

What if you treated even your energy as sacred? Do not let any of your sacred energy leak out for unnecessary reasons. Those little leaks impair your thinking and deplete the energy that you could otherwise use towards important things. You must assess where your energy is going and where it is given or taken away.

Your energy is the most sacred essential thing you have! Notice when you are feeling low on energy how hard it is to show up for your friends and family that way you'd like to? You must remove stress and negativity to keep your energy sacred.

Do not participate in unnecessary outputs of energy! These energy leaks diminish your spirit and can physically age you. Your brain secretes the hormone cortisol in your blood when you're under stress, which causes inflammation and muscle and collagen loss and weakens the immune system.

Little incidents should not send you into a state where you treat the people you love badly. Examples of unnecessary outputs of energy are flying off the handle easily, road rage, and snapping at a loved one. All of these actions poison your body and diminish your spirit. Where is your power given or taken away? Where do you get involved with unhealthy patterns or boundaries?

A question for road ragers (I know because I used to be one!): do you notice how anyone driving faster than you is crazy and anyone driving slower than you is an idiot? We all know that most people don't pay super close attention to things, which causes them to drive like idiots, right? I'm pretty sure this is a widely known fact. So why would you be upset when you can just expect it? Maintaining a calm, cool, collected demeanor allows you to drive defensively and be ready for any and all sudden changes and you'll avoid all those Cortisol shots!

Generally, when I used to experience road rage, I was the only person that was upset. Most of the time the other driver didn't even look at me while I flipped them off. They didn't care or even have a clue how angry I was. Why would I waste my time, energy, and health on someone that made a stupid mistake? When I had that realization, it just didn't make sense for me to get upset and fly off the handle anymore. I now consciously choose to expect erratic driving and am pleasantly surprised when drivers are thoughtful and considerate. Coincidentally, this has also made me a better driver.

> **"Well, everything is at stake, it makes it hard to concentrate. And there are men who see a war and see a paycheck. Such different programming—to live so fearfully. Terror this and terror that—terrible reality. There is no medicine on the television, so turn it off and turn yourself around"**
> **~ Nahko & Medicine for the People ~ (Lyrics from "Manifesto")**

GO ON A MEDIA FAST

Go on a media fast for a month or more. If a month seems difficult, try cutting out TV and movies for at least a solid week each month. I know that you have been wanting to make positive changes for a long time, so substitute doing that instead of watching a screen.

We live in an information world with any data at our fingertips. It is really easy to become overwhelmed by the vast amounts of information being flooded and forced onto us. By choosing to cut out daily programming for one week, you allow your spirit's voice to be heard that you may not have been cognizant of before. You also remain in control of what you are feeding your brain. Watching television can make people lazy and complacent.

Humans are so easily influenced by things around us and the people we surround ourselves with. It's a wonderful opportunity to allow that time for your spirit to be heard instead of zoning out. Take the time you'd normally spend watching a program to do something you have always wanted to do—meditate, get into nature, make a special meal, or get creative. Do *anything* other than stare at a screen and you'll see some positive shifts in your life that will enliven your spirit.

I like to go on media fasts for the duration of any new project I'm working on or when I'm starting a new habit. It's really wonderful to have quiet time to think about my project so I can initiate and activate accordingly. You'd be surprised by how much you can get done in the time wasted sitting on your butt watching the tube. Even thirty minutes a day working towards your goals instead of watching other people live their dreams will enrich your life and bring you closer to your goals.

SPIRIT HACKING

You have the ability to tap into limitless source energy when your spirit is heard and honored by your obedience. Start by listening to your spirit and all the little signs it gives you along the way. Keep your spirit clean and free from toxic energy. No gossip or spreading rumors, ever!

Use your time wisely and intentionally. Talk about dreams and goals or things that will elevate you or others. Don't complain. Complaining actually lowers your vibration and the vibration of those who listen to you and those you complain about.

Don't let others complain in your ear space. It is toxic. Complaining is talking judgmentally about something or someone without having a solution in mind. Complaining is the ego's way of being right and keeps you powerless over your life. Complaining makes you to out to be the victim and dims your spirit. I suggest reading Christine Lewicki's Best-Selling book, "I Quit Complaining." It's genius and very informative.

When you have several spiritual practices and play games that fill up your cup, you become more aligned with your soul's purpose and life becomes more effortless. Commit to your big beautiful spirit and feed it with the juiciest nutrients you can by not giving in to unnecessary negative emotion or energy. Be free to be free. I also suggest reading Shaman Durek's book "Spirit Hacking" for his full shamanic download.

POSITIVE ATTRACTION PALACE & SANCTUARY

Begin to pay attention to the organization or lack thereof in your life, especially the key areas of home, finances and health. Is the space you live in organized or full of clutter and unnecessary items? Too many material possessions weigh you down.

Are your finances in order? Disorganized finances can bog you down and stop you from achieving your goals, financial and personal. It's good to take a hard look at where you are spending your money and create plans to save.

Prioritize your life around your health—make it easy for you to be successful on your path to wellness. Take the time to organize yourself and your life in ways that save you time and energy in the future. Being disorganized can easily overwhelm you and waste a lot of time. Start small and be patient.

There is a reason they say "Cleanliness is next to Godliness." When you treat your home as a palace, it's available for you to positively attract what you want. Often we hang on to items that don't work for us anymore and take up our valuable mental and physical space. Clearing the clutter is a powerful tool that honors your space as if it is a holy sanctuary.

Only keep items in your home that give you a positive charge. If it's not contributing to you, it's taking away by cluttering your mind and space. This doesn't mean you should throw away things you need just for the sake of clearing an area. If it serves a purpose or makes you happy, keep it. If it's something you don't need, give it to someone who does or sell it. Either way, get rid of the things that you're not excited about.

Being organized is more efficient and saves you so much time. You have no idea how much time can be lost that you will never get back looking for items. Everything that exists is made up of atoms, which is also energy. Everything is energy.

Being organized means having all of your energy working for you, not against you. Start with something easy. Test every pen in your house and get rid of the ones that don't work so all you have are working pens. In doing this exercise, you are training your mind to find what's not working and remove it from your life. Start with the junk drawer.

Practice makes perfect. The places in which you spend the majority of your time are the most important spaces to make into a perfectly energized palace or sanctuary for yourself. This way, you can be rejuvenated just by being in the spaces where you spend most of your time. Check our Marie Kondo for organizing techniques that will change your life.

~ YOUR BODY ~

"Take care of your body, it's the only place you have to live." - Jim Rohn
"Protect & take care of Terra—it's the only place we *all* have to live." - Me

PROPER NUTRITION

Give your body all the things it needs to run optimally.

When you commit to health in potent ways you see the results faster, giving you the strength and encouragement to keep going. Health is wealth. Food is either medicine or poison. Proper nutrition is chemistry and science. Feed your body back into health. You literally *are* what you eat!

Give your body a fighting chance to heal and regenerate itself properly by giving it the best fuel. Most people treat their cars better than they treat their own bodies. You would never put the wrong type of fuel in your car, yet we regularly shovel into our bodies foods that don't fuel us or actually hurt us. You'll have several cars in your lifetime but only one body! Treat it like it has to last a lifetime, because it does.

Poor food choices lowers your immune system, which makes it harder for your body to heal itself. You can literally heal yourself through proper nutrition and detoxification. Our bodies are designed to heal without you thinking about it. Imagine what happens when you start putting all your conscious energy into healing as well!

We are made up mostly of water and is crucial we get enough daily replenishment and from a pure source. Drink the best water available to you—ALWAYS! Most city tap water has arsenic, chlorine, lead, and other toxic ingredients. Get a filter of some kind so you are not drinking straight from the tap, there many to choose from. If the tap is your only choice, you can at least boil it to evaporate the chlorine and kill some of the other organisms floating in there.

Avoid drinking water from plastic bottles as much as possible. Most bottled water is really just tap water. Avoid brands like Dasani, which is owned by the Pepsi company and has salt added to their water which dehydrates you so you have to drink more. I wouldn't trust a company that sells soda pop as a good source of drinking water. Use glass bottles whenever possible. I like to go to the thrift store to get the ones with the hinge flip top lids so I have several for all the rooms I frequent most as well as in the car.

Alkaline and fresh pure spring water are good choices too. There is hydrogen water you can get in tablets to drop in your glass or a machine that dispenses it. It has been helpful for a faster recovery by reducing inflammation, it has also been shown to improve gut health and lower oxidative stress. I really love my Echo Ultimate™ because it offers all four different types of water dispensed: hydrogen, alkaline, filtered, and acid water. You can get 10% OFF using my link https://synergyscience.com/OracleJ

REDUCE TOXINS PUT INTO YOUR BODY

The Earth and its atmosphere sustain and protect human life but it can only do so much. When we poison the air with ozone-depleting aerosols and burning fossil-fuels, the ozone layer thins in parts of the world like Australia and New Zealand. Our bodies are just like a planet. When we put toxins inside it, either mentally, spiritually, or physically, we may create irreparable sickness.

Fear is a toxin that negatively impacts the entire holy trinity temple. Good nutrition is the best place to start. We have blindly trusted corporations to create our food but they have not been looking out for our health. The food system has been broken for far too long. The only thing really looking out for us and our well-being is Mother Earth. We must return the favor. We are of Terra. We must protect the mother of all mothers and start with ourselves!

READ EVERY INGREDIENT LIST

Read the ingredient list on all your foods so you know what you are really eating. If you can't pronounce it, you shouldn't put it in your body. Packaged and processed foods should be avoided altogether, or at the very least heavily reduced.

Eating whole organic non-processed foods is healthiest for you. You'll want to eat foods that look as close to how they were grown, which means at a grocery store you would mostly shop on the perimeter of the store and avoid the packaged food aisles. The best things to eat are items that don't come with an ingredients list because they are made by God and come from the earth.

REMOVE HEAVY METALS FROM YOUR BODY

Heavy metals are toxic and need to be removed from your body as soon as possible *and* on a regular basis. They are everywhere, from microparticles sprayed into the air you breathe to most vaccinations. Some of us have metal in our bodies from a surgery or in our mouths from a dentist.

If you have that type of dental work, it would be wise to get it removed. My grandmother claimed she heard radio stations in her head which we found out later was due to conductive metal in her mouth, we thought she was starting to go crazy. Heavy metals need to be cleansed out of your body once a year at the very minimum.

There are several cleanses you can find online to facilitate this process, but a really great and simple protocol is to eat a parsley and cilantro salad every day for 30 days (approximately one cup of chopped leafy greens each serving), sit in an infrared sauna 3 times a week, and give yourself an enema two to three times week during the cleanse. Heavy metals stored in the body are one of the biggest contributors to the inability to use all the parts of our brain.

Reduce and then stop drinking out of aluminum cans and cooking using aluminum foil. Aluminum is the leading cause of dementia and Alzheimer's and is what many people in my family have died from. Our body's natural defense mechanism tries to protect us from the damage heavy metals and toxins wreak by storing it away until it can be released safely, but then it's up to us to release it through cleansing.

Fish are known to have heavy metals so it's important to consume only the ones with the lowest mercury levels. Shark, swordfish, king mackerel, tilefish, marlin, orange roughy, ahi, bigeye tuna, and farm raised salmon should be avoided because they have the highest levels. I, personally, have become a vegan to avoid all the heavy metals and Fukushima radiation poisoning in all the fish from our west coast and I have never felt better. Plus my body is super fit and I am back to my highschool weight.

Whenever I ride my motorcycle in Los Angeles I wear a protective breathing mask to avoid breathing the heavy metals and toxins in the air. I suggest doing this when riding your bike if you live in a major city. When you are in, around, or near major fires, you should wear a breathing mask every time you go outside.

When I was in China the air quality was so bad that it was commonplace to always wear breathing masks anytime one is out and about. It was challenging where I lived because they kept raising the allowable toxic chemicals ppm (parts per million) in the air in order to claim that Los Angeles's smog levels have gone down over the years. Although, now with the corona most people are wearing masks most of the time.

AVOID EXCESS SUGAR

Cut out excess sugar from your diet. It is essential to be aware of the serious harm that results from eating too much sugar. It comes in beautiful, tasty, lovely packages given to you by the people you love—it's everywhere!

There is nothing sweet about excess sugar. It's hard to stop a sugar addiction, but doing so is one of the best things you can do for your health, even if you do it for short periods of time throughout the year. There are many alternatives you can use which come in both liquid and powder. I bring my bottle of Stevia with me everywhere so I have it whenever I need it. Monk fruit is another great option that is very tasty and delicious. I use it for baking.

Sugar is a mild neurotoxin that harms our organs and disrupts the body's normal hormone cycles. Eating it in excess leads to weight gain, problems with blood sugar regulation, and depression, and increases your risk of heart disease. Sugar has been linked to acne and may accelerate the skin's aging process. There is much research and several studies on the effects of sugar, although my grandmother, bless her soul, showed me by her poor example all I needed to know about its dangerous effects. It was enough to keep me off the stuff as an adult.

Even after she was diagnosed with diabetes, my grandmother would still make her favorite dessert, a bowl of three tablespoons of peanut butter and one cup of sugar mixed together like a paste. She would hide it in her drawers so we couldn't find it and had stashes of cookies and candy everywhere. It was her drug. She made the BEST coffee cake in the world, and no one in our family ever wrote her recipe down before she got Alzheimer's. I saw her health decline right before my eyes every time she'd go on a sugar binge.

DETOX & CLEANSE YOUR ENTIRE BODY

Your body is your temple and you only have one. Like I mentioned before, I bet you treat your car better than you do your body. How often do you get your oil changed in your car? We change the oil when it becomes too dirty for our cars every three to five months. When is the last time you detoxed your body? Detoxing your body is like doing an oil change on your car. You must get that filthy dirt out too!

Toxins are everywhere, especially if you live in a major city. If you don't allow your body to get rid of these toxins every year, your body keeps storing them. Over long periods of time those areas of storage get overloaded and mutate the cells, which can cause cancer and other horrible diseases. Eastern culture believes you can pretty much put anything into your body as long as you get it out, which is why bath houses and spas are very popular in Asia. They sweat toxins out on a daily and weekly basis.

You regularly cleanse the outside of your body by showering and bathing, but how often do you cleanse the inside? You are dirtier on the inside than the outside. Most disease happens between your mouth and your anus which is your entire digestive tract. Build-up anywhere along this path could become a permanent fixture in your body. Prevent permanent damage by doing some sort of digestive tract cleanse at least once a year. If you cleanse and detox your body often it will be easier to stay healthy and manage your health as you age.

Mucoid plaque builds up in your intestines because most people do not go on regular cleanses. Imagine you used the same dishes to eat for several years without washing them. By then it would be almost impossible to clean off the built-up sludge and bacteria.

Now imagine those unwashed dishes as your intestinal tract. This layer of mucus builds up into a plaque that prevents your colon from absorbing all the nutrients in your food, so you end up eating more and more to satisfy your craving for real sustenance but are still starved of the nourishment you need. The extra food gets stored as fat and is a leading cause of obesity. Get your digestive tract back on track with a cleanse and you will notice a real difference in your energy that doesn't come in a coffee cup or teacup.

ENEMAS AND COLONICS

Speaking of coffee, try a coffee enema while you're cleansing. If you are squeamish doing it on your own, I suggest an open-system colonic (hydrotherapy) instead. There are so many little hidden pockets in the intestinal walls and colon that store massive amounts of bacteria where a series of good flushes (colonic/enema) will set you straight, especially while you are doing any type of cleanse. I suggest you consult your doctor if you have health problems to make sure any method won't cause harm or exacerbate your issues (e.g., a perforated colon if you're giving yourself an enema).

After that, you'll want to cleanse the major organs that do most of the filtration for your body. Your kidneys, liver, gallbladder, and skin (your largest organ), also needs to be cleansed. Consider doing cleanses for your entire body once a year if you really want to give your entire body an upgrade. Consult your physician before doing any such cleanse. If you can cleanse quarterly or even twice a year, do it!

WAKE UP WITH APPLE CIDER VINEGAR OR LEMON JUICE IN THE MORNINGS

Have you ever seen calcium buildup from water that comes out of your faucet? It's extremely difficult to get it off if it sits for a long time, but if you clean it with vinegar every couple of months it's much easier to manage. The same is true for the human body. Every morning I drink a shot of Organic Apple Cider Vinegar or Organic lemon juice in 16oz of Alkaline water upon waking. It's a mild cleanser and lubricates the body to a full waking state without caffeine.

REMOVE TOXINS FROM YOUR HOME

Replace toxic cleaning chemicals with natural earth-friendly cleaners without dyes. I find they clean better and are safer to use. Try borax, baking soda, peroxide, and vinegar instead of bleach. You can buy or make biodegradable soaps for all purposes and it's safe for children and pets as well as the environment.

REDUCE RADIATION EXPOSURE

One of the biggest toxins is a silent killer: radiation. It's everywhere technology is. Now with 5G wi-fi being introduced nationwide, we will experience a whole new level of toxicity. Some people are more sensitive to electromagnetic smog than others. I am one of them. Protecting yourself from radiation is simple when you have the right tools. I have become an ambassador for these special Qi Technology waveform protection devices because of my sensitivities and have made it one of my missions to protect others from harm. Reduce your personal radiation exposure and get 10% OFF using my personal link https://synergyscience.com/OracleJ

Steve Jobs knew about the dangers of radiation poisoning from touching your phone, which is why he hid it in a clause on all iPhone terms of service. The clause indicates that you should NEVER touch your phone to any part of your body or come within 5/8 inch of it. They count on the fact that people simply don't read those things. I am the type of person who is always looking for more information on any subject I deem important. There is always something behind the surface and we can choose to look or not. It's our choice.

RADIATION EDUCATION

Safety is the most important thing as we move into 5G. Turn off wi-fi and Bluetooth if you keep your phone in your pocket or next to you when you sleep. Electric and magnetic fields (EMFs) are invisible areas of radiation energy caused by electric power. All electronics and forms of technology cause radiation.

The federal government is aware of the dangers of cell phone radiation, which is why they have been using things like EMF protection protocols. Protect yourself and your family from EMF radiation. I personally use the Qi-Shield EMF Protector that is designed to protect bedrooms, offices, apartments, vehicles, and very small houses, and can be taken on an airplane. It's the size of a Bluetooth speaker and easy to carry with you wherever you go.

You can have peace of mind knowing you are protected from harmful and damaging EMFs while on the go! The Qi-Shield has an effective torus field size of 16 x 16 feet and can be purchased at https://www.synergyscience. com/OracleJ. I personally also carry the 8 X 8 foot protection with me everywhere I go, even in the car, while the larger one stays put in my home.

EMF DETECTORS & BLOCKING FABRICS

You can get EMF detectors online for about $100, though you'll have to search for the best deal on the fabric. You can pool your resources with several friends or co-workers or people in your family. I sewed a sleeve for my phone from this fabric, so anytime it's in my fanny pack/purse and close to my body, I am protected. I tested it in the EMF sleeve and it was not nearly as toxic.

Without it, I learned my personal phone is one of the most crazy toxic ones on the market and radiates out much farther than other phones. Each phone is different and radiation may be coming from an outside unknown source, which is why having a detector is handy. The farther away you are from it, the better. I lined my laptop carrying case with that fabric as well.

MINIMIZE TOUCHING TECHNOLOGY

Minimize touching your computer and phone with your fingers. Use a stylus to touch your phone. It's ergonomic and more accurate than my fat finger tips. I use a stylus to touch the screen and operate it. It's like I'm hand-writing again, which is a dying art form these days.

Laptops are *never* for your lap! If you have a laptop, stop putting it directly on your lap, unless you are a male who wants to lower your sperm count, because it has been scientifically proven to kill cells. You want and need all your cells to be healthy and the computer won't differentiate between just sperm and other healthy cells.

Your phone, computer, iPad, kindle, or whatever tech device you are obsessed with should never be touching you. If you have a laptop, it's best to have an external keyboard and mouse to operate it with. Ladies, stop putting your phone in your bra, unless you want breast cancer! Find a protective phone case or you can purchase an EMF protection purse/sleeve from my online shop https://www.etsy.com/shop/DiatomaceousLove.

I use a selfie stick or phone stand to hold my phone to keep it a safe enough distance away from me. People may laugh and make fun of me, but I know I am protecting myself by reducing the radiation toxicity. I have to be on my phone all the time for business and I get this weird electric shock feeling and burning pain sensation in my fingers anytime I touch the screen. After doing research, I started doing things differently. Steve Jobs and Bill Gates didn't let their kids touch cell phone or computer screens due to all the radiation, which is more toxic and dangerous for children and the elderly.

HEATED SALT LAMPS

Get a heated Himalayan salt lamp for every room in your home. They reduce the positive ions in the air. Positive ions are molecules that have lost one or more electrons so they are floating around trying to attach to whatever they can to regain structure, causing destruction wherever they attach. When they attach to you, they damage your cells.

Negative ions are oxygen atoms with extra negatively charged electrons and are scientifically proven to neutralize free radicals in the body. Himalayan salt lamps can boost blood flow, improve sleep, calm allergies or asthmatic symptoms, and increase levels of serotonin in the brain. You can purchase a small one for around $20. They look beautiful in the home and are great night lights, too. And if you ever run out of salt in your kitchen you can just go lick your lamp!

REMOVE RADIATED FOODS FROM YOUR DIET

Know where your food comes from. Read all packaging, labels, and nutritional information. Radiation is already in our food sources. Many of our foods are radiated (pasteurized) to prevent bacteria or mold, but it also kills the live enzymes in the fruits and veggies. I used to wonder why every bag of Trader Joe's avocados would have black spots all throughout them and why their produce goes bad fast, and found out they radiate many of them.

Find out where your fish, rice, seaweed, etc. comes from. Anything coming from Japan should be avoided. The radiation from the Fukushima disaster has already reached our west coast thanks to underwater ocean currents. It has hit Seattle and Western Canada especially hard. Their coastlines have been testing positive for radiation since 2016. The research is out there if you are willing to look.

MOVE YOUR BODY

If you don't use it, you lose it. A really great way to get your body in alignment and have your body working for you is to become active, even if it's just walking a little bit every day. Each time the bottom of your foot hits the ground, it sends a message to your brain to create stronger bone density. Get a little trampoline for daily jumping. Benefits include improved motor skills, balance, and coordination while also stimulating the lymphatic system.

Exercise is amazing for so many reasons. It increases blood flow and circulation and brings oxygen to your brain and body. It speeds up your heart rate so you sweat out toxins. It strengthens your entire cardiovascular system, which is equivalent to keeping your battery in your car working well. It helps with depression, improves memory, reduces inflammation, and releases growth chemicals in the brain that create new brain cells and blood vessels in the brain. It prevents and helps manage type 2 diabetes by improving the way the body processes blood sugar.

Exercise improves coordination and reflexes and makes you stronger. Then there's the good old vanity piece to it, making you look and feel good, which increases confidence and boosts your moxie or mojo. When you feel sexy and confident you become unstoppable. Notice how everything works out and how things just come to you when you are in that sexy state of mind?

PAMPER YOUR BODY

If you were to do only this one thing every day for yourself it would change your entire life for the better! No matter who you are, we can always pamper our bodies! You deserve to be pampered and are the best person for the job because you know exactly what you like and how you like it.

Treat your body like the holy temple it is. You'll be sorry you didn't start sooner. Massage yourself or get regular massages. I like to do trades with friends where we each take an hour to massage one another. It's a great excuse to connect and visit while providing that magical healing touch.

GET PROPER SLEEP

The amount of sleep you need to repair both your body and mind is crucial to how you feel the next day, how fast your brain works, how clear your thinking is, how much patience you have, and how much joy you experience. The first part of your sleep cycle repairs your body, while the mind can only repair in REM sleep. The longer you sleep, the more REM cycles you can go through. You want to have three to four cycles each night in order to maintain optimum health. Most people get less than that.

If you have a really hard time sleeping, like I do at times, you can create a bedtime ritual to set the mood. My nighttime ritual consists of making a cup of dream tea and running a hot bath with Epsom salts to relax my muscles and mind. Sometimes I get a massage right before bed so I can just drift off to sleep when it's over.

Do whatever it takes to create a sacred container for rest. I had to invest in a really nice expensive bed that has changed my dreaming life. Depending on your body type, health and preference you may want a softer or firmer bed.

Do not eat after 7PM, otherwise your entire digestive tract and brain cannot rest or repair because your body is busy breaking down the food you just ate. Do not work where you sleep. Do not watch screens an hour before bed, including phone, TV, and computers. Put your phone on airplane mode during sleep and unplug your router/modem so the radiation waves will not disrupt your brainwaves preventing you from going into full REM sleep.

The time you go to sleep is more important than trying to catch up on missed hours. Ever heard the saying "Early to bed, early to rise, makes a person healthy, wealthy and wise"? Well, come to find out through science that it is actually true. Each night our bodies systematically go through and repair each part of our body at different times of the night until early morning. Two hours of sleep before midnight is better than four hours after. This process begins at 11pm, so you'd have to be in bed two hours before that to reach REM because our bodies can only heal in this deep sleep, unless you are on a completely different schedule.

The exact times our bodies heal are based on circadian rhythms or your meridian clock. Our bodies change our meridian clocks/circadian rhythms according to time zones we live in or times we are most active. Travelers crossing multiple time zones experience jet lag, which is when their internal clock is thrown off causing a myriad of issues. Maintaining a regular sleep cycle super boosts your healing and strengthens your immune system. Major studies all over the world conclude you can die from lack of sleep.

You can train yourself to be a night person or a morning person by shifting your circadian rhythm or meridian clock. Our bodies are magical, powerful, and most of all, adaptable. Getting enough good sleep helps your body heal itself naturally, before you get sick or, goodness forbid, get a terminal illness that you'd have to fight.

The amount of time needed to sleep differs person to person and we need less the older we get. Babies sleep all the time, whereas adults can be perfectly healthy with anywhere from five to ten hours of sleep. You will know what amount of time works for you by keeping track of your sleep over the course of 30 days. You can store the info in your notes section of your phone or in a sleep journal, where you can also track your dreams!

MINDFUL BREATHING TECHNIQUE

This is a great exercise to reduce stress, anxiety, and negative emotions, calm your temper, and sharpen your concentration skills. Find a nice, quiet, and comfortable seated position, keeping your back and spine straight. It may be easier for you to sit against a wall or in a chair.

Close your eyes and begin to breathe deeply. Bring your attention to the weight of your body on the ground and the air touching your skin. Relax any areas of tightness or tension in your body as you focus on your breathing. Feel the natural flow of each inhale and exhale. Notice where your chest or stomach expands and what parts of the body are activated in this breathing.

If your mind wanders, that's okay, it's natural to have thoughts come in. When this happens, think or say out loud "mind" and then softly bring your awareness back to your breathing. After five to ten minutes of this, shift your focus again to your body's sensations and your connection to the ground, and send some love and appreciation to yourself for giving yourself this special time. Fill your body with gratitude and self-love.

To close this mindful breathing technique on your last breath, breathe in as deeply as you can and hold it for ten seconds. Exhale all the air through a tight round mouth (as if you had a straw between your lips) and send that love into the world. Take your time to come back and slowly blink your eyes open.

BALANCED BODY

Everything in nature comes back to a state of equilibrium eventually. Our bodies will, too, if we let them heal and stabilize. The problem is that our environments are so toxic, even if you have a perfectly clean diet you'll still have to deal with the air or water quality. It's a good thing that there are many powerful tools to help us.

Stress is the major concern for any health related situation. When your body is in a state of stress it is not able to heal itself. Bring your body back to balance so you can live a more effortlessly healthy life. There are many techniques you can use, from methods dating back to ancient times to new scientific discoveries. Ayurveda has been practiced for over 5,000 years according to recorded history and has many helpful techniques and information for living a healthy life.

AYURVEDA
Definition: //A·yur·ve·da// //äyrvād// ~Noun
1. The traditional Hindu system of medicine, which is based on the idea of balance in bodily systems and uses diet, herbal treatment, and Yogic breathing. (www.OxfordDictionaries.com)

BALANCED LIFESTYLE

Living in balance and getting in sync with those natural cycles is what the Ayurvedic lifestyle is all about. Almost everything in Ayurveda is a body hack. It is the science of life and was the very first medicinal practice. It is a method to get you back in touch with your own nature, which is what this book is all about. It originated in India and is still the current traditional way of medicine there. *Aya* means life and *Veda* means knowledge. It's important to be connected to the natural cycles of nature on this planet. It's the only way we can maintain health and our own existence.

Living your life in balance will leave you waking up feeling refreshed, where we don't have cravings and we can finish our day with the same energy we had when we got up. We only get one body and one life to live. The more body hacks you adopt, the healthier, longer, and happier life you will live.

BODY HACKS

The body hack with the fastest results is to exercise and move your body every day! The thing that causes your body to store more toxins is not being active. Alter the blood flow in your body for ten to thirty minutes every day. You can try dancing in your living room, any type of cardio, headstands & handstands, hanging upside down, or jumping on a rebounder (mini trampoline), as long as you are getting plenty of air in a well-ventilated room or fresh outdoor air.

Here are some more hacks:

MOUTH:

- Every day when you wake up, drink a large glass of warm water. This will stimulate everything and get your digestive system going. Like I mentioned previously, you can add an ounce of organic apple cider vinegar or organic lemon juice into a huge cup of water and chug it first thing in the morning. Over the course of a week or two you will see belly fat melt off you! No joke!
- n the morning wash your face, brush your teeth, and scrape your tongue to start your digestion.
- For breakfast have a nice, slow, relaxing meal, preferably with some berries, cherries and grapefruit, or foods that will detoxify.
- Do not eat anything from breakfast until lunch.
- Make lunch a relaxing meal, then nothing until supper.

- Have an early supper, no later than seven p.m., and get to bed before ten p.m. For those of you on different sleeping schedules, don't eat three to four hours before bedtime.
- Cleanse your digestive tract, kidney, liver, gallbladder, lymphatic system, etc. at least once a year.
- Go on a fast each season. Ask your doctor before trying this for the first time to ensure you are healthy enough and avoid if on prescription medications.
- Eat foods according to the seasons. Realize that nature is doing its best to detoxify us by what is being grown at that time. It is essential to our lymphatic system and to our health.
- Your own breath has the ability to heal your body. Nasal breathing exercises detoxify the body. Try doing the Wim Hoff breath or Kundalini Yoga.
- While cleansing or fasting, do two enemas or colonics per week.

SKIN:

- Exfoliate your skin to improve lymphatic drainage, circulation, and the quality of your skin.
- Dry brush before your shower or before your oil massage. Always brush towards your heart.
- After your shower, give yourself a nice oil massage to calm your nervous system.
- Take a hot Epsom salt bath each week.
- Sauna and sweat it out for 30 minutes every week or daily if you have the opportunity.
- While cleansing or fasting, take a hot Epsom salt bath every night. Use about a quart of Epsom salt for about twenty minutes, in water as hot as you can stand it, so it will trigger your skin to start detoxing. Start every day with a skin brushing followed by an oil massage and sip hot water every ten to fifteen minutes for the duration of your detox.

REST:

- Get good sleep every night and as often as you can so your body can repair itself. At 10 p.m. the body starts detoxifying, so if you're awake, your body is unable to perform those cleansing actions unless you are on a different circadian rhythm or sleep cycle.
- Get routine sleep. Go to bed at the same time every night or as often as possible so you don't throw off your circadian rhythm.
- Black out all forms of light while sleeping so as to not disrupt your body's healing. All light (except red light) seen through the eyelids triggers the brain to be alert and on the watch. Red light allows you to go deeper and faster into sleep.
- Meditate every day. No exceptions.

~ YOUR MIND ~

Our brains were the first computers. That's how we were able to make a computer in the first place. We have the ability to access new parts of our brain by expanding our consciousness, strengthening our intuition, getting healthy, and tapping into spirituality. Doing those things eradicates the negative aspects of the ego which keep the mind sick and stuck. You must get your mind healthy and in good shape if you want it to work properly for a long period of time, hopefully until you leave this physical plane.

MASTER YOUR MIND WITH MUSIC

The corpus callosum is the white matter that connects your left hemisphere and the right hemisphere together. People who are avid musicians have a stronger corpus callosum. It's been thought that if you are a musician you are more right brained, but in actuality it means that you are more "whole brained."

Learning to play a musical instrument or a new song strengthens your corpus callosum because it uses both the right and left hemispheres of your brain. Playing or writing music requires both sides of your brain to be proficient in function and processing. Being a musician or becoming a musician keeps your mind healthier longer. It's time to pick up an instrument!

MASTER YOUR MIND WITH MEMORY

Everyone has a different method of remembering things. Some people are great at remembering names or dates. Others never forget a face, or a song. Maybe you remember things experientially or linearly.

If you ever lost something, you'd look for it in areas where you think it might be. In an organized home you can immediately find what you're looking for because the scissors are in the kitchen drawer right where they belong. If you took the time to organize that area you would have been able to find them right away. This same organization is important for remembering information.

Organizing information is different than knowing, memorizing or using the information. When you organize information before you try to memorize it you will be able to find it later. There are many ways to go about doing this.

In ancient Greece, messengers needed to remember massive amounts of information and names. They would memorize all the names of the town members and officials to introduce them at the banquet before they delivered news. That feat ensured they could be trusted. I have compiled several different exercises and games in this chapter for you to enhance your memory. I encourage you to play them with your friends or make new ones at www.polrliving.com.

There is no one single part of the brain that stores all your memories. Memories trigger electrical signals throughout many different parts of the brain and body, even when recalling only one experience. Two separate people recalling the same incident will have different parts of the brain and body light up due to the way they process information. Memory recall is affected by a person's brain cognition, upbringing and emotional charge.

When you have important information you want to remember, treat it as such. Information combined with emotions becomes stored in your long term memory. For faster learning you need three states to commit something to memory:

1. Playfulness
2. Focus
3. Confidence

Ever wonder why you have a hard time remembering names? When you don't value someone's name as information that you hold dear and important by properly organizing it, you chalk it up to just being "bad with names." You give yourself an excuse not to treat that information as sacred and important and this excuse gets you off the hook for not remembering their name. But when you devalue their worth in this way, you give your subconscious the message to devalue your own self-worth as well.

Properly organizing this personal piece of information about them in your mind allows you to "Walk in like a Baller-Boss Rockstar" and remember people's names. Would you like to have a couple of ways to remember people's names and make them feel special, which makes them see you as special in return? How do you feel when someone remembers your name? It will boost your self-confidence so much that it will also be a way for you to remember other things in your life like birthdays, grocery lists, and such.

REMEMBERING NAMES

It is really helpful to have a word or image associated with the name of the person to help you remember. You can invent a relationship between the name and a physical characteristics of the person or come up with a rhyming word. If you have someone you care about in your life with the same name, you can use that loved one's image to create a wild variation or sensation along with it. Once you've associated an image to it, it's best to repeat the name three times to yourself in your head and then three times out loud in the conversation with that person.

HAPPINESS IS CONNECTED TO INTELLIGENCE

Pleasure is reflected in your body's electrical currents and stimuli, which increases your performance. That is why you want to be in a state of pleasure when remembering information. You have a higher IQ, your reflexes are faster, and your premonitions are stronger when you are in a blissful state. Also, when you are having fun it makes it more likely that you'll want to repeat the experience. You can bring a sense of fun and joy to remembering information by making a game out of it. Practicing these games improves your memory.

ENHANCED REMEMBERING

When I attended The American Academy of Dramatic Arts, I had to memorize massive amounts of text at a time. We had three-page monologues from several classes plus dialogue for partner scenes to remember each week. In order to not fall behind in any of my classes I had to work extra hard on memorization. I am a visual person and love to tell stories, so I opted to use imagery and stories to help remember my lines.

These techniques will help you learn, organize, and connect information with key words or letters to recall the information later. People often say they have a bad memory when they simply don't have the tools to help them remember something in a specific manner. When you understand how to get your brain to cooperate, you can appropriately organize any set of information to recall at another time. It feels good for the brain to perform at optimum levels. If you don't use it, you lose it. You can enhance your ability to recall information by using any of the following strategies below.

NUMBER RECALL

This is great for remembering combination locks, phone numbers, addresses, dates, and any sequence or string of numbers. You break the sequence up into sections to build a story with images so it cements it in your brain. For example: The combination to my storage lock is 2139812. You can break it down several different ways as long as it has meaning for you. 213 is an area code in Los Angeles, 98 is about as old as you get, and 12 is a dozen eggs. When you have images and a story in your mind for each section of numbers, you can easily recall the full sequence.

I imagine a busy street in L.A.(213-area code) with cars zooming past this cute little 98-year old woman walking with a cane. Her shoulders all rounded forward, she's holding a dozen eggs with a smile on her face. Now every time I unlock my storage I have granny visions that make me laugh. The key is to make your story personal.

Choose things, people, and places in your life to make it vivid for you. I'll break it down another way to demonstrate a number of ways to go about this. 21 is the legal drinking age in California, 39 was my favorite age, 8 feels like the number of days in a week I work, and 12 is the number of people on a jury that would find me innocent for having a drink after working 8 days a week.

Using images for numbers also enhances your ability to remember them. The stories and images will come easier the more you practice it. Try breaking it down a couple different ways in the beginning until you get the hang of it.

ACRONYM RECALL

Invent a combination of letters with each letter acting as a cue to an idea to remember each item on your list. For example, say you want to remember a ten item grocery list of carrots, toilet paper, rice, aluminum foil, bread, orange juice, butter, flour, ice, and pickles. I read the full grocery list several times out loud to get familiar with it. Then, I write the first letter of each item together and see if I can spell any words or come up with a phrase. I came up with this phrase: TCB FOR PABI to remember each item. This may take longer for the first few times you do it, but I assure you that it does get much quicker with practice.

RHYMING RECALL

This is a two-step process using a pre-memorized number-word association such as (one-bun, two-shoe, three-tree, four-door, five-hive, six-sticks, seven-heaven, eight-date, nine-wine, ten-hen) as a base. You can come up with your own image words for each number so you can lock it in. You then create a story with imagery by adding each of your items on your list to each pairing that makes sense. Visualize these next images and add details.

Using the same ten item grocery list of: carrots, toilet paper, rice, aluminum foil, bread, orange juice, butter, flour, ice, and pickles. I came up with one-bun wrapped in aluminum foil (hot on the grill), two shoes kicking flour(white powder going everywhere), three trees drinking orange juice (sticking straws in each others' oranges), four doors made out of butter (melting fast), five hives made of rice (my new favorite vegan sushi dish), six sticks each sporting a roll of toilet paper (this one is very easy to imagine), seven loaves of bread in heaven (with wings), eight dates with rabbits eating carrots (so this is how rabbits multiply so fast), nine glasses of iced wine (sorority party that didn't have time to chill the wine), ten hens eating pickles (I see ten hens all surrounding one pickle while pecking it).

STORY RECALL

This is a story you already know by heart and can recall to a tee, or you can create one by describing one of your regular routines or rituals. Set the word or items you have to remember throughout your story to cue you to the next one to recall. You can also build word associations throughout your story to remember items in a specific order.

You can also use simple nursery rhymes such as "Twinkle Twinkle Little Star." As you say each line, you add your information to the story, creating strong visuals to help you remember. For example, using my regular nightly routine to remember the ten items from the last recall would go something like this:

- I turn off all the lights in the house. I visualize the windows covered in aluminum foil.
- I bring my dog in my room and put her on my bed. I visualize luring her in with carrots which are her favorite!
- I go to the bathroom. I visualize the toilet paper.
- I wash my face. I visualize using only flowers (flour) to wash my face.
- I brush my teeth. I visualize my cringing face from drinking orange juice after brushing my teeth.
- I use a water pick. I visualize an icepick.
- I put creams and lotions on my skin. I visualize butter as the face cream.
- I stimulate my scalp. I visualize my fingers as pickles tickling my head.
- I meditate for twenty minutes to an hour. I visualize being in the east, meditating, and eating rice.
- I go to sleep. I visualize my bed made out of bread, soft and warm.

LEARNING NEW LANGUAGES

Take the sound of any foreign word to see what it is closest to in the English language and imagine a story or image around it to help you remember the foreign word. For instance, when I was learning Spanish, the phrase for "I'm sorry" is "lo siento". I imagined I was in a crowded area and accidentally stepped on someone's toe. "Low, I see unto your toe" sounds like "lo siento." I created a story and an image around the sounds of the phrase to help recall the meaning. Get creative—the more fun you have, the easier it is to remember.

ACROSTIC ASSOCIATION

This is an invented sentence, poem, or word puzzle where the first letter of each word is a cue for an idea you need to recall. If you're a musician or have taken a music class before you have heard of the acrostic way to remember the order of the notes on sheet music: E,G,B,D,F. EVERY GOOD BOY DESERVES FUN.

You'll find that you may never forget something when you categorize it the right way. When learning the directions in school for the proper order of North, East, South, and West, we used NEVER EAT SOGGY WAFFLES. I have also heard NEVER EAT SHREDDED WHEAT and NEVER EAT SOUR WATERMELON. It's amazing how imprinted in my brain it is. I am confident I will always be able to recall it.

KILL YOUR TV

TV stands for Tell-A-Vision. It tells us what to think and what to look at. Television programming is set up to program your subconscious in a myriad of ways. They are all for financial gain and are controlled by major corporations, businesses, CIA, and even the government. Check out the documentary called "Out of the Shadows" for a deeper understanding on the how and why they control the media.

We didn't use to have a protagonist or an evildoer depicted on the screen. Now, it's all set up as a story of revenge where one person is always to blame. And we wonder why people often don't take responsibility for themselves. It's because we are programmed to point the finger at someone else—it's their fault. Then we want to retaliate.

But what they don't tell you is that in revenge, everyone dies in the end.

I haven't had a TV in my home for twenty years and I can honestly say it's been one of the best things I have ever done for myself. I am not beholden to the programming and thoughts the media wants me to think to feel insecure or live in fear so I go right out and buy their brand new, super improved products that won't make me happy. TV pretends to know the solutions to life's problems. The TV says we are just one more product away from true joy. Only in America does a person die from being trampled by a mob of shoppers. Still think TV doesn't affect you?

In my opinion, only programs that educate and elevate are worthy of my full attention. Our focused energy and attention is the greatest gift we can give anyone. We have been blindly listening to information put out by people that do not have our best interests in mind. What we give all of our attention to should be held the most sacred out of all.

TV ZOMBIES

Have you seen the photos of the children watching TV and how zombied out they look? They lose all sense of self and personal expression. Some kids are babysat by the TV 20+ hours a week. I daresay that almost every parent at least once in their life has used TV as a babysitter and my mom was no different. Watching TV trains us not to think for ourselves and to look outside ourselves for answers. We blindly trust the programming crafted by the very people who want to control where and how we spend our money. We have become a culture of complacency. We believe everything presented to us in our information bubble and nobody steps back and asks why.

Program your own mind, or someone else will.

PROGRAM YOUR MIND

You can teach yourself to do almost anything or you can take a course or find a mentor who will show you how. If you don't take the time to program your own mind, someone or something else will. Look how the media and the news are already doing it.

Programming trains your mind to think a certain way. Bias is everywhere. It puts things in the programmer's favor and not in your best interest. It's impossible not to be affected by the things we watch, people we surround ourselves with, and anything that comes into our periphery. Surrounding yourself with people who are already doing the things that you want helps you get there faster.

If you have children, you are aware how important it is for them to avoid hanging out with the wrong group of kids because they will most likely be influenced by them. Just because we are adults doesn't change anything. We are influenced by everything, everywhere, and in every moment. Our brains are like tiny little sponges absorbing information every millisecond. You can choose to control what you watch and select things that inspire or lift you up, or choose not to. The choice is yours. It always has been.

My favorite time to program my mind is at night just before bed, either before or after my meditation. I like to come up with mantras (words or phrases often of spiritual nature) to repeat in my head for twenty minutes or more. I create counterbalance using a mantra for any limiting belief or block I am currently working through. I will often use three to five mantras, repeating them over and over again, but change them every night according to how I feel that day or what I need at that moment.

THE LAW OF ATTRACTION

By focusing on either positive or negative thoughts you will bring positive or negative experiences into your life. The "Law of Attraction" term was coined by Abraham Hicks, although the idea has been around since the early 17th century and there are even several references to this law in the

Bible. You can find them in Matthew 9:29 and 21:22, Luke 17:21, John 10:30, Mark 9:23, Proverbs 23:7 and Romans 12:2.

To be a confirmed Catholic you were required to read the Bible all the way through and study it intensely in a separate after-school program called Confraternity of Christian Doctrine (CCD). Throughout the year, I had more questions for the teachers than the entire class combined. I was made fun of because I was the nerdy kid with all the weird questions. It's a good thing I didn't focus on what the kids thought of me then or I would have attracted more of that. I was hyper focused on knowing the meanings behind all the teachings in the Bible.

I recommend first starting with anything at www.abraham-hicks.com, the Abraham-Hicks Publications website, where you will find their Law of Attraction teachings. Authors that use this philosophy in their specific field, with their spin on it, are Napoleon Hill in "Think and Grow Rich" (1937) and Louise Hay in "You Can Heal Your Life" (1984). My mother had this book while I was growing up, which she read often. The movie, "The Secret" explains this law and is fun to watch, although people think it's a quick fix to all your problems. The film discusses the conscious practice of awareness and the act of taking responsibility for all the things in your life.

LEARN NEW THINGS

Changing your beliefs and outlook for your future also extends your lifespan. When you learn new information it creates new brain cells to store the information. Axons and dendrites form in the brain to create the circuitry that connects specific parts of your brain.

When you learn something new, you create a new neurological pathway. Every time you practice the new skill it creates stronger circuitry. You create strong neural networks by doing activities regularly.

Do something every day to exercise and stretch your mind or it will get out of shape. It's easy to learn something new with the Internet at our fingertips. It's nice to share information with those appropriate to share with.

Explaining it to or teaching someone else furthers your own understanding of it. For instance, in one of my daily "Learn Something New" practices I discovered that all rice is covered in talcum powder to prevent it from sticking together in the bag. If you don't rinse it first your water will be super white. I had been drinking talcum powder my entire childhood-YUCK!

Do something differently than you normally would to beef up your brain. Try switching out your dominant hand for simple tasks such as brushing your teeth or controlling the computer mouse. If you go hiking or jogging, switch up your route.

For those of you who work out, switch up your routine or your body gets used to the exercises and you will eventually plateau and stop seeing results. You can always do the same routine in a different way to keep things sharp. Visualize new ways to do things.

VISUALIZATION
Definition: //vis·u·al·i·za·tion// //viZH(oo)lzāSH()n// ~Noun/Verb
1. The representation of an object, situation, or set
of information as a chart or other image.
2. The formation of a mental visual image of
something. (www.OxfordDictionaries.com)
3. The act or process of interpreting in visual terms or of
putting into visible form. (www.Merriam-Webster.com)

CREATIVE MENTAL VISUALIZATION

The best way to achieve goals, learn something new, or change anything in your life is through visualization. It also improves your memory. When I was acting, the night before every performance I visualized all my blocking (stage action) on the stage throughout the entire play. I went through each piece of choreography in my mind so that the night of the show I was ready to go. This is also how Olympic athletes train. We have learned we can change anything using our thoughts. You must visualize it for it to happen. If you cannot see it, you cannot have it.

Set aside personal quiet time to prime your brain and visualize each of your goals. What direction do you need to point yourself to begin? Who do you need to become in order to attain it? Visualize yourself becoming that person and achieving your goal. Watch yourself succeed in your mind's eye. Envision any obstacles falling away with grace and ease. Before I had the courage to start writing this book, every night for six months I would stand in front of the mirror holding someone else's book in my hands. I closed my eyes and visualized that it was my completed best-selling book. It allowed me to move through my blocks and prepare myself for the future.

I use creative mental visualization in many of my meditations because of how effective it is. I never start a new project without doing this visualization first. People have been flabbergasted at how quickly I learn things. If I had one superhero power it would be "copycat" because I am a very visual person. I can learn new skills by watching exactly how another person does something and visualizing myself doing it instead of them. Then when I do it for the first time it's just like I saw it in my mind only now I'm doing it in person.

HEART-MIND LISTENING

The connection between the heart and the mind is such a profound one. When you listen with both at the same time, you make better decisions. There have been many scientific studies on the heart-mind connection. This heart-mind connection is an ancient technological advancement for humans. Go to www.heartmath.com for all the leading technology and scientific information on this practice.

Practice heart-mind listening whenever deliberating an important decision. Sit in a quiet space where you will not be disturbed with your eyes closed and your hands on your heart. Breathe slowly and deeply for about ten breaths. Presence yourself with the question that's presently at issue for you while keeping your hands on your heart, and wait for the answer.

When having an uncomfortable conversation with someone you can place one hand over your heart as you speak so that you are present to your heart's voice. It helps you stay calm and focused, especially when delivering difficult information. You can also sync your breathing to someone else's breathing, which also syncs your heartbeat to theirs. You can actually enter another person's energetic field when your breathing and your heart rate is at the same pace as theirs. That is how you begin Tantra with your lover or in duo yoga practices.

MIND HACKING

The power you gain from the simple act of making a decision changes your life. You can reset both your software and hardware, which determine your mindset. Learn a language. Take a cooking class. Take a dance class. Sign up for a workshop that you've wanted to try. Garden.

Remove the word "should" from your vocabulary. This word implies that you or the other person is wrong, and causes guilt and blame. The more accurate word to use instead is "could."

A great way to boost your brain is to read every day. I usually have an audiobook as well as two or three physical books I'm reading at any given time. I keep an ongoing list of books to read in the notes section of my phone. I also like to ask people I admire what their favorite books are so I can read them too. Check out the resources section on www. POLRLIVING.com to see some of my favorite reads.

You can also practice memory games either online or on your own. I like to randomly pick ten words out of any book to memorize in 30 seconds. I also flip through the dictionary and pick new words to learn and use throughout my day when writing emails or texts.

SPIRIT, BODY, & MIND IN SYNC

All in all, when your spirit, mind, & body are all in sync, you will have better results at anything you're working towards. Do yourself a favor and help you help yourself by getting your Holy Trinity Temple in sync. Listen to the signs you receive from them to grow your intuition and share results with friends. Follow your excitement, live your dreams, and fulfill your purpose.

CHAPTER 12

MOVING FORWARD

"*DO* THE ROBOT. DON'T *BE* A ROBOT."
~ Tyson Eberly

Well, this is where we say goodbye for now. I have to say it has been a splendiferous pleasure getting these channellings out on paper for you. I do love you. I am grateful you took the time to read this book, not only for me, but for YOU! You matter! What you care about matters and you have the ability to help others by the sheer act of healing yourself. I used these tips and tricks to heal the deepest pain and traumas in my life and I hope they help in your personal healing journey.

I know we've covered a lot in this book. Some of it may be stuff you already knew but needed to be reminded of because we are human, after all—we came here to remember it all over again. Here at the end of the road—which I hope is the beginning of a wonderful journey for you as you put into practice what you've learned and remembered—I'd like to reiterate some really important things to keep at the forefront of your mind.

Most of us move throughout our lives on autopilot. Even those who regularly practice mindfulness and meditation daily still succumb to the repetitive movements and patterns in life. It's very easy to get hypnotized back into our sleepwalking state of autopilot living. My one hope for you is that you will actually use one or more of the gems in this book and pass it on.

I highly recommend not overwhelming yourself by trying to change everything in your life at once. It took almost half a century for me to acquire all the tools in this book and I continue to learn more everyday. Adopt one or two new concepts or practices for at least two weeks before adding more.

Unless you have a coach, in which case, you can pretty much go full steam ahead because you'll have someone there during all the breakdowns. Your coach will help you progress faster than you can on your own. You can find one at https://www.polrliving.com/. Also, it is advised to reread this book from time to time as you will have a deeper understanding of these concepts as you evolve and one section that you didn't resonate with before may actually become your new favorite!

The most important thing to remember is that you have a choice in every thought that you think and every feeling that you invoke. Your body awareness and consciousness will direct you where to proceed when you pay attention to the signs that your body gives you. Your body is a tuning fork, so listen for the "ring of truth" that your body resonates to. And if you don't like a situation it's up to you to change it, or it will keep showing up.

No one is going to save you except you. You are the one that you have been waiting for. We must all do it together or none of us are free. Apologize and make things right—do the repairs necessary to make up for what has been done. And go forward armed in truth, with compassion, power and love.

And when you change it—*everything shifts*. Each process of healing uncovers a different Light frequency and you go to a higher, more all-inclusive state of consciousness. So you begin to have more Unity within your own system (Spirit, body, & mind) and you have more value for yourself. Not having an awareness of value as a human is fragmentation and causes destruction.

You are like no other species in this creative realm. Each person alive on this planet today is unique unto themselves and plays a special role in the universal refinement of consciousness taking place now by healing their fragmented self. We all chose to come here at this time because our special superhero powers are needed to shift the consciousness on this planet. For the first time in history the whole world has stopped (Covid-19) to give us this time for us to get back on track and into alignment with all the aspects of ourselves—the Holy Trinity.

YOU ARE A SUPERHERO

It is *super* imperative that you understand that you are a creative being &
what you create in the now is actually reflected in your reality. What are
your thoughts that you're having that consistently give your body a specific

energy? It's up to you to bring this awareness into your body through investigation and then take the necessary actions towards refinement.

Make it your job to manage your "states" (being proactive instead of reactive) so that you will have the most joy and opportunity in every experience. You can't create from a place of survival or feeling less than. If you are feeling stressed, fearful, or out of balance you must take time for yourself.

Make a list for the important things, set due dates and get into action. Download the TA-DA! LIST on www.POLRLIVING.com to get started writing your goals down and crossing things off that list. Each time you cross something off, jump into the air and make a landing pose as if you were a gymnast while saying "Ta-Da!" out loud.

Get up an hour earlier each day to make time to center yourself. Get up another hour earlier to use that time for something creative, catching up on reading, or working on your personal goals until you start seeing positive shifts. Take time to ground yourself and love yourself every single day! Get into action on a daily basis starting right now.

Nourish yourself. Schedule it into your planner and put it on your priority list. What is it that really feeds you and gives you energy? If you're having a hard time loving yourself *this is the best way to learn how*—by doing it! Just do it and you will love yourself. It's that simple. When you practice loving yourself you learn how to do it better and better! When you love yourself you will be more whole (holy) and connected to source.

My last questions for you are "Why?" and "What are you waiting for?" Do you have a powerful enough "why" to take action? Do you see how misalignment and fragmentation have held you back?

Do you have a vision of how good your life will be when you have united your Spirit, Body & Mind? Can you keep that vision before you like the banner an army marches behind? With that vision in mind, will you take action now?

Are you willing to take the steps required to eliminate this fragmentation from your life? Recognizing the Divine within yourself removes this fragmentation from human form and your emotional body so that you can be confident in your creations, have hope, and look forward to enjoying the rest of your life.

This unity within yourself and love in your heart is your birthright! Stay open and focus on love. In trying times always ask yourself "What would LOVE do?"

I know you can do it. I have faith you will. I believe in you.

Love Always,

Jesselynn Desmond
Los Angeles, California
Monday September 21, 2020